USING X
TROUBLESHOOTING THE X WINDOW SYSTEM, MOTIF AND OPEN LOOK

ERIC F. JOHNSON
KEVIN REICHARD

A Subsidiary of
Henry Holt and Co., Inc.

First Edition—1992
ISBN Book 1-55828-212-2

Printed in the United States of America
10 9 8 7 6 5 4 3

MIS:Press books are available at special discounts for bulk purchases for sales promotions, premiums,
fund-raising, or educational use. Special editions or book excerpts can also be created to specification.

For details contact: Special Sales Director
                         MIS:Press
                         a subsidiary of Henry Holt and Company, Inc.
                         115 West 18th Street
                         New York, New York 10011

TRADEMARKS:

Throughout this book, trademarked names are used. Rather than put a trademark symbol after every
occurrence of a trademarked name, we used the names in an editorial fashion only. Where such
designations appear in this book, they have been printed with initial caps.

DEDICATION

From Kevin:
As always, to Penny. And, as always, to Geisha.

Contents

ix

Introduction

X Marks the Spot

The X Window System is a standard wrapped in an enigma. As a successful technical accomplishment and stable programming environment, it defies most attempts at categorization. Is it a UNIX shell? No. Is it the all-singing, all-dancing graphical system that will cure all your computing woes? Not yet. Has it become a standard? Yes, although some vendors—most notably workstation giant Sun Microsystems—have been brought into the X fold kicking and screaming. Is it a workable business-oriented environment? Yes.

Why use the X Window System, and why should you care about it? Because it works, and it works well. Sophisticated X, Motif, and Open Look applications are now available for the business world. The X Window System is a network-independent, operating-system-independent window system. Sitting on top of various operating systems (UNIX, DOS, Macintosh operating system, AmigaDOS, VMS), X Window shields both the user and the programmer from the messy details of specific displays, operating systems, and networks. With X, a systems designer can apply consistent interface designs across a wide variety of hardware, operating systems, and networking schemes.

Make no doubt about it: The X Window System can be a very challenging environment. Add in the complexities posed by the Motif and Open Look window managers and specifications, and you have a very complex milieu for users, system administrators, and programmers alike.

This book addresses some of the basic, procedural problems posed daily by the X Window System. We cover the basics of X Window usage, beginning with actually starting X, through using Xterm and window managers, ending up with a trouble-shooting section that helps you solve your X problems.

Early in the design process, X's designers (Robert Scheifler, James Gettys, and the rest of the people who have worked for or are working for the MIT X Consortium) traded flexibility and the ability to run on just about any computer system for a dramatic increase in complexity, and we're all living with that complexity today. In many ways X offers the ultimate in flexibility. You can customize many more things under X than you can with the Macintosh (for example). On the Mac, however, customization is not a *necessity*. On X, it is.

This book is partially based on columns we've written for *UNIX Review* since January 1991. Because these columns and articles were written with the programmer in mind, not the end user, we have reoriented that material for a totally different audience.

Who Should Read This Book

Most X, Motif, and Open Look books are geared for programmers, including three previous works by the authors (*X Window Applications Programming, Advanced X Window Applications Programming*, and *Power Programming Motif*—all MIS:Press). This has not been a bad thing. After all, for the first few years of its existence, X belonged almost totally to the world of programmers or highly advanced users who managed to integrate some programming into their daily usage.

Using *X* is different. We've seen a great need for a book geared to the increasing number of X Window System, Motif, and Open Look users who must deal with X and these variants on a daily basis. Regular end users who may have little or no programming experience will pick up a lot from the beginning chapters, where we cover basic X usage. System administrators and UNIX site administrators should gain some insight from the trouble-shooting sections. And programmers should learn from the entire book—finding out, for instance, how their applications can have sometimes-unintended effects on end users.

Even though this is not a programming book, there is some discussion of X programming. Don't worry. We don't expect you to sit down and churn out C code after reading this book.

What You'll Need

Obviously, you should be using the X Window System, Motif, or Open Look, or be actively evaluating its use in your business or school. We assume that you have some familiarity with computing and the operating system of your choice.

In the course of writing this book, we used several hardware and software applications: Desqview/X, SCO Open Desktop, IBM AIXwindows, Sun OpenWindows, Silicon Graphics Irix, Hewlett-Packard HP-UX, Interactive UNIX, Mach 386, and, of course, the X Window System as distributed by the MIT X Consortium.

Typographical Conventions

Anything you must type into your computer; commands, programming functions, file names, and so forth, are noted by the **monospaced** font. New ideas and concepts are noted by **bold** type.

Assumptions We Make

X is not an environment for the meek, nor is it an environment for those totally new to computing. In our collective mind's eye we pictured you, dear reader, as a computer user who likes a challenge, who is fairly familiar with the UNIX operating system—at least enough to know what we mean when we discuss "shells" and the like—and who's interested in X/Motif/Open Look as operating environments in which to perform specific jobs. This is not a treatise on operating systems, nor is it a programmer's guide to X.

Finally, we mundanely assume that you are using a mouse with three buttons. While X supports up to *five* buttons, we have never seen a five-button mouse, and most workstation and PC users will be using a three-button mouse. Instead of using X button descriptions (Button 1, Button 2, Button 3), we've stuck to the clearer left-mouse button, middle-mouse button, and right-mouse button.

Using This Book

This book is divided into eight sections, which are designed to expose users gradually to the key ideas of X and to provide hands-on tips that will make X easier to use. In Section I, we introduce the X Window System, Motif, Open Look, OpenWindows, and several entry-level applications, such as **xterm**. In Section II, we cover various topics essential to successful X computing: how a user can be in two places at once, setting up command-line parameters for applications, customizing applications and setting up the system fonts. In Section III we describe the three major window managers: Motif, Open Look, and Tab. In Section IV we go over actual X usage, from running X applications to changing the system colors. In Section V we highlight several common problems for X users and convey relatively simple solutions. In Section VI we discuss Motif and X programming. In Section VII we discuss X administration, from installation and configuration to optimization. In section VIII we discuss Motif and Open Look usage. Finally, in Appendix A we explain how to acquire X, Motif, and Open Look, and we also cover some essential X programming books.

Each chapter ends with a summary of the chapter's concepts.

How to Contact the Authors

We welcome your comments about *Using X*. You can reach us via UUCP mail at **kreichard@mcimail.com**; via Compuserve mail addressed to user ID 73670,3422; via MCI Mail to kreichard; via America Online to KReichard; or via conventional mail addressed to 1677 Laurel Av., St. Paul, MN 55104.

I

Introducing X

This section introduces you to the basics of the X Window System, including its history and underlying philosophy. You will then move on to some basic X Window functions, including:

- Starting and stopping X.
- How to use xterm, probably the most commonly used X Window program. It offers a command-line interface to UNIX shells such as sh, csh, and ksh.

## Chapter 1

The Joys of X

X is a **graphical windowing system**. Instead of merely providing lines of text on your screen (as DOS or UNIX do), X provides you with multiple windows (run by multiple applications), windows that form the building blocks of a graphical user interface (or GUI, to use a popular and trendy term).

A graphical user interface provides immediate benefits for the end user. If you're using a publishing package like FrameMaker, for example, the document in the window looks exactly the same as it does when it's printed. This property is called **what-you-see-is-what-you-get** (WYSIWYG)—and that's an important property in modern computing.

Older operating systems, like DOS and UNIX (in the traditional text mode), lack the ability to display WYSIWYG windows of any sort. Many modern applications, ranging from data analysis to publishing to word processing to computer-aided design, benefit from WYSIWYG. Several studies clearly indicate that a well-designed graphical interface cuts down on corporate training time and increases worker productivity.

X is not the only modern attempt at providing a graphical user interface. Microsoft Windows and the Macintosh operating system are two very popular graphical interfaces. So why use X? Because Windows and the Macintosh operating systems are tied to specific hardware implementations; X Window allows the programmer to transcend those limitations. X will run with virtually any operating system (UNIX, DOS, AmigaDOS, Macintosh, VMS) and on hardware configurations ranging from PCs, Amigas and Macs, to VAXes and Cray supercomputers.

Providing the building blocks of a graphical interface is merely one element of X. This system also contains the tools necessary to compute effectively on a network. How? The X Window System divides computing into two parts, based on a **client-server relationship**. This relationship can be rather confusing, but it offers the ability to distribute applications over a network efficiently.

In the mini and micro worlds, a **server** is usually a hardware device (a VAX, an AS/400, a Novell file server) running at the center of a network, distributing data and processing power to networked workstations and terminals. Because other systems on your network have access to your display, the X server cannot be thought of in the same way a file server on a local-area network is. With X, the role of the **server** (sometimes called a **display server**) is reversed. The server is a program that runs on your local machine and controls and draws all output to the **display**. Your local machine, no matter if it's a PC running Desqview/X or a Sun SPARC station running OpenWindows, is called a **display**. The server draws the images on your physical monitor (or monitors—X supports multiple monitors on a workstation), tracks client input via your keyboard and pointing device (usually a mouse), and updates windows appropriately.

The server also acts as a traffic cop between clients running on local or remote systems and the local system. Clients are application programs that perform specific tasks. (In X, the terms clients and applications are used interchangeably.) Because X is a networked environment, the client and the server don't necessarily compute on the same machine (although they can and do in a number of situations). That's how X features distributed processing. For example, a personal computer running Desqview/X can call upon the processing power of a more-powerful Solbourne host within a network, displaying the results of the Solbourne's computations on the PC's monitor. In this case, the client is acutally running on the remote Solbourne, not your local machine—thus distributing the processing across the network. The idea is simple: The actual computing should take place on the machine with the network's greatest computing power, not necessarily at the computer that a user happens to be using.

The server tracks input from the display and passes information to the clients. In X, such inputs are called **events**. When you press on a key, that's an event; when you let it back up, that's another event. Similarly, when you move the cursor with a mouse, that's an event, too. These events are delivered to applications through an event queue.

A **window manager** is a program that defines how the interface (that is, the actual look of the programs) appears and acts on the screen. X does not provide the specific look and feel of these windows—that is, the specific arrangement of elements on a screen (scroll bars, title bars, and so on). As we noted before, X provides the building blocks for a graphical interface. The user is free to layer any look and feel on top of X. (Two popular user-interface specifications, Motif and Open Look, do just that. We'll explain both a little later.)

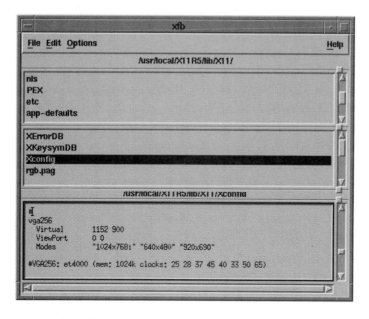

Figure 1.1 The Motif window manager.

From the beginning, X designers have worked with a goal of **mechanism, not policy**. The designers have been concerned with providing general-purpose portable tools, not with religious issues concerning the merits of various interfaces. This sane and simple philosophy has served X designers well, helping to maintain a focus within X that is lacking in other unwieldy, do-everything environments. The "mechanism, not policy" credo is central to understanding X. This separation of mechanism and policy can be confusing sometimes, but it provides one of the great strengths of X. We'll return to this concept regularly as we explore the many functions of X.

X provides the mechanism for creating a user interface, while a window manager enforces a specific policy. There are several window managers available. The generic X, as shipped by MIT, includes several window managers, including twm, the Tab (or Tom's) window manager. OSF/Motif, as defined by the Open Software Foundation, includes the mwm window manager. Open Look, as defined by AT&T and Sun Microsystems, includes the olwm window manager.

Motif and Open Look

Since the X Window System doesn't mandate a user interface, you are free to layer a particular look and feel on top of it. And, indeed, most X users don't deal directly with X; they deal instead with vendor-supplied solutions. And that's where **Motif** and **Open Look** come in.

If you are using a Sun SPARCstation, there's a good chance you aren't using the X Window System directly; you're probably using OpenWindows, a product that conforms to Open Look specifications. If you're using an IBM RS/6000, you're probably using the Motif window manager, which conforms to Motif specifications.

Even though you may use the terms "Motif applications" and "Open Look applications" in casual conversation, those beasts really don't exist, because, strictly speaking, there are no such things as products named Open Look and Motif. Instead, there are products that conform to the Open Look specifications, as defined by AT&T and Sun Microsystems (such as Sun's OpenWindows), or Motif specifications, as defined by the Open Software Foundation. Both Motif and Open Look provide a style guide with a particular look and feel. Both provide toolkits that allow programmers to create applications that conform to the style guide easily. And both provide window managers that allow applications to take advantage of the features unique to the Open Look and Motif style guides.

An example: Sun's OpenWindows is the sum of many products: the Open Look window manager (olwm), three toolkits (OLIT, XView, and tNt), and a server that supports both the X and NeWS windowing protocols. OpenWindows menus include a pushpin at the top of the menu. This allows you to keep the menu permanently on your screen; it won't disappear when you're finished with the menu. Your work is centered around a Workspace menu (or the root menu), which provides access to other menus (Programs, Utilities, and a Properties editor, as well as an Exit choice). Several programs (mail, calendar, icon editor, and others) come with OpenWindows.

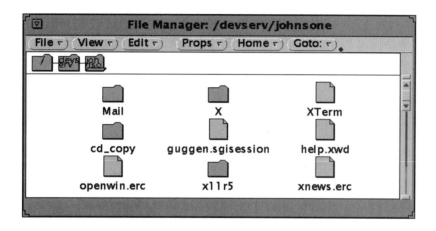

Figure 1.2 An OpenWindows window.

The computing press likes to play up an imagined battle between Motif and Open Look to see which specification has garnered the most users. This is a false battle, we feel, as the two styles are not contradictory. There are basic similarities to the Open Look and Motif specifications. Both support horizontal and vertical scroll bars, for example. Both support the basic functions as defined by the X Window System. Contrary to popular belief, you can run Open Look programs on a Motif system, and vice versa, without any fancy vendor-supplied solutions. The Motif program running an Open Look–based window manger won't have the benefits of the full Motif interface and window manager, but it will be able to run just fine. The same goes for Open Look programs running under a Motif system, although you'll probably lose those spiffy Open Look push pins in the process. It is a naive and technologically weak argument that one style must "win" at the expense of the other.

The real battle goes on for the hearts and minds of vendors, who find that because of economic and logistical limitations they are forced to commit to one style guide or the other when developing commercial applications. And, indeed, it is these vendors who will determine (to a great extent) whether you use Motif or Open Look window managers. Sun has done an excellent job of seeding the marketplace with Open Look–compliant applications, but the Open Software Foundation's diverse and powerful membership (DEC, IBM, Hewlett-Packard) means that some mighty marketing muscle will be devoted to Motif-compliant applications. If your particular computing needs are filled only by Open Look–compliant applications, you will be an Open Look user. And if your particular computing needs are filled only by Motif-compliant applications, you will be a Motif user. Most advanced users end up using both window managers at some point.

X Today

First and foremost, you will be an X Window System user. While you don't need to be an X programming whiz in order to use X, it's a good idea to be familiar with the basic X Window System.

The generic X Window System as shipped by MIT consists of the X graphics subroutine library (known simply as Xlib), the X network protocol, an X toolkit, and several window managers.

Xlib is a low-level library providing access to X graphics and interface functions. Unlike most DOS-based graphics, however, these low-level routines don't directly access the hardware. While this library may not seem optimal for performance, it does provide X's much-vaunted portability. Xlib provides functions and macros for drawing lines, creating windows, displaying text, and defining colors. Xlib hides most of the gory details about making a connection with an X server, maintaining network links, and the actual format of X fonts. (When things go wrong, though, it will be up to you to solve the problems, as you'll see in several chapters later in this book.)

Xlib contains about 400 routines that map to X Protocol requests or provide utility functions. Xlib converts C function calls to X Protocol requests that implement display functions, such as **XDrawLine()** to draw a line. These functions include creating, destroying, moving, and sizing windows; drawing lines and polygons; setting background patterns; and tracking the mouse. Xlib allows a programmer to access windows in a number of ways, including overlapping and allowing simultaneous output to multiple windows. It supports multiple fonts, raster operations, line drawing, and both color and monochrome applications.

These capabilities allow X to be portable—that is, a program should look the same on a Sun workstation as it does on an IBM PS/2 running SCO Open Desktop. This is a situation where users, system administrators, and training specialists win. There's no need to retrain users if they have to move to different hardware platforms during the course of normal work.

Above X sits many toolkits (as discussed earlier). X toolkits are program subroutines that can make programming easier. They are prewritten graphic routines; you can put together different parts to form a program. Toolkits are under constant revision from different vendors. These toolkits (after a steep initial learning curve) can speed the creation of X applications. We find, however, that programmers still need a thorough grounding in Xlib and how it operates in order to create quality, commercial-grade applications.

X research is now directed by the X Consortium, whose members include IBM, DEC, Apple, Hewlett-Packard, Sun, and several other industry heavyweights. In March 1988, MIT officially issued Version 11, Release 2. Later that year Release 3 was issued. In January 1990, Release 4 appeared. Release 5 appeared in the middle of 1991. Release 5 is important because it provides the framework to deal with many perennial problems with X, such as internationalization, scalable fonts, and 3-D graphics.

To what extent should users care about these X parts? Not much. One of the goals of this book, we hope, is to take the power of X out of the hands of the programmers and system engineers and put it into the hands of everyday X users. Although X users still tend to be on the advanced side, they aren't necessarily programmers or engineers anymore. Throughout this book, we hope to bring the power of X to you, proving that X can be as accessible an environment as the more-popular graphical user interfaces.

Actually Using X

The first step in empowerment is actually getting your hands on X. Unfortunately, the X Window System is not a package you grab from the shelf of your neighborhood software store—yet.

If you're a workstation user, you probably are already utilizing X or have it available for use. Workstations from Sun, DEC, Hewlett-Packard, Silicon Graphics, and IBM all feature X as a central part of their operating environments—but not, sad to say, necessarily the latest versions of X. Most commercial vendors, as we write this, still include only Release 4 of the X Window System, even though Release 5 has been available since the middle of 1991 to the vendors. Several vendors offer X Window under their own proprietary monikers: DEC offers DECwindows, IBM offers AIXwindows, and Sun offers OpenWindows. Each implementation has its own quirks. We cover the major problems, but unfortunately we can't cover all of them here.

If you're a PC user, you probably aren't using X. However, several new products, as well as advances in the UNIX world, are bringing X to the PC desktop. Desqview/X from Quarterdeck serves both as X client and server, and it can be either integrated into an X network of some sort or used as a free-standing X development system. Several products (eXceed from Hummingbird Systems, for example) allow X servers to run under DOS and Microsoft Windows, as long as there's another powerful machine on the network already running X. Destiny or UnixWare from Univel (the joint Novell-UNIX System Laboratories venture) will bring a slimmed-down UNIX to the Intel platform, with a custom X interface as well as standard Open Look and Motif window managers. Solaris from Sun will also bring a newer UNIX and the Open Look window manager to PCs, while SCO Open Desktop is attempting to merge many different programs (UNIX running DOS applications and X) into a coherent desktop package.

If you're a Mac user, you can access X via standard windows and MacX in Apple's A/UX (its UNIX implementation), or you can buy a third-party product (like White Pine Systems' eXodus) that runs X clients in a window connected to a network.

If you're already working in a networked workstation environment, or work with a VAX/VMS system running DECwindows, you may be familiar with X. A way to bring the power of X to additional users, without the expense of additional workstations, is through X terminals. An X terminal is more than a dumb terminal but less than a full workstation. X terminals have enough horsepower to run a local server, but they rely on machines elsewhere on the network for most of their computing power. Other drawbacks include limits on the sophistication of the window manager; generally, X terminals feature proprietary servers that may not allow you to take advantage of the entire OpenWindows interface if you hook an X terminal to a Sun workstation. (This scenario should never occur, according to Sun, the last major workstation vendor not to offer an X terminal.) NCD and Tektronix are the leading vendors of X terminals.

And if you're a Cray supercomputer user...well, you probably know more about X than we can teach you.

Summary

The X Window System provides a rich, graphical windowing environment to end users.

At the same time it allows corporations to avoid being tied to a specific hardware scheme.

As a user, you should be familiar with many of the buzz phrases surrounding the X Window System. You should know that a server in the LAN world means something totally different from a server in the X world. You should know what a display entails. You should know the significance of Motif and Open Look specifications and how they are significant in your computing plans. You should be aware of X's basic structure. And, most of all, you should be excited about your further adventures with the X Window System, as we guide you through twenty-three chapters covering everything from basic X usage to advanced troubleshooting. Good luck!

## Chapter 2

Starting and Stopping X

The logical place to start our coverage of X usage: How do you start X? Surprisingly enough, starting X is a difficult task, much more difficult than it should be. Similarly, stopping X is also a difficult task. This chapter will cover many of the different ways to start and stop X.

Because the processes are so difficult, many vendors have already installed their own mechanisms for starting and stopping X. In many cases, all you have to do is log in to get X started on your system. If you're already using a vendor-supplied solution, by all means use that method until you feel confident enough with X to cause some damage with your own customization.

As UNIX workstations become commodities, hardware vendors are doing more to add value to their products, such as setting up proprietary X-based user environments like Hewlett-Packard's **VUE** and Silicon Graphics' **ToolChest**. These environments add many nice features, but they also limit you to the vendor's machines, which is the whole point. All of these environments, though, are based on the X Window System; so, while we don't cover every nook and cranny of the proprietary features, the techniques shown here should help you better understand the way your X environment is put together.

Starting X

Before you can run any X application, you need to start the X **server**. The X server takes over control of a display: the keyboard, a pointing device (usually a mouse), and at least one video monitor (sometimes more in multiheaded systems). This means the X server must engage in a form of voodoo to convince your UNIX system to give up control of those devices. It also must communicate with a variety of proprietary graphics controllers and other assorted hardware.

An X server alone isn't worth much—all you get is a cross-hatch pattern and an X cursor. You'll also want to start a number of X applications, including a window manager, when you start up the X server. The applications are important; the X server merely provides the infrastructure.

Start the X server with the **xinit** program. Normally, **xinit** can run without any arguments:

```
xinit
```

Xinit starts the X server, a program named **X** that's normally stored in **/usr/bin/X11**. Many systems link a particular server to the file named **X**, depending on your graphics hardware. On a Sun workstation the X server process is called **Xsun**. A symbolic link ties **Xsun** to the file **X**. On Intel-based systems, you may see X servers named **Xvga**, **Xega,** or **X386**.

After starting the X server, **xinit** executes the programs listed in the file **.xinitrc**, which is located in your home directory. This file lists the programs you want to start when you launch X. It usually includes a graphical clock, at least one **xterm**, and a window manager such as **twm**, **olwm**, or **mwm**.

Because **.xinitrc** is a shell script, all the programs it launches—except the last—should be run in the background with an ampersand (**&**) trailing the command. Commands that execute quickly and then exit, like **xsetroot**, need not be run in the background.

When **.xinitrc** terminates, **xinit** kills the X server. This, in essence, is how you stop X.

If you run every program in **.xinitrc** in the background, then **.xinitrc** will quickly terminate, and so will your X server. Run the last program in **.xinitrc** in the foreground, as the example **.xinitrc** file shows below:

```
xterm -geom 80x40 &
xterm -geom 80x40+300+300 &
oclock -geom 120x120+900+10 &
xsetroot -solid bisque2
exec mwm
```

Obviously, you'll choose a program that you intend to keep around for your entire X session. Like the example above, most users end their **.xinitrc** file by running a window manager—**mwm**, for example. There are two main reasons for this. First, you want a window manager running during your entire X session. Second, most window managers provide a menu choice that allows you to exit. This menu choice is an easier (and easier-to-remember) way to quit X than typing **Ctrl-D** in an **xterm** window or using **kill** to terminate the X server. Using the example above, exiting the window manager also exits X.

Whatever program you choose, this last key placeholder process controls when X exits. When this process exits, X does, too.

If **xinit** fails to find an **.xinitrc** file, it merely starts the X server and one 25-line **xterm** window.

The .Xinitrc File

Let's go over our example **.xinitrc** file line by line.

```
xterm -geom 80x40 &
```

starts an **xterm** window. **Xterm** is a VT102 terminal emulator, certainly nothing flashy. This is the most commonly used X program, in our experience, even though X is such a ballyhooed graphical environment. In this case, we start an **xterm** window with a geometry of **80x40**—80 characters wide by 40 lines tall. This command is run in the background. Note that **xterm** describes width and height in *characters* (based on the size of **xterm**'s font), while most other X programs specify width and height in *pixels*. This distinction can be confusing.

```
xterm -geom 80x40+300+300 &
```

also starts an **xterm** in the background. This **xterm** is started at the same size, but the location is set to **300, 300**, which is 300 pixels across from the left-hand side of the screen, and 300 pixels down from the top.

The origin in **X** is the upper-left corner. Values increase in the **x** direction moving right. Values increase in the **y** direction going down.

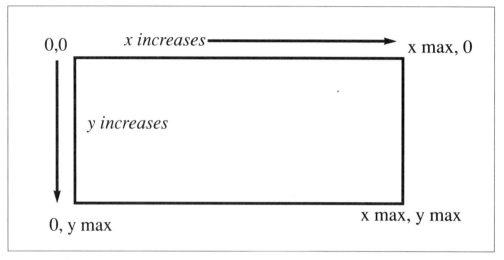

Figure 2.1 Basic X geometry.

(We show how to control **xterm** in the next chapter.)

oclock -geom 120x120+900+10 &

starts a graphical clock, **oclock**. Since most computer users are Type A personalities, they all want to know what time it is—all the time. There are two main X clocks: **xclock** and **oclock**.

Oclock provides a rounded window on systems that support the **SHAPE** extension to X. **SHAPE** provides for odd-shaped windows rather than boring rectangular ones.

xsetroot -solid bisque2

sets the color of the screen background. We find that the color *bisque2* forms a pleasing background. You can experiment with many solid colors, or you can even set your background to a bitmap. Other programs allow you to use a graphics file, such as a GIF image, for a screen background. (See Chapter 12 for more on color and Chapter 13 for more on **xsetroot**.)

Figure 2.2 Oclock.

Figure 2.3 Xclock.

Note that we started **xsetroot** in the foreground. **Xsetroot** executes and completes in a short period of time, so there's no need to run it in the background.

exec mwm

launches a window manager, **mwm**, in the foreground. Window managers control the layout of windows on the screen, allowing you to move windows, iconify them, and change their sizes. Window managers also give the window title bars a certain look, such as the Motif or Open Look style. We use **exec** to launch **mwm** because **exec** will overlay the shell process with the **mwm** process, saving compute cycles, and we all know X grabs far too many cycles.

Xinit Command-Line Arguments

Xterm accepts three forms of command-line options: **xinit** options, X server options, and options to control the starting X client program (which is optionally started in place of **.xinitrc**).

For **xinit** options, you can pass a display name, with the **-display display_name** option. (See Chapter 4 for more on display names.)

xinit -display nokomis:0

After a display name you can specify an X program, such as xterm, to run in place of **.xinitrc**:

xinit xterm -geom 80x24

X server options begin after a double dash (--). Any options that follow are passed to the X server started by **xinit**. The first option passed usually determines which X server to run, such as:

xinit -- Xsun -1

Any options following the X server name, such as **-1**, are passed to the X server.

You can also specify options for the X server in a file named **.xserverrc** in your home directory.

Other Ways to Start X

Xinit is not the only way to start X. In addition to **xinit**, some vendors provide their own customized means. And X comes with a few more methods itself.

The script **startx** acts as a front end to **xinit**. On some older systems, though, **startx** acts differently, launching the programs in a file named **.startxrc**, not **.xinitrc**. The purpose of **startx** is to determine which X server to start, to find system or user **.xinitrc** files, and then to begin **xinit**. On 80386/486 systems using **X386**, **startx** determines which X server to start based on an **Xconfig** configuration file.

OpenWindows uses the program **xnews** to start the merged X11/NeWS server (see below). This server supports both the NeWS (Network-extensible Windowing System) and X Window protocols.

The **X Display Manager**, or **xdm**, provides an X-based log-in screen and controls the X server. **Xdm** is an advanced topic, which we cover in Chapter 22. If you login your workstation and see an X-based log-in screen, you're probably running **xdm**. You can also check by listing the running processes with the **ps** command and searching for **xdm**. On Berkeley-based UNIX systems, use **ps -aux**; on System V–based UNIX systems, use **ps -ef**. Note that **xdm** is normally run by the root user.

If your system does run **xdm**, *don't* run **xinit**, since they conflict. Also, on **xdm** you won't edit a **.xinitrc** file but an **.xsession** file. The **.xsession** file acts much like **.xinitrc**, but you normally have to add more commands. (See Chapter 22 for further information.)

Starting OpenWindows

Under OpenWindows **xnews** starts the X server instead of **xinit**, **startx**, or **xdm**. To make life easier, you can run the **openwin** script, which starts **xnews**, the Open Look window manager (**olwm**), and a number of X programs from Sun's DeskSet.

Before calling **openwin**, set the **OPENWINHOME** environment variable to the location of your OpenWindows directory, usually **/usr/openwin** or **/home/openwin**:

```
setenv  OPENWINHOME  /usr/openwin
```

You'll also want to set up the **LD_LIBRARY_PATH** to point to the OpenWindows library directory:

```
setenv  LD_LIBRARY_PATH  $OPENWINHOME/lib
```

If you have problems connecting to the OpenWindows X server, you may want to run **openwin** with the **-noauth** (no authorization) option. Otherwise, you shouldn't need any command-line parameters for **openwin**:

```
openwin
```

The **openwin** script will start **xnews** and then run the commands in **.xinitrc**, if you have such a file in your home directory. If not, **openwin** looks for a file named **.openwin-init** in your home directory and executes the commands in that file. The **.openwin-init** file is created by saving your workspace from **olwm**. This allows you to restart an X session like the one you last ran.

Setting Up an Account to Run X

You can set up your user account to run X on login by placing the **xinit** or **startx** commands in your **.login** file, assuming you use the C shell, **csh**. If you run the Korn shell, **ksh**, you'll need to edit your **.profile** file instead of **.login**.

You'll want to start X if you log in at the system console, your local machine. If you log in over a serial line or via **rlogin** or **telnet** over a network link (using an X terminal or a PC running X server software), you *don't* want to start X. In this case, the X server is already started, so you don't need to, and shouldn't, run **xinit**.

Your `.login` file needs to check whether you're running at the console before starting X. It also needs to set up the path to include **/usr/bin/X11**:

```
set path = ( $path /usr/bin/X11 )
if ( `tty` == "/dev/console" ) then
xinit
logout
endif
```

The first line sets the command path to include the directory **/usr/bin/X11**, and the **if** statement checks whether the process is run at the system console.

Troubleshooting Your Startup

The above example highlights a very common error experienced by new X users: trying to run **xinit** on a system already running an X server. Powerful computers can run more than one X server at a time, but each X server needs its own monitor, keyboard, and mouse. For example, if you're sitting in front of an X terminal or running X under Microsoft Windows, then the X server is already started, so you don't need to—and shouldn't—run **xinit**.

Another problem occurs when **xinit** doesn't seem to read in your **.xinitrc** file. Systems may be configured to skip your **.xinitrc** file, either in a configuration file in **/usr/lib/X11** (as is the case with Data General Aviions), or through an environment variable such as **XINITRC**.

X silently ignores many errors, so many times you're just not sure whether your change was actually used. If you copy a complex system default file into your **.xinitrc**, you might not know whether the file is set up properly to run the commands you want. In this case, we typically place a command in the **.xinitrc** file that is *very* easy to spot on the screen. The whole idea is to set up something that's obvious to see whether or not your file is going to run. Here's an example command:

```
xclock -bg red -geom 500x500+1+1 &
```

After adding this command to your **.xinitrc** file, log out and restart X. The command should start a big red clock on your display (assuming your display supports color). If you don't see it, you know that none of your commands is executing and that your **.xinitrc** file wasn't read in properly.

OpenWindows Keyboard Problems

If you're running under OpenWindows or running X on a Sun SPARCstation, you can experience keyboard problems after quitting X. To prevent that, we always run the **kbd_mode** program after exiting X:

```
kbd_mode -a
```

In fact, we usually place this command on the same command line as **xinit**:

```
xinit ; kbd_mode -a
```

If you fail to do this, your keyboard can get locked up. This requires you to log in from another terminal and kill some processes.

Setting Up the Proper Paths

One problem that might plague your system: not being able to find the executable programs in your command path. If you get a **command not found** error, this is probably the case.

The default location for X Window binary executables is in **/usr/bin/X11**. Make sure your path includes the directories where your X programs reside. With OpenWindows, the default location for X programs is in **/usr/openwin**.

Here's a list of the X executables in Release 5 on a 386/486 platform, from **/usr/bin/X11**:

X	fstobdf	showrgb	xcutsel	xkill	xrdb
X386	ico	startx	xditview	xload	xrefresh
appres	imake	twm	xdm	xlogo	xset
atobm	listres	viewres	xdpr	xlsatoms	xsetroot
auto_box	lndir	x11perf	xdpyinfo	xlsclients	xstdcmap
bdftopcf	makedepend	x11perfcomp	xedit	xlsfonts	xterm
beach_ball	maze	xauth	xev	xmag	xwd
bitmap	mkdirhier	xbiff	xeyes	xman	xwininfo
bmtoa	mkfontdir	xcalc	xfd	xmh	xwud
bsdinst	oclock	xclipboard	xfontsel	xmkmf	
editres	plbpex	xclock	xgas	xmodmap	
fs	puzzle	xcmsdb	xgc	xon	
fsinfo	resize	xcmstest	xhost	xpr	
fslsfonts	showfont	xconsole	xinit	xprop	

The Display Environment Variable

Another possible problem when starting X is the failure of applications to connect to a certain X display. In that case, the most likely cause (on your local machine) is that the DISPLAY environment variable is not set up correctly. (You might also have a problem with authorization; see Chapter 17 on Troubleshooting.)

You can look in Chapter 4 for more on the **DISPLAY** environment variable, but for now you need to set the variable to a local default name. If you're running X11 Release 4, set **DISPLAY** to **unix:0** as a default. If you're running X11 Release 5, set **DISPLAY** to **:0**. In the C shell, **csh**, for example, you can use the following command for R5:

```
setenv DISPLAY :0
```

This is one place where you need to know which version of X you're running. The best way to determine this is to check your vendor documentation or the online manual pages. Checking the manual page for X (**man X**) should help you determine your system's default-server name.

Stopping X

What good is a window system that you cannot leave? Again, just like starting X, there are many ways to get out of X.

The key to stopping the X server is to stop the key last process in the chain of X applications. For example, if you start X using **xinit**, the last process in the **.xinitrc** file is the **key process**. Normally users make a window manager, such as **mwm** or **twm**, this last, key process. Sometimes, you may have a session manager as the last process, but the concept is the same.

When you exit the window manager (from a Quit or Exit menu choice), the window manager exits. When the window manager exits, then the **.xinitrc** shell script exits. When that happens, **xinit** exits, taking the **X** process—the actual X server—with it. Of course, you can configure a different process to be the last X application in the sequence.

Stopping X on Hewlett-Packard Systems

Many Hewlett-Packard systems use a **.startxrc** file instead of the **.xinitrc** file, ending the **.startxrc** file with a command to wait for a very long time, where long is measured in years. In this configuration, the X server will effectively run forever. You stop the HP X server by pressing Control-Shift-Reset (all three keys) at the same time. If you use VUE, this won't be a problem. Your HP documentation should have more information on this.

Summary

Starting and stopping the X Window System can be a confusing process. Before you can run any X application, you need to start the X server. The X server takes over control of a display: the keyboard, a pointing device (usually a mouse), and at least one video monitor.

You start the X server with the **xinit** program. **Xinit** starts the X server, a program named **X** that's normally stored in **/usr/bin/X11**. After starting the X server, **xinit** executes the programs listed in the file **.xinitrc**, which is located in your home directory. This file lists the programs you want to start when you launch X. We cover the contents of an **.xinitrc** line by line.

There are many potential problems when starting X. The most common is trying to run **xinit** on a system already running an X server. One problem that may plague your system is not being able to find the executable programs in your command path. Another possible problem when starting X is the failure of applications to connect to a certain X display. In that case, the most likely cause (on your local machine) is that the **DISPLAY** environment variable is not set up correctly. We also cover common errors faced by OpenWindows users.

Stopping X is somewhat simpler, but it's still a somewhat hazy process. The way to stop the X server is to stop the last process in the chain of X applications. For example, if you start X using **xinit**, the last process in the **.xinitrc** file is the key process.

## Chapter 3

Using Xterm

Despite all the fuss over the X Window System's value as a graphical user interface for UNIX, we find the most frequently used X program to be **xterm**, a text-based DEC VT102 terminal emulator. **Xterm** follows most of the VT102 escape sequences, as well as Tektronix 4014 line graphics and a few extra sequences.

After all is said and done, most users still need to enter in UNIX commands at a command-shell prompt, mainly because X tools simply aren't advanced enough to hide the command prompt completely and obsolete the shells.

A **shell** in UNIX parlance is a command-line interpreter. With UNIX, you can choose which shell you want to use. These shells, such as the C shell (**/bin/csh**), the Bourne shell (**/bin/sh**), or the Korn shell (**/bin/ksh**), appear in an **xterm** window and act as if you log in to UNIX from an ASCII terminal. **Xterm** manages the interface to X so that all your old text-based programs, like the **vi** text editor or the **elm** electronic mailer, work fine inside **xterm**.

23

It seems odd to use a graphical windowing system merely for command-line windows, but **xterm** provides more than a simple command line:

- You can control **xterm**'s window size and location, fonts (and font size), as well as the foreground and background colors.
- You can have multiple **xterm** windows on screen at the same time and copy and paste between them.
- **Xterm** provides a handy scroll bar to review previous commands or the long output of complex programs. In fact, our standard X environment includes two or three very large **xterm** windows on the screen. This provides the base for a very productive software-development environment on UNIX.
- The **xterm** application is a fine X training tool, covering most of the concepts users need in order to run X effectively.
- If you like the standard 80-column-by-25-line text display, then you'll like an 80-column-by-46-line text display much better, particularly if you can have two of these side by side—a better set-up than multiple 80x25 character virtual screens.
- **Xterm** works great when editing program source files, since you can normally see a lot more of the file than a 25-line terminal allows. In addition, you can watch the status of a program while you edit text in another window. **Xterm** even has a tiny font, so you can reduce the size of the window while **make** builds your software.

This chapter concentrates on **xterm**: how to launch it, how to use it, and what can go wrong. We'll also introduce resource files and show you how to customize **xterm**. First, to take advantage of these features, you need to start up **xterm**.

Starting Xterm

You can start an **xterm** window (normally from another **xterm**) with the following command:

```
xterm &
```

This will start the **xterm** in the background. For this to work, you must be running the X server. Normally, you'll start the **xterm** in the background so you can continue to work in your current terminal. You may want to arrange your X start-up configuration to launch more than one **xterm** window—all in the background.

Xterm Shells

When **xterm** starts, it begins a UNIX shell, like **csh**, **sh**, **bash**, or **ksh**. You can change this behavior to run any UNIX program inside the **xterm** window. The default will be your preferred shell, the shell you get when you log in to UNIX.

Between the shell and **xterm** sits a **pseudo terminal**. This ensures that the UNIX shell sees the **xterm** window as a dumb terminal. Remember, **xterm** emulates a VT102 terminal. This emulation isn't perfect. If you have problems with text-based software in an **xterm** window, try changing your **TERM** environment variable to **vt100**. The following command does this in **csh**:

```
setenv TERM vt100
```

Most modern versions of UNIX and application software should handle the terminal-type **xterm** just fine, though.

Font Control

Like most X applications, **xterm** will accept a font-name command-line argument. Use either **-font** *fontname* or **-fn** *fontname*:

```
xterm -font fontname &
```

where *fontname* is the valid name of an X font installed on your system. Use **xlsfonts** to get a list of the available fonts installed on your system:

```
xlsfonts
```

If your system is fully configured, you'll see a listing of hundreds of fonts. Here's a sampling of the most common:

```
-adobe-courier-medium-o-normal—12-120-75-75-m-70-iso8859-1
-adobe-helvetica-bold-r-normal—14-140-75-75-p-82-iso8859-1
-adobe-new century schoolbook-bold-i-normal—10-100-75-75-p-
          66-iso8859-1
-adobe-symbol-medium-r-normal—24-240-75-75-p-142-adobe-
          fontspecific
-adobe-times-bold-i-normal—14-140-75-75-p-77-iso8859-1
-b&h-lucida-bold-r-normal-sans-14-140-75-75-p-92-iso8859-1
-b&h-lucidatypewriter-medium-r-normal-sans-0-0-75-75-m-0-
          iso8859-1
```

```
-bitstream-charter-bold-r-normal—19-180-75-75-p-119-iso8859-1
-daewoo-gothic-medium-r-normal—16-120-100-100-c-160-
        ksc5601.1987-0
-dec-terminal-medium-r-normal—0-0-75-75-c-0-iso8859-1
-jis-fixed-medium-r-normal—16-150-75-75-c-160-jisx0208.1983-0
-schumacher-clean-medium-r-normal—10-100-75-75-c-50-iso8859-1
-sony-fixed-medium-r-normal—16-120-100-100-c-80-
        jisx0201.1976-0
-sun-open look glyph—-10-100-75-75-p-101-sunolglyph-1
12x24kana
12x24romankana
6x13
6x13bold
8x13
8x13bold
9x15
9x15bold
cursor
decw$cursor
decw$session
fixed
variable
```

We find that a good font for regular use is:

-adobe-courier-medium-r-normal—12-120-75-75-m-70-iso8859-1

This is a fixed-width font (see Chapter 7 on fonts and decoding the long font names). We find this font more attractive than the small font named **fixed**, the default **xterm** font.

You must use a fixed-width font for regular usage with **xterm**. Variable-width fonts confuse **xterm**, resulting in poorly displayed output.

Most users don't want to type in that very long font name for every **xterm** they start up—we sure don't. There are three solutions:

- Use only the default font.
- Set the long font name into a shell-script or window-manager file.
- Change the default font name **xterm** uses to your desired name, and then use the new default font.

Setting Up an Xterm Resource File

You can change xterm defaults by using a resource file (see Chapter 6 for an in-depth introduction to resource files). You can place a file named **XTerm** in your home directory—normally with **$HOME/XTerm**. In that file, put in the following two lines:

```
*font:     -adobe-courier-medium-r-normal—12-120-75-75-m-70-
           iso8859-1
*scrollBar:  True
```

The ***font** changes the default **xterm** font. We can also change the bold font with ***boldFont**. The ***scrollBar** tells **xterm** that we always want a scroll bar, which allows you to look back over the previous output—a very handy feature when dealing with errant programs. We always use scroll bars with **xterm**.

Common Xterm Resources

Xterm supports all the core X Toolkit resources (described in Chapter 6 and a specific set unique to **xterm**). The most important ones are shown below. You can look up the rest in the **xterm** on-line manual pages. The most common **xterm** resources include:

man xterm	Calls the **xterm** main page.
iconGeometry	The size and position of the icon. Window managers may not support this.
iconName	The icon name. Defaults to the application name.
sunFunctionKeys	If *true*, **xterm** uses Sun escape codes rather than the default codes.
tek4014.height	Gives the height of the Tektronix window in pixels.
tek4014.width	Gives the width of the Tektronix window in pixels.
title	Sets the window title.
utmpInhibit	Set to *false*, **xterm** won't write a user entry into **/etc/utmp**.
vt100.allowSendEvents	If *true*, xterm accepts synthetic events sent by other programs; defaults to *false*.
vt100.autoWrap	Enables auto-wrap mode if *true*, the default.

vt100.boldFont	Names a font to use for bold text.
vt100.background	Sets the vt100 window's background color; defaults to *white*.
vt100.foreground	Sets the vt100 window's foreground, text color; defaults to *black*.
vt100.cursorColor	Sets the vt100 window's cursor color; defaults to *black*.
vt100.eightBitInput	Turns on or off eight-bit character input; useful for European languages.
vt100.eightBitOutput	Turns on or off eight-bit character output; useful for European languages.
vt100.font	Names the normal font; defaults to *fixed*.
vt100.pointerColor	Sets the foreground pointer color.
vt100.pointerShape	Names the pointer shape; defaults to *xterm*, but we prefer *gumby*.
vt100.reverseVideo	If *true*, simulates reverse video; defaults to *false*.
vt100.scrollBar	If *true*, turns on a scroll bar; defaults to *false*.
vt100.visualBell	Turns on or off the flashing visual bell; defaults to *false*.

Xterm Command-Line Options

In addition to the resources you can set in a resource file, **xterm** takes a number of command-line parameters. These parameters, when set, override whatever an X resource file contains. We introduced the **-fn** and **-font** parameters above. The more common parameters are listed below. Look in the **xterm** on-line manual pages to see the full set.

Table 3.1 Xterm command-line options.

Option	Meaning
-132	Allows 132-character mode.
-bd *color*	Sets border color; defaults to *black*.
-bg *color*	Sets background color; defaults to *white*.

Table 3.1 continued...

Option	Meaning
-bw *border_width*	Sets border width, in pixels.
-C	Tells **xterm** to take over console output.
-cn	Turns off cutting of newlines in line-mode.
+cn	Turns on (default) cutting of newlines in line-mode.
-cr *color*	Sets color of text cursor.
-cu	Turns on a mode to work around a bug in *curses*.
+cu	Turns off (default) the curses work-around.
-display *display_name*	Names which display (X server) to connect to.
-e *"program [arguments]"*	Runs the given program instead of a shell.
-fb *fontname*	Sets the bold-text font to *fontname*.
-fg *color*	Sets foreground color; defaults to *black*.
-fn *fontname*	Sets normal-text font; defaults to *fixed*.
-geometry *geometryspec*	Sets window size and location; see Chapter 5.
-help	Prints *help* message.
-iconic	Starts program as an icon.
-j	Turns on jump scrolling.
+j	Turns off jump scrolling.
-l	Logs all text output to a log file.
+l	Turns off logging.
-lf *filename*	Sets the log file to *filename*.
-ls	Turns the shell into a log-in shell.
+ls	Makes the started shell *not* a log-in shell.
-mb	Turns on margin bell.
+mb	Turns off margin bell.
-name *name*	Sets application name for grabbing resource values.
-rv	Turns on reverse video.
-sb	Turns the scroll bar on.
+sb	Turns the scroll bar off.

Table 3.1 continued...

Option	Meaning
-t	Starts in Tektronix mode rather than VT102 mode.
+t	Starts in VT102 mode, the default.
-title *title*	Sets window title.
-ut	Disables writing **/etc/utmp** entries.
+ut	Enables writing **/etc/utmp** entries.
-vb	Turns on visual (flashing) bell.
+vb	Turns off visual bell.
-xrm *resource_command*	Sets the given resource, just as if the command were in a resource file.

We often use the **-C** option to display messages sent to **/dev/console**. Without it, many systems (such as Sun's) will paint console messages across the bottom of the screen and scroll them up, which moves all the screen's pixels and messes the entire X display in the process. The usual procedure is to make a small **xterm** window to display any console messages:

```
xterm -C -geometry 80x5+1+800 -font 6x13 &
```

You can place this command in your **.xinitrc** file. You can use another program called **xconsole** to do the same thing:

```
xconsole -geometry 400x50+1+700 -font 6x13 &
```

Note that **xconsole** treats the **-geometry** width and height in units of *pixels*, not *characters*, as **xterm** does. The **6x13** font is one of the smaller fonts available under X.

On some System V UNIX platforms, especially 386 and 486 systems, **xconsole** and **xterm -C** won't work. We find that **xconsole** works better than **xterm -C** in most cases.

Running Other Programs with Xterm

The **-e** option, which runs a named program instead of a shell, adds a lot to **xterm**. For example, if you want to run the **elm** electronic-mail program and enter the **gui** mail folder, you could use the following command:

```
xterm -e elm -f=gui &
```

When you quit **elm**, the **xterm** window will also exit. Any command-line parameters following the **-e** will be passed on to the program you intend to run under **xterm**—in this case, **elm**—so the **-e** option must come last on the **xterm** command line.

If you just want to edit a file named **foo.txt**, you could use the following command:

```
xterm -e vi foo.txt &
```

We tend to use the **-e** option to **xterm** when on the screen we have an icon that calls up a program. If we don't have an X-based program to call up, we can call up an **xterm** window with our text-based program inside. When the text-based program exits, so does the **xterm**. For example, Silicon Graphics offers a program called **mailbox** that presents a picture of a mailbox on the screen. When the user clicks on the mailbox picture, **mailbox** launches a user-specified program to read the mail. Since we like the **elm** mailer, we specify a command to **mailbox** like the following:

```
xterm -e elm
```

Many other programs, such as VUE from HP or Looking Glass from Visix, allow you to launch programs from picture-based pushbuttons on the screen. Most window managers, like **mwm** or **twm**, allow you to launch programs from a menu. In all these cases, the **-e** option to **xterm** allows you to launch text-based programs under your X environment.

Logging On Remote Systems with Xterm

You can log on remote systems by extending the ability to run other programs under xterm. Simply run the rlogin program from xterm with the **-e** option. The following command runs an **xterm** window that logs in to a machine named **nokomis**:

```
xterm -e rlogin nokomis &
```

In this example, if you are computing on a machine named **nicollet**, the **xterm** process is computing on **nicollet**, as is the **rlogin** process. The **rlogin** daemon (the receiving end of **rlogin** requests) and a shell, such as **csh**, both compute on machine **nokomis**.

If you want to run any X-based programs on the remote machine **nokomis** and have them display on your local machine **nicollet**, you'll need to set the **DISPLAY** environment variable. See the next chapter for more on this topic.

Resizing Xterm Windows

When you resize an **xterm** window, the number of lines and columns are likely to change. Unfortunately, most text-based software you run inside the **xterm** window won't detect this change. Some systems send a **SIGWINCH** signal, but you cannot depend on this. You must therefore run the **resize** program after you've resized an **xterm** window.

Resize outputs the shell commands, so you normally need to **alias resize**. In the C shell, you can use the following:

```
alias rs 'set noglob; eval `resize` '
```

Note that we placed a space after `resize` and before the single-quote (`'`). After resizing the window, run the alias:

```
rs
```

If you run the Bourne shell, **sh**, you can use the following commands:

```
resize -u  > /tmp/foo
 . /tmp/foo
```

Two more rules to follow when resizing **xterm**s:

- Virtually all UNIX text-based programs assume a width of 80 characters. If you intend to run text-based software inside an **xterm** window, you should keep the width at 80 characters.
- Few text-based programs seem to detect the **SIGWINCH** signal on those systems that send it, so you should be at a shell prompt before resizing an **xterm** window. If you're running the **vi** text editor, you should quit **vi** before resizing the window. Restart **vi** after running the **resize** program, as shown above.

Xterm Variants

Xterm isn't the only X-based program that provides a command-line shell. IBM pushes **aixterm**— many **aixterm**s, in fact—one of which acts like **xterm**. Hewlett-Packard has **hpterm**, Sun **cmdtool**, SCO **pcterm**, and Silicon Graphics **xwsh** (or just plain **wsh**). These programs provide compatibility with previous windowing systems and theoretically add value to the vendors' workstations. We find these programs problematic, because they can be considered standard on one platform only, and normally they don't work well with **xterm**. **Xterm**, in contrast, runs on *every* UNIX-based X platform.

The bottom line: Use whatever you see fit. We recommend using a straight **xterm** instead of the proprietary equivalents.

Setting Xterm's Title

As you populate your X screen with more and more **xterm** windows—some computing on your current workstation, some computing on various machines across the network—it's easy to get confused as to what's what. One method to identify your windows is to set the title (shown in the window manager's title bar) to display the current directory, user name, and hostname. You can set the **xterm** title by using an escape sequence. Normally, when **xterm** changes its title, the window manager will then update the title bar. There are three **xterm** title-setting escape sequences:

Table 3.2 Xterm escape sequences.

Escape Sequence	Meaning
<ESC>]0; *string* **<BELL>**	Set xterm icon and window name to *string* x
<ESC>]1; *string* **<BELL>**	Icon name only x
<ESC>]2; *string* **<BELL>**	Window name only x

In the above chart, **<ESC>** is the escape character (ASCII 27), **<BELL>** is the bell character (ASCII 7), and **_string_** is whatever text string you want for the title.

We usually set up an alias in our **.cshrc** file (in the C shell, obviously) to set up the **xterm** title. We call the alias **xcd**, to differentiate it from the normal **cd**. (We could alias **cd**, but this causes problems if you log in over a text-only link, such as **telnet**, or via a serial line. The **xterm** title-changing escape sequence also seems to lock up an OpenWindows program called **cmdtool**.)

The **xcd** alias changes your current directory (just as **cd** does), then displays the current user name (the result of **whoami**), the machine name (from **hostname**), and the current working directory, from **$cwd**. As you log onto other machines over a network, it becomes tough to keep track of which **xterm** window is running on which machine, so the title bar really keeps things clear. (Some versions of UNIX do not support **whoami**. Also, you may need to use **uname** rather than **hostname**. If you have problems, you'll need to tune this alias to your system.)

Here's our alias in the **.cshrc** file:

```
alias xcd      `cd \!* ; echo -n "^[]2; `whoami`@`hostname`  $cwd^G" `
```

Entering the Escape sequence and **^G** in most text editors can be tough. In **vi**, go into insert mode, then type **^V** (Control-v), then Control-*[* (^*[*) for escape. You can do Control-G (bell) the same way: Type Control-V, then Control-G.

Setting the Title Bar in Cmdtool

OpenWindows on Sun SPARC machines comes with an **xterm**-like program called **cmdtool**. **Xterm** simply doesn't fit the OpenWindows style; in fact, OpenWindows hides **xterm** in the **demo** directory, **/usr/openwin/demo**. **Cmdtool**, based on its SunView roots, uses a different escape sequence to change its title.

Note that the **xterm** title sequence seems to lock up a **cmdtool** window. The proper **cmdtool** sequence is:

```
<ESC>]l string <ESC>\
```

Type Escape, **]**, lowercase *l*, your **string** to set the new title to, then Escape, \.

Copy and Paste with Xterm

We find that using **xterm** with **vi** works fine for general-purpose text editing. (Of course, use **emacs** or **epoch** or whatever is your cup of tea.)

While **vi** doesn't have the perfect interface, the ability to paste chunks of text dramatically improves **vi** and any other text-based UNIX program. **Xterm**'s copy-and-paste ability sits on top of any text-based applications. To your applications, pasting text looks just like the user typed in that text very quickly. This is both a boon and a problem. It helps because you don't have to modify any of the older programs, like **vi**, to accept pasted text. However, since the programs run under the shell (under **xterm**), they don't know about the X pointer (mouse) and don't understand about copying and pasting.

Thus you sometimes have to play a few tricks. With **vi**, for example, don't paste until you're in insert mode. Once in insert mode, you can press the middle mouse button to paste any selected text. **Vi** reacts just as if you typed the text into the window.

Selecting Text

Select text by dragging the mouse with the left button held down (**xterm** displays this text in reverse video). With the X Window System's active copy and paste, only one area on the screen can own the **PRIMARY** selection at a time. Only one area will be highlighted with reverse video.

Open Look applications such as **cmdtool** normally use the **CLIPBOARD** selection, which makes it tough to copy and paste between normal X applications (including Motif programs) and XView applications. The program **xclipboard** can help you translate from one selection to the other. If you're brave, you can also configure **xterm** to use the **CLIPBOARD** selection rather than the **PRIMARY** selection (see below).

To select a long section of text, hold the left-most mouse button down and drag. Double-click to select one word. Triple-click to select a whole line. In Motif applications, at least, quadruple-click to select all the text. (These are the default configurations. As with most things in X, you can change them.)

To paste, move the mouse into the destination window and then click the middle mouse button. If you selected text that went to the end of a line, you'll get a carriage return in the pasted text. This makes a difference when you're pasting text to form a UNIX command. That embedded return may cause an incomplete command to be executed, so watch out.

With many 386 versions of UNIX, if you try to paste more than four lines, you may overrun the streams buffers and lock up your **xterm** window. (You can modify a kernel parameter to allocate more space to the streams buffers—and we recommend this—but you cannot always guarantee that this system-administration task has been done.)

Copy and Paste in OpenWindows

The X Window System's active copy and paste is based on **selections**. Each selection in X has a name. The selection that's used most often for copy and paste is called **PRIMARY** (the name is all uppercase), as we mentioned above. There are a few other selections commonly used for copy and paste.

The selection **SECONDARY** is used when you need to swap the **PRIMARY** selection with something else. The **CLIPBOARD** selection is supposed to be used by a clipboard application, such as **xclipboard**, to store multiple selections. But many OpenWindows programs use the **CLIPBOARD** selection in place of the **PRIMARY** selection for regular copy and paste. If you run primarily under OpenWindows, you may want to change **xterm** to use the **CLIPBOARD** selection. This is generally easier than changing all the OpenWindows programs to use **PRIMARY**, because many OpenWindows programs cannot be changed at all.

You can place the following resource-setting commands in the **XTerm** file described above—that is, in **$HOME/XTerm**, the file named **XTerm** in your home directory:

```
XTerm*VT100.translations: #override\n\
Shift <KeyPress> Select: select-cursor-start() \
                        select-cursor-end(CLIPBOARD,
         CUT_BUFFER0) \n\
Shift <KeyPress> Insert: insert-selection(CLIPBOARD,
         CUT_BUFFER0) \n\
  ~Ctrl ~Meta <Btn2Up>: insert-selection(CLIPBOARD,
         CUT_BUFFER0) \n\
  <BtnUp>:  select-end(CLIPBOARD, CUT_BUFFER0)
```

To convert back to using the **PRIMARY** selection, replace the word **CLIPBOARD** with **PRIMARY** in the above example.

Note that **xterm** should copy and paste just fine with Motif applications.

N O T E

Using Xclipboard

When you need to copy and paste more than one selection at a time, X provides a useful program named **xclipboard**. **Xclipboard** holds multiple **CLIPBOARD** selections, only one of which is active at any one time.

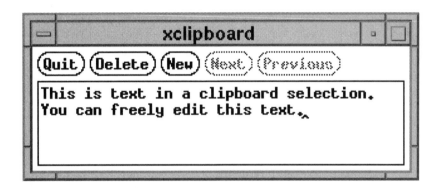

Figure 3.1 The xclipboard.

With **xclipboard** you can paste the text you selected from an **xterm** window. Then you can use **xterm** to select other text. Whenever you need to use the first text again, you can select it from the **xclipboard** window. Thus you can cycle through multiple selections of text.

The New button in **xclipboard** allows you to get a fresh (blank) area on which to paste text. You can also edit text directly in **xclipboard**. The Next and Previous buttons allow you to cycle through all the chunks of text that **xclipboard** holds.

Xterm Menus

Xterm provides four pop-up menus that allow you to change its settings while **xterm** is running. You call up these menus, by default, by holding down the Control key along with a mouse button. Most of the menu choices are self-explanatory. The ones that aren't are usually so obscure that most users never need to use them.

The Ctrl–left mouse button calls up the **Main Options** menu.

Table 3.3 Choices on the Main Options menu.

Secure Keyboard	Allow SendEvents
Log To File	Redraw Window
Send STOP Signal	Send CONT Signal
Send INT Signal	Send HUP Signal
Send TERM Signal	Send KILL Signal
Quit	

The Ctrl–middle mouse button calls up the **VT Options** menu.

Table 3.4 Choices on the VT Options menu.

Enable Scrollbar	Enable Jump Scroll
Enable Reverse Video	Enable Auto Wraparound
Enable Reverse Wraparound	Enable Auto Linefeed
Enable Application Cursor Keys	Enable Application Keypad
Scroll to Bottom on Key Press	Scroll to Bottom on Tty Output
Allow 80/132 Column Switching	Enable Curses Emulation
Enable Visual Bell	Enable Margin Bell
Show Alternate Screen	Do Soft Reset
Do Full Reset	Reset and Clear Saved Lines
Show Tek Window	Switch to Tek Window
Hide VT Window	

If you want to run Tektronix 4014 graphics, you'll find the *Show Tek Window* option useful. The options that are enabled will have a check-mark in the left margin.

The Ctrl–right mouse button calls up the **VT Fonts** menu.

Table 3.5 Choices on the VT Fonts menu.

✓ Default	Unreadable
Tiny	Small
Medium	Large
Huge	Escape Sequence
Selection	

The VT Fonts menu is the most useful menu provided by **xterm**. A very common use of this menu is to change the **xterm** font to a very small font, either **Unreadable** or **Tiny**, when executing a long software build process using **make**. With the **Tiny** font you can still read the output.

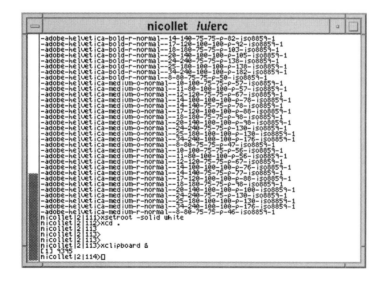

Figure 3.2 Xterm's Tiny font.

With the **Unreadable** font, though, you merely see marks for characters; you cannot read individual letters. Most programmers quickly recognize good and bad **make** output, though, so you can shrink down an **xterm** window and look at just the shape of the output. The following output shows a good build with **make**.

Figure 3.3 Make under xterm.

The following output, however, shows that **make** detected some error.

Figure 3.4 Make with errors under xterm.

Using this technique, you can save on-screen real estate and still watch your programs build.

Inside the Tektronics window, the Ctrl–middle mouse button calls up the Tek Options menu:

Table 3.6 Choices on the Tek Options menu.

Large Characters	#2 Size Characters
#Size Characters	Small Characters
PAGE	RESET
COPY	Show VT Window
Switch to VT Window	Hide Tek Window

Summary

The most frequently used X Window program is **xterm**, a text-based terminal emulator. Most X users still need to enter in UNIX commands at a command-shell prompt, as most X tools aren't advanced enough to hide the command prompt completely and obsolete the UNIX shells.

Xterm provides many advantages for the X user: multiple **xterm** windows can be used for multiple editing sessions, and a scroll bar can be used to review previous commands.

After starting an **xterm** window (**xterm &**) in the background, you can run any number of UNIX shells (**csh**, **sh**, **bash**, or **ksh**). You can change **xterm** defaults by adding a separate resource file. We use this file to set the font and add scroll bars as the default.

In addition to the resources you can set in a resource file, **xterm** takes a number of command-line parameters. These parameters can override whatever is in an X resource file. Many are very handy; for instance, the **-e** option runs a named program instead of a shell. Using this option, you can log on remote to systems by extending the ability to run other programs; simply run the **rlogin** program with the **-e** option.

When you resize an **xterm** window, the number of lines and columns are likely to change. You must therefore run the **resize** program after you've resized an **xterm** window.

Xterm isn't the only X-based program that provides a command-line shell. IBM pushes **aixterm**—many **aixterm**s, in fact, one of which acts like **xterm**. Hewlett-Packard has **hpterm**, Sun **cmdtool**, SCO **pcterm**, and Silicon Graphics **xwsh** (or just plain **wsh)**. We advise using the straight X **xterm** unless there are compelling reasons to use the proprietary equivalents.

When computing across a network with multiple windows running on various machines, it's easy to get confused as to what's what. One method to identify your windows is to set the title (shown in the window manager's title bar) to display the current directory, user name, and hostname.

When editing files, the ability to copy and paste between **xterm** windows greatly enhances productivity for the end user. We covered the main methods for copying and pasting within X, Motif, and OpenWindows (Open Look).

When you need to copy and paste more than one selection at a time, X provides a useful program named **xclipboard**. **Xclipboard** holds multiple CLIPBOARD selections, only one of which is active at any one time.

Xterm provides four pop-up menus that allow you to change their settings while **xterm** is running. You call up these menus, by default, by holding down the Ctrl key along with a mouse button. Most of the menu choices are self-explanatory.

II

Conquering X

This section concentrates on the areas in X that present the most problems for beginning and intermediate X Window System users:

- Logging onto remote machines on a network;
- Customizing applications with command-like parameters;
- Customizing applications by setting resources; and
- Creating, installing, and using fonts.

Chapter *4*

Being in Two Places at One Time

G etting X programs to run can be daunting. Getting X programs to run across a network can seem nearly impossible, especially when you see the dreaded **X Toolkit Error: Can't Open display** message.

The whole notion of running programs on one machine, while displaying (and interacting with) programs on another machine, confuses many who first approach X. Yet the ability to run applications across a network is one of X's greatest strengths. This ability is something that Microsoft Windows and the Macintosh don't support. Really, though, these programs are not all that hard, just confusing at times. (Remember: If X programs didn't actually work, most X terminals couldn't function at all.)

The basic idea is simple: You can run X applications on other remotely networked machines and yet interact with these programs while sitting at your desk, working with your keyboard, monitor, and mouse. That is, you can sit at a Sun SPARC-2 (running X, of course) and execute programs on an IBM PS/2 running Desqview/X. If you set it up correctly, the PS/2 programs will display on your Sun monitor, and you can type input into the program with your keyboard.

Even on a stand-alone workstation, X divides up the tasks for graphical windowing among a number of processes connected over a "network." (Why the quotes? Because in this case the traditional notion of a network doesn't apply, as you're doing all the work on one workstation.) The Xserver process draws the dots on your monitor and reads the mouse and keyboard for input. Your Xapplication processes, called clients, connect up to the X server over some form of networking (or interprocess communication) stream, and ask the server to draw particular dots in particular places. You're always using at least two processes: the server and at least one client.

The next step is to divide the tasks over the actual network. Instead of running FrameMaker on the Sun at your desk, you can run it on a Data General Aviion— but you don't have to get up and walk over to the Aviion. You can remain at the same keyboard. Some people go to extremes and even run their remote X applications in another country.

The trick, now, is that you have to tell the programs that compute on the Aviion to connect to the X server on the Sun, *not* the server (or servers) on the Aviion.

Normally you must run at least one of these distributed processes at your desk, on the X server itself. If you sit at a workstation or X terminal, the X server must access the actual frame buffer and other proprietary hardware on your desk. (Although it may seem fun to attack someone else's frame buffer directly, this usually isn't considered proper etiquette.) This is why you usually run a program like **xinit** (which starts the X server) on your local machine and not remotely. You run clients, like **xterm** or **xclock**, on the remote machine. Using an X terminal makes all of this easier, since most X terminals don't run anything more than the server locally, as all X clients are normally remote to an X terminal.

Generally, you need to figure out the name of the X server you want to connect to, and then you tell your X programs that name.

Naming Names

Most X servers are named with the hostname of the machine running the X server:

hostname:server_number.screen_number

If your workstation has a hostname of **nokomis**, the standard X server display name will be:

nokomis:0.0

The single colon (**:**) denotes Ethernet-style networking with TCP (or UNIX domain) streams. Two colons (**::**) denote DECnet protocols. The **0** stands for the first X server on machine **nokomis**.

The optional **.0** tells the computer to use the first screen on the given display or X server. Screens can be confusing, but a screen is really just a physical monitor. Most workstations have only one monitor, so you almost always use the screen number **.0**. A single X server, however, can control a number of monitors at once. These systems are often referred to as **multiheaded** systems.

The word display, too, is poor terminology, since display seems to mean the same thing as a monitor or screen, but in X jargon a display (X server) is at least one screen (CRT monitor) along with a keyboard and a pointing device (usually a mouse).

The Display Environment Variable

The **DISPLAY** environment variable contains the name of the default X server. This is the X server name used by most X programs, unless you explicitly state otherwise (see below). Normally, this should be the name of the machine that sits on your desk. To set the **DISPLAY** environment variable to the first server and the first screen on a machine named **nokomis**, you can use the following command (in the C shell, **csh**):

setenv DISPLAY nokomis:0.0

Many systems allow a sort of generic name, **unix:0**. This usually means you have a workstation and are running X applications locally. (Programmer's note: The **unix:0** display name tells the **XOpenDisplay** function to connect using UNIX domain streams, so don't expect the **unix:0** name to work across networks.) With Release 5 of the X Window System, the default generic name switched from **unix:0** to a simple **:0**.

Passing Display Names on the Command Line

You can also pass the name of an X server on the command line. Most X programs recognize the **-display** option. For example, here's how you tell the **xterm** program to appear on the X server on machine **nokomis**:

```
xterm -display nokomis:0.0
```

Automatically Setting the Display Variable

You can set the **DISPLAY** environment variable automatically on a remote machine when using the remote shell, **rsh** (also called **remsh** on some System V-based systems, to avoid confusion with the restricted shell). **Rsh** launches a shell on the remote machine and can run an X application from that shell. To run an **xterm** on a remote machine, but have the **xterm** appear on your display, you can use a command like:

```
rsh -n xterm -display $DISPLAY
```

This tells **rsh** to run the command **xterm -display $DISPLAY**, where **$DIS-PLAY** is the value of your local **DISPLAY** environment variable. Once this **xterm** is running, you can easily launch programs on the remote machine from that **xterm**, since the **xterm** has a shell on that machine, which will connect up to the X server on your local machine. (Really!) To run this command successfully, though, you may need to mess with files like **/etc/hosts.equiv** and **.rhosts** to set the proper permissions. (Check your UNIX manual for details.)

In addition, the shell on the remote machine might not know where the **xterm** program resides, so you might need a command like:

```
rsh -n /usr/bin/X11/xterm -display $DISPLAY
```

The **xterm** program is normally placed in **/usr/bin/X11**, but it might not be on your system, especially if you're running X on a 386/486-based UNIX system. Under OpenWindows, **xterm** is located in **/usr/openwin/demo**.

When you use **rsh** to spawn a shell on the remote system, you are using a good chunk of that system's resources. First, you have a shell on that machine, and then you add in an **xterm**. There's a great debate over whether this is more or less efficient than simply using **rlogin** or **telnet** to log on to the remote machine from a locally run **xterm**. There are persuasive arguments on both sides of the issue, so choose whatever method you can most easily use.

What Can Go Wrong

To connect you to an X server, your X programs need the proper permissions. Luckily, security in X generally follows the typically lax UNIX model. X servers have a list of machines (hostnames) that are allowed to connect. To allow X programs on a remote machine to connect to your local X server, you need to run the **xhost** program locally. The command:

xhost nicollet

will allow X programs computing remotely on the machine named **nicollet** to connect to your *local* X server, the X server at your desk.

As in the UNIX community, some users are finding they need more security, and there is an X authorization system that uses the program **xauth**. Ask your system administrator for more information if you use this or a more restrictive means for security.

Summary

One of X's most wonderful features is its ability to run programs on any machine on a given network. In this chapter we reviewed the process of logging onto a remote machine:

- Set the **DISPLAY** environment variable;
- Pass the name of an X server on the command line;
- Set the **DISPLAY** environment variable automatically on a remote machine when using the remote shell, **rsh**.

We also discussed the various things that can do wrong when trying to connect to remote machines.

## Chapter 5

X Command-Line Parameters

B ecause X Window System designers adopted a philosophy of mechanism, not policy, virtually everything within X can be configured by the end user (as well as the programmer and system administrator). To that end, there are literally hundreds of options available within X. In an effort to simplify the conceptual load on X users who may want to make global changes, most X applications accept a standard set of command-line parameters. (In theory, end users should worry about the application, not the underlying framework.) These parameters deal with colors, sizes, locations, fonts, and icons.

Yes, there are X programs that also accept parameters that deal with program-specific options. The OpenWindows **cmdtool**, for example, still uses the command-line parameters of the older SunView **cmdtool**. The Silicon Graphics **wsh** still accepts the older 4-D command-line parameters, although SGI does offer **xwsh**, which accepts the X command-line parameters.

To determine whether a program requires a toolkit-specific parameter, though, the user must determine what toolkit was used to create an application and then determine what options are standardized for a given toolkit. This, quite frankly, is an annoyance. Yes, vendors want to maintain backward compatibility with programs created before X became a standard, but at some point users have to draw a line in the sand and demand a standard set of command-line parameters. We advise users to ignore toolkit-specific parameters, we advise system administrators to avoid configurations where toolkit-specific parameters are necessary, and we advise programmers to avoid toolkit-specific parameters.

Instead, follow the lead of most X programs (including Motif programs) and support the standard set of X command-line parameters.

X Command-Line Parameters

Most X programs accept a standard set of command-line parameters, as listed in Table 5.1.

Table 5.1 Standard command-line parameters.

Parameter	Meaning
-background *color*	Sets window background color.
-bd *color*	Sets window border color.
-bg *color*	Sets window background color.
-bordercolor *color*	Sets window border color.
-borderwidth *border_width*	Sets window border width, in pixels.
-bw *border_width*	Sets window border width, in pixels.
-display *display_name*	Names which display (X server) to connect to.
-fg *color*	Sets foreground color.

Table 5.1 continued...

Parameter	Meaning
-fn *fontname*	Sets font.
-font *fontname*	Sets font.
-foreground *color*	Sets foreground color.
-geometry *geometryspec*	Sets window size and location.
-iconic	Starts program as an icon.
-name *name*	Sets application name for grabbing resource values.
-reverse	Turns on reverse video.
-rv	Turns on reverse video.
-selectionTimeout *timeout_value*	Sets the amount of time to wait, in milliseconds, for copy-and-paste operations between programs.
-synchronous	Turns on synchronous debugging mode.
-title *title*	Sets window title.
-xnllanguage *language[terr][.code]*	Sets language, and optionally territory and codeset for current locale.
-xrm *resource_command*	Sets the given resource, just as in a resource file.

We described the **-display** parameter in the last chapter. We'll cover color names in Chapter 12, and X resource-setting commands, with the **-xrm** parameter, in the next chapter. For now, the most complex command-line parameter is the geometry specification.

Setting the Window Geometry

A window's **geometry** is its size and location. You can start X programs at a certain location with a given size. To do this, use the **-geometry** command-line parameter, which you can also abbreviate as **-geom**. The **-geometry** parameter should be followed by the desired geometry for the window. This geometry is specified in a stylized manner, as follows:

[=][Width x Height][{+/-}XOffset{+/-}YOffset]

The use of the leading equal sign (=) is now considered obsolete and is officially discouraged. (Older systems may still use the equal sign, though.) The width and height values are normally measured in pixels. **Xterm** is one exception; it uses characters as a measurement. The pixel size is then determined by the size of **xterm's** default font.

The best way to figure out these geometries is though examples. Typical geometries include the following:

-geometry 300x200+15+5

For a 300-by-200 pixel window, place the window at coordinates x = 15, y = 5, from the upper left corner (origin) of the window.

-geometry 450x200

Make the window 450 pixels wide by 200 pixels high.

-geometry 100x200-35+5

Here, the negative *x* coordinate means to position the *right* edge of the window 35 pixels from the *right* edge of the screen. A positive *x* coordinate means to position the *left* edge of the window *x* pixels from the left edge of the screen.

The *y* coordinate is positioned using similar rules. A positive *y* value means to position the top of the window *y* pixels from the top of the screen. A negative *y* value means to position the *bottom* of the window *y* pixels above the bottom of the . screen.

This leads to some odd contortions when specifying the corners of the display, as seen in Table 5.2.

Table 5.2 Specifying the corner of the display.

Geometry	Meaning
+0+0	upper left corner
+0-0	lower left corner
-0+0	upper right corner
-0-0	lower right corner

Examples with Xlogo and Xterm

The best way to master the X Window System's strange set of command-line parameters is to play with some examples. We'll use a simple X program called **xlogo**. **Xlogo** has nothing to do with the programming language Logo; instead, **xlogo** displays the logo of the X Window System, a stylized letter X. You'll recognize it immediately; vendors seem to think that no one will recognize the X Window System unless an X logo is present on a display, so every product shot involving X Window-related hardware and software includes an **xlogo** running.

The following example starts **xlogo** with a very wide window and changes its colors:

```
xlogo -geometry 500x60  -foreground yellow -bg black &
```

Figure 5.1 The first xlogo example.

The next command starts **xlogo** as an icon:

```
xlogo -iconic &
```

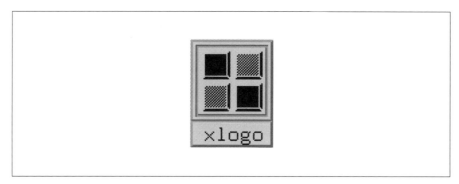

Figure 5.2 Xlogo as an icon.

The last example starts an **xterm** window in reverse video mode (white text on a black background) and sets this window's title:

```
xterm -rv -title "This is in Reverse Video" &
```

If you're not sure how these command-line parameters work, we suggest you experiment until you feel confident. These command-line parameters are especially useful when creating X start-up files.

Summary

There's really not much to summarize, is there? Command-line parameters allow you to customize your X applications. We have listed the most common parameters and have guided you through a few examples to familiarize you with the process.

## Chapter 6

Customizing Applications with Resources

One of the oft-ignored features of the X Window System is the high amount of customization possible through the use of **resources**. X resource files provide a powerful means to customize X applications *without* any programming.

The designers of X must have liked the term *resources*, as it means a great many things in X documentation. In this book, though, we'll describe resources as a handy means to change the default settings of an X program. These resources apply to programs built with the X Toolkit (Xt) Intrinsics, such as **xterm**, **xclock**, and other Athena widget programs, Open Look applications built with OLIT (but not XView), and all Motif programs. A few other toolkits also support X resources.

As we've pointed out in previous chapters, X is still to a great extent a programmer's windowing system. The user of resources is just one more example. There's really no way for users to discover exactly which toolkit was used to build an application, unless you have that application's source code. Yet these X resources may not apply at all for X programs built with certain toolkits. You can make some good guesses, though, and most X applications do accept resource-setting commands in resource files.

Application vendors should document the resources that are available for customization. If your vendors haven't taken this basic step, complain *loudly* to them.

Resources are a means to control applications from the outside, at the so-called user level, without resorting to programming. Setting resources externally has many advantages, but it gets really confusing when you try to figure out the dizzying array of options you have available for setting resources values. (When your head starts to spin, don't say we don't warn you!)

Widgets and Resources

X programs built on top of the Xt Intrinsics, such as the ones mentioned above, are made up of widgets—interface elements like scrollbars, menus, pushbuttons, and text-entry areas. Every one of these widgets is controlled by a set of resources that modify its behavior. These resources tell the widget the color of the text, the font size, whether scroll bars appear (and where they appear), how wide borders around objects should be, and so on.

You can customize each widget's resources. Most X applications are made up of hundreds of widgets, though, so you don't want to customize every one. Instead, you can customize classes of resources and set values at a global level for a given X application. For example, you can set the font used by the ubiquitous **xterm** by using the **font** resource.

Every widget has a **name** and a **class**. If you know the name of a widget or its type (class), you can modify that widget's resources, customizing the application. You can set resources in an application using either method, or both. (The best way to determine what resources are available for changing is to look up an application's documentation.)

The neat thing about these resources is that you can change them without having access to any source code. In addition, you can change the customizations every time you run applications—on the fly, so to speak.

You can also use resources to maintain systemwide consistency between applications. Perhaps you want the foreground and background colors to be inverted. Perhaps you need to use very large fonts for better visibility. Perhaps you want different colors instead of the defaults. (Motif, for example, defaults to blue backgrounds.) It's all possible.

Five Ways to Set Resource Values

There are five basic ways to set resource values:

1. In a **user-resource file**. This is a text file that contains resource-setting commands. These files are called user-resource files, since they are usually set up by the user. These files can reside in a number of places, which we'll go into later. The resource-setting commands in these files can apply to any X application.

2. In a **class-resource file**. This is also a text file that contains resource-setting commands. However, these commands apply just to one application class. For example, XTerm is the class name for the **xterm** application. Usually, these class-resource files are used to set resources on an application-wide basis. That is, you may want to set up all **xterm** programs to act in a certain way. To do so, you could use a class-resource file. System administrators may want to set up class-resource files to establish systemwide standards and make life easier for the users.

3. In the **RESOURCE_MANAGER property** on the root window, or the **SCREEN_RESOURCES property** (for color information). These properties are created by the standard X Window program called **xrdb**. You can use **xrdb** to add the resource values you want to this **RESOURCE_MANAGER** property. You may want to use **xrdb** if you're using an X terminal that doesn't have its own file system.

4. In **command-line parameters** passed to the program.

5. **Inside a program**, by hard-coding the resource values. This is a topic that programmers need to deal with. Look in Appendix A for a listing of X programming books.

Setting Resource Values

There are a number of ways to set resource values. All resource-setting involves identifying the resource to set and then providing the new value for that resource.

A colon (:) separates the two parts. This will become clearer as you look at the line below.

```
name_what_we_want_to_set : value_to_set
```

All resource-setting is done using text strings. Sounds easy, right? Yes, it is—but if you make a mistake, the X toolkit just doesn't care. Most resource errors are silently ignored. If you make a mistake, you could have a very hard time figuring out what went wrong. This makes the already tough process of resource-setting tougher. Some relief is available in X11 Release 5, though, and we will cover that below.

Another tough part is naming exactly what you want to set. The key here is finding the name of the resource you want to set. Then you need to find the acceptable values for that resource.

Naming the Resources You Want to Set

Most X applications should come with a documented list of available resources. Finding this list is not always easy, but normally you can use the UNIX **man** command to view the on-line manual pages. The program **xterm**, for example, lists a number of resources, such as **font**, **background**, **foreground**, **cursorColor**, **pointerShape**, and **scrollBar** in the **xterm** on-line manual pages. Other sources of information include documentation-browsing programs, such as IBM's InfoExplorer and Sun's AnswerBook, as well as other manuals that came with your system. (When in doubt, read the manual.)

Setting Resources for the Xterm Program

With **xterm**, you can change the normal foreground (black) and background (white) colors. The resource-setting commands would be:

```
xterm*background:  lightgrey
xterm*foreground:  red
```

Xterm*background represents what we want to set, and **lightgrey** is the value we want the resource to take.

The above example, as you've probably guessed, sets the background color to lightgrey and the foreground color to red. (See Chapter 12 for more on X color names.) The asterisk (*) is a wildcard. The result: For applications with the resource name *xterm*, set all foreground resources to *red*. (Remember the **-name** command-line parameter from last chapter? This can be used to change the resource name for X applications. The default resource name is usually the program name, such as **xterm**.)

We used the wildcard, since we don't know all the widget names buried in the **xterm** program, nor do we really want to. (Otherwise, we could fully specify the names of the widgets.) To do this, you need to specify the whole naming hierarchy with a period between each name. For example:

```
app_name.child_widget.grandchild.resource_to_set:     value
```

Normally, you won't know (or be able to find out) all the widget names buried in an X program, so you'll need to use wildcards. Use wildcards with care, since you can easily change more than you want to. The following example sets the **foreground** resource to red—for *everything*:

```
*foreground: red
```

Of course, it isn't as simple as this, since the above resource-setting command may appear only in a class-resource file, which would then apply only to all applications of the given class. If you placed the above command in your **.Xdefaults** file, every foreground would be red. Bottom line: Be careful with wildcards in setting resource values.

Resource names themselves also have class names. The class names are usually the resource name with the first letter capitalized, such as **Foreground**, the class name for the resource **foreground**.

```
xterm*Foreground:    red
```

Specific names—"lowercase," for example—take precedence over the class names. The following list goes from general to specific:

```
*foreground:         red
XTerm*foreground:    blue
xterm*foreground:    green
```

With this set of resource-setting commands, **xterm** will start with a green foreground.

Resource Files

How do we get **xterm** to recognize our resource-setting commands? We create a resource file, which contains resource-setting commands.

A resource file is an ISO Latin-1 (an extension of ASCII) text file that contains resource-setting commands. To be useful, a resource file needs to be located in a place where your Xt-based applications will look for it. What isn't so obvious is where all the possible resource files can reside. The following are traditional places your applications will search. (In addition to resource files, you can place resource-setting commands on properties on the root window and in command-line parameters.)

Possibility #1:

```
/usr/lib/X11/$LANG/app-defaults/Class, or
/usr/lib/X11/app-defaults/Class
```

Class is the name of an application class. **$XFILESEARCHPATH**, if set, overrides **/usr/lib/X11/app-defaults**.

Possibility #2:

```
$XUSERFILESEARCHPATH/Class
$XAPPLRESDIR/$LANG Class
$XAPPLRESDIR Class
$HOME/$LANG/Class
$HOME/Class
```

Class is the name of an application class, such as **XTerm**.

Possibility #3:

RESOURCE_MANAGER property on the root window, or, if not present, **$HOME/.Xdefaults**

Possibility #4:

$XENVIRONMENT, or if not set,

$HOME/.Xdefaults-*hostname*

Possibility #5:

Program command-line parameters, such as the **-xrm** parameter.

The files are searched in the order above. If the same resource is set more than once, the last value remains. In addition, resource commands that use direct names have precedence over class-resource values.

$LANG is used for internationalization. **$XFILESEARCHPATH** should be a path name. So should **$XUSERFILESEARCHPATH** and **$XAPPLRESDIR**. **$XAPPLRES-DIR** must end with a slash character, /. An example: **/users/erc/resources/**.

The above list demonstrates that there are many different locations to remember. We therefore strongly advise you not to use the X environment variables unless you really need to. These environment variables often serve only to complicate matters. They become useful in very specialized circumstances, so, unless you really need them, avoid them.

RESOURCE_MANAGER and **SCREEN_RESOURCES** properties can override the **$HOME/.Xdefaults** file. Many installations, though, use the **xrdb** program to load in the contents of the **.Xdefaults** file into the **RESOURCE_MANAGER** property, negating the difference.

Class is the name of an application class. The class of the **xterm** application, for example, is **XTerm**. (Most class names start with an upper-case letter, and ones that start with X usually have the first two letters in uppercase.)

Since everyone's X system is different, we're not going to cover all the possible resource files and locations in detail. We're going to concentrate instead on the syntax of resource-setting commands. You can then use these resource-setting commands with any resource files you care to set up.

Class-Resource Files

There are two basic types of resource files, class-and user-resource files.

Class-resource files pertain to applications of the same class. This really means that class-resource files pertain to separate applications, since most applications have their own class. For example, the **xterm** application that most X users use all the time has a class of **XTerm**.

A class resource file for the *XTerm* class would only pertain to the **xterm** application. For example, say you wanted all **xterms** to use a different font. You could set up a resource file that contains the following line:

```
xterm*font:   9x15
```

Name this file **XTerm** (that is, the class name is the filename) and place it in your home directory. Since this file is a class-resource file, the following commands would all act the same:

```
*font:        9x15
XTerm*font:   9x15
```

The first command sets all resources named *font*—for all applications—to have the value of *9x15*, which happens to be the name of a font. Since this appears only in a class-resource file, no other X applications will see the resource-setting command.

The second command sets the resource for applications with the class name *XTerm*.

Motif applications use the resource **fontList** to set font names, while Athena widget programs (which include the standard X programs like **xterm** and **xclipboard**) use the resource **font**. It's easy to confuse **fontList** with **font**, so watch out. Athena programs, like **xterm**, also use the **label** resource for changing the text displayed in a pushbutton. Motif applications use the **labelString** resource for the same purpose.

Here's another example. In the resource file, an exclamation mark indicates a comment (to the end of the current line). Comments are ignored when the resource file is loaded in. Add the following resource-setting commands to the **XTerm** file:

```
! The "!" character starts a comment to the end of the line
!
! Set the colors
xterm*background:      lightgrey
xterm*foreground:      red
!
! Set up a font
xterm*font:            9x15
!
! Set the text block cursor to magenta
xterm*cursorColor:     magenta
!
! Use the gumby shape for the mouse cursor
xterm*pointerShape:    gumby
!
! Yes, we want a scroll bar
xterm*scrollBar:       True
```

The **cursorColor** resource (note the capitalization) sets the color of the block text cursor used by **xterm**. On a color system, we guarantee you'll notice the magenta. The **pointerShape** resource sets the mouse cursor to use a Gumby shape (this is our favorite standard X cursor), and the **scrollBar** resource is set to *True*. This means that, yes, we do want a scroll bar. After you create this file, you'll need to launch a new **xterm**, because once an X application starts, it no longer checks for new resource definitions.

This resource file applies only to one class of X applications, in this case **XTerm**. Thus we could use straight wildcard commands like the following:

*scrollBar: True

If this command is placed only in a class-resource file, it will apply only to applications of that class. This limits the effect of ***scrollBar**, which normally would apply to every application. Since many applications don't support scrollbars anyway, it wouldn't affect those programs.

Formal Resource File Syntax

These resource-setting commands make a form of primitive programming language and follow a strict syntax. According to the online manual page for *X*, the pseudolanguage for resource-setting commands is formally defined by the following Syntax:

Table 6.1 Resource-setting commands.

ResourceLine	=	Comment | IncludeFile | ResourceSpec | <empty line>
Comment	=	"!" {<any character except null or newline>}
IncludeFile	=	"#" WhiteSpace "include" WhiteSpace FileName WhiteSpace
FileName	=	<valid filename for operating system>
ResourceSpec	=	WhiteSpace ResourceName WhiteSpace ":" WhiteSpace Value
ResourceName	=	[Binding] {Component Binding} ComponentName
Binding	=	"." | "*"
WhiteSpace	=	{" " | "\t" }
Component	=	"?" | ComponentName
ComponentName	=	NameChar {NameChar}
NameChar	=	"a"\-"z" | "A"\-"Z" | "0"\-"9" | "_" | "-"
Value	=	{<any character except null or unescaped newline>}

In the table above, the vertical bar character, |, divides alternate values. The curly braces, { and }, surround zero or more repeated entries. Square brackets, [and], surround optional elements. Quotes, " and ", surround literal character strings.

You can include files in resource files, but only if a program supports the **#include** directive. The **xrdb** program, for example, does, but many X applications don't.

In a **ResourceSpec**, all white-space characters that come before the name are ignored, as are all white-space characters that come before or after the colon. Special characters include:

"\ " for a leading space

\t for tab

\\ for a single backslash

\n for a new line

To extend a resource command onto the next line, end the line with a single backslash, ****. (Make sure a newline character comes right after the backslash to end the line.) You can encode special characters with their ISO Latin-1 (extended ASCII) values, using **\nnn**, where **nnn** is the character number, in octal.

A question mark (?) matches a single component name as a wildcard. That is, a question mark can replace a class name or other single component.

This syntax applies to all resource-setting commands in any resource file.

Where Do Class-Resource Files Reside?

Most class resource files reside in the directory **/usr/lib/X11/app-defaults**. This is typically where system-wide application-default files (that is, class-resource files) are stored. (Look at the chart above for variations on this.)

Normally, a regular user doesn't have permission to change these files, as they are meant to apply system-wide and are usually set up by system administrators. In multilingual systems, you might have a number of directories under **/usr/lib/X11**. In that case, the class-resource files are located in **/usr/lib/X11/$LANG/app-defaults**, where **$LANG** is the value of the **LANG** environment variable.

Here are some example files you will find in **/usr/lib/X11/app-defaults**:

Table 6.2 Example files.

Resource File	Use
XTerm	for the **xterm** application
XCalc	for the **xcalc** calculator application
XLoad	for the **xload** application
XClock	for the **xclock** clock application

If your X Window System isn't installed in the standard directories, your system may have the **app-defaults** directory somewhere else. If you suspect this (and you should if you don't find a **/usr/lib/X11/app-defaults** directory), ask your system administrator.

You can create a local applications default file (that is, a class-resource file), such as the **XTerm** example above, in your home directory. Your X applications will recognize that file as well.

The Xapplresdir Environment Variable

If you're feeling particularly ambitious, you could use an environment variable, **XAPPLRESDIR** (which stands for X APPLication RESource file DIRectory). The **XAPPLRESDIR** environment variable provides another place (a directory) to find your class-resource files.

Let's say that your class-resource file is located in the directory **/users/erc**. In that case, the environment variable **XAPPLRESDIR** would be set to **/users/erc/** (note the trailing slash character). In the UNIX C shell, you could use the following command:

```
setenv XAPPLRESDIR /users/erc/
```

User-Resource Files

User-resource files contain resource-setting commands for anything you care to set. While class-resource files apply to just one application class, user-resource files apply to any application under X.

Inside one of these user-resource files, though, you place the same resource-setting commands. The only difference is that these commands can apply to all application classes (that is, to all applications), so you need to be very specific about which application resources you choose to set. Maintain some discipline and be very careful with the use of the wildcard asterisk. A good rule to follow: Never start an X resource-setting command with an asterisk.

The traditional user-resource file is the **.Xdefaults** file in your home directory. You can set resources for any and all your X applications in this file. You probably already have a file named **.Xdefaults** in your home directory.

You can also use host-based **.Xdefaults** files. In such a case, the resource file for a machine named **nokomis** would be:

.Xdefaults-nokomis

Most users work with just one **.Xdefaults** file, though.

The Xenvironment Variable

In addition to the **.Xdefaults-*hostname*** file, user-resource files can be located anywhere. What you need to do, though, is tell your X applications where the resource file is. You can do this with the **XENVIRONMENT** environment variable. **XENVIRONMENT** is the full, complete pathname for a resource file.

For example, if you create a user-resource file named **foo** in the **/users/erc/resources** directory, then you should set the **XENVIRONMENT** environment variable to **/users/erc/resources/foo**.

In the UNIX C shell, you can use the following command:

setenv XENVIRONMENT /users/erc/resources/foo

XENVIRONMENT points to a file, while **XAPPLRESDIR** points to a directory in which to look for files.

Setting Resources with Command-Line Parameters

You can set some common resources with standard X Window command-line parameters, as we described in the last chapter. For example, **-fg** stands for the foreground color. You can set the foreground color (usually the color in which the text is drawn) of **xterm** to green with the command:

```
xterm -fg green
```

Look back to the last chapter for coverage of these options. Most of these are obvious, but the real interesting one is the **-xrm** parameter.

Using the Xrm Command-Line Parameter

You can set resource options of an application from the command line by sending the values to the X resource manager with the **-xrm** command-line parameter. For example, to set a value of the **font** resource, the syntax in a resource file would be:

```
*font:      variable
```

The command line, using the **xterm** application, would be:

```
xterm -xrm "*font: variable"
```

The above command runs **xterm** and sets its **font** resource to the font **variable**. The syntax ***font:** usually sets the font for all applications, but resources set with the **-xrm** parameter affect only the application receiving the command-line parameter. This limits the scope of the resource-setting command, much like class-resource files.

With the **-xrm** command-line parameter, you can basically set any resource values that you can in a resource file, only you don't need to create a resource file to do it. Unfortunately, you do need to be a very good typist. If you have more than a few options, you'll probably want to create a resource file.

Translations

With all the strange X terminology, you may think you need a United Nations translator to figure out what's going on. X commandeered the term **translations**, much like X staked its claim to resources. Translations in X are a means to customize the way keystrokes and mouse actions interact with X programs, using resource-setting commands.

Each widget, such as a scroll bar or pushbutton, has an internal **translation table** that defines how that widget handles input events like keystrokes and mouse clicks. The translation table maps input events to internal functions (we told you X was a programmer's windowing system). These internal functions are often called **actions**, especially as references in a program's online manual entry.

All translations for a given widget are grouped together in a table, and this table is set with one X resource command. The basic syntax for each entry in the translation table is:

<Event> : action()

The event appears between angle brackets, followed by a colon and the name of the action (function) to execute. Some action routines can also accept parameters, such as the **bell** action that is part of the **xterm** program. For example, if the user presses the first mouse button, the event can be abbreviated as:

<Btn1Down> : action()

Keyboard keys, like letters of the alphabet or function keys, use the following syntax:

```
<Key> F1 : action()      \n\
<Key> E : action()       \n\
<Key> 6 : action()       \n
```

Every line uses a **\n** to end the translation for a given key, and all but the last have a **** to allow the resource command to extend over multiple lines.

To start a translation table, you must first find the widget name or class to set the **translations** resource. In addition, translation tables need a **#override** starting command, which tells the X translation manager to use your commands to override any previous commands for the same events.

The following example sets the F1 function key to ring the bell for **xterm**'s **vt100** widget:

```
*vt100*translations:  \
#override \n\
        <Key>F1:bell(100) \n
```

This multiline resource command sets the ***vt100*translations** resource. This resource is set to a translation table that overrides any entries already defined for the named events. Only one event is set up for the F1 key. When this key is pressed, the bell action is executed, passing 100 as a parameter.

Translation Modifier Keys

You can set up translations to work only when certain modifier keys are held down, such as the Shift key, Control key, or Meta key (often labeled Alt on your keyboard). The syntax for this follows:

```
Shift Ctrl Meta <Btn2Up> : action()
```

In the above example, the Shift, Control, and Meta keys all must be held down when the event—the middle mouse button—is released. You can mix and match modifier keys.

If you *don't* want a modifier key, you can use the Tilde (~) character, which means "not" to C programmers:

```
~Shift <Key> F5 : quit()
```

The above example means that if the user presses the F5 function key while the shift key is not held down, the **quit** action routine will be called.

The translation manager executes only the *first* action that matches an event. This means that general rules should go at the end, and specific rules at the beginning, of a translation table. The second action, shown below, will not be called, since the first translation will trap all F8 key presses.

```
<Key> F8 : action_a()
Ctrl <Key> F8 : action_never_called()
```

Now place the second translation *before* the first:

```
Ctrl <Key> F8 : action_will_get_called()
<Key> F8 : action_a()
```

X applications should document the list of default actions, which shows what actions will be accepted by a given application. Most users, though, don't want to bother with translation tables and we agree: The syntax is cryptic, to say the least, and debugging is problematic.

Debugging Resource Commands

X handles resource-setting errors in the traditional X manner: Most errors are silently ignored. This makes debugging resource commands burdensome, especially if you define some of the many X environment variables.

Some resources, like fonts or colors, can generate error messages, but most don't. Other resource values can stop a program dead in its tracks. Setting the **scrollBar** resource to *Bozo*, instead of the proper *True* or *False*, makes **xterm** freeze for a long time, then crash.

X11 Release 5 adds new support for debugging resource commands. You can set the **StringConversionWarnings** resource to **on**, which will print error messages if problems occur when trying to convert the text (strings) in a resource file into actual values. These messages, while somewhat cryptic, can help debug resource files.

```
*StringConversionWarnings:   on
```

Listing the Resources for an Application

In addition, you can use a program named **appres** to list the resources that an application is set up to load. This won't tell you all the resources available, but will tell you how an application is customized. **Appres** looks in all the standard places for resource files (listed below), as well as at the **RESOURCE_MANAGER** and **SCREEN_RESOURCES** properties, and then prints out what resources have been set in all those places. You need to pass the resource-class name and an instance name, if you wish, to **appres**. For example, the **xterm** resource-class name is **XTerm**.

Users can customize **xterm** using either the *xterm* or the *XTerm* monikers, or both. For best effect, use the following command to determine what resources have been set for **xterm**:

```
appres XTerm xterm
```

The voluminous output of this **appres** command looks like the following (which we edited down considerably for space):

```
xterm*borderWidth:     2
XTerm*fontMenu.Label:  VT Fonts
XTerm*VT100*font1:     nil2
XTerm*VT100*font2:     6x10
XTerm*VT100*font4:     9x15
XTerm*tekMenu.Label:   Tek Options
XTerm*vtMenu*reversewrap*Label:      Enable Reverse Wraparound
*font:  -adobe-courier-medium-r-normal—14-140-75-75-m-90-iso8859-1
*scrollBar:            True
*vt100*translations:   \
```

```
#override \n\
        <Key>F1:bell(100)  \n
xterm*background:      ligthgrey
xterm*foreground:      red
xterm*font:            9x15
xterm*cursorColor:     magenta
xterm*pointerShape:  gumby
```

In the above example, note that some of the commands started with *xterm*, while most of the rest started with *XTerm*. This is why we used both names on the command line. The commands that start with an asterisk are the ones from a class-resource file.

Because of the huge amount of output **appres** prints out, you can ask for the resource customizations for just a particular widget, or a smaller portion of the widget tree. An example from the **appres** online manual follows:

```
appres Xman.TopLevelShell.Form xman.topBox.form
```

Two other programs lists resources, but are mainly of use to programmers (and a limited number of programmers at that). **Listres** lists all the resources available for a given widget, using the freely available Athena widget programming library. **Viewres** presents a graphical view of the same data as **listres**. If you have access to the sources for the X Window System, you can customize **listres** and **viewres** to display Motif widget resources. Otherwise, only the Athena Toolkit can use them, so they don't add much value.

Using Xrdb and the X Resource_Manager Database

The **RESOURCE_MANAGER** property is stored on the root window (of the first screen) of a display and contains, in text format, resource-setting commands that apply to all X clients on that display. This property (a named collection of data) then acts much like the **.Xdefaults** file described above. This may seem like yet another XWindow attempt at complexity, but storing resource-setting commands only in files doesn't always work.

Two cases where resource files don't work are X terminals and where you run X programs on multiple machines and display them on your workstation. None of the resource files will pertain to programs running on another machine unless that machine, and your user account on that machine, share the same resource files and configuration.

You could, for example, set up similar resource files on every machine you log on, or you can use the **RESOURCE_MANAGER** property.

Normally, a program called **xrdb** uploads a file called **.Xresources**, creating the **RESOURCE_MANAGER** property from this file.

With X11 Release 5, **xrdb** also manages the **SCREEN_RESOURCES** property. This property contains resource commands that pertain to a specific screen, such as color settings. (You could, for example, have a two-screen display, with one monochrome screen and one color.)

Many users configure their X systems to run **xrdb** at startup. **Xrdb** then creates the **RESOURCE_MANAGER** property from a resource file, using the **-load** command-line parameter.

The standard way to run **xrdb** follows:

```
xrdb [options] filename
```

To load a file named **.Xresources** in a user's home directory and override any existing **RESOURCE_MANAGER** property, use the following command:

```
xrdb -load $HOME/.Xresources
```

If you run **xrdb** as part of your X startup, you don't have to worry about overwriting preexisting commands in the **RESOURCE_MANAGER** property. If you run **xrdb** later on, you may want to preserve the resource commands that are already in the property. If so, use the **-merge** command-line parameter.

```
xrdb -merge my_resource_file
```

The term *merge* is a bit of a misnomer, as **xrdb** performs an odd "lexicographic sorted merge of the two inputs," according to the online manual.

Xrdb runs your resource file through **cpp**, the C-compiler preprocessor, allowing you to use constructs like **#ifdef** and **#include** (which should be familiar to all C programmers). With X, you typically use **cpp** directives for separating monochrome and color resources. For example, you can use the following layout to define a set of resources for color and monochrome screens. **Xrdb** will define the symbol **COLOR** if you have a color screen.

```
#ifdef COLOR
!       ... color resources
xterm*foreground:   white
xterm*background:   lightgrey
#else
!       ... monochrome resources
xterm*foreground:   black
xterm*background:   white
#endif
```

The **#ifdef COLOR** directive is especially useful for Motif and Open Look programs, because the three-dimensional effects of these two interfaces require special values on monochrome systems.

Common **xrdb** command-line parameters include the following:

Table 6.3 Common xrdb command-line parameters.

Parameter	Meaning
-nocpp	Don't run resource files through **cpp**, the C preprocessor, which is mainly used for include files and separating color from monochrome resources.
-query	Returns the contents of the **RESOURCE_MANAGER** property.
-load	Replaces the **RESOURCE_MANAGER** property with the new file's resource-setting commands.
-merge	Merges the resource-setting commands in the passed file with those already in the **RESOURCE_MANAGER** property.
-remove	Removes the **RESOURCE_MANAGER** property.
-edit	Works backwards. This option places the resource-setting commands in the **RESOURCE_MANAGER** property into the given file.

Editres and the Future

Up to now, we've edited every Xresource file by hand with a text editor, such as **vi** or **emacs**. With X11 Release 5, though, a new program named **editres** allows you to edit resource files with a graphical front end.

Editres queries an existing application for the set of resources and widgets it supports. It can also change an application's resources on the fly, but only if the application was compiled with support for **editres**. Programs shipped with X11 Release 5 should work fine with **editres**, but older Motif and Open Look applications probably won't.

Until all applications are compiled with special support for the **editres** protocol, you're likely to have problems with **editres**. In addition, **editres** can write out a set of resource commands to a file, but it is very likely to overwrite your existing resource files.

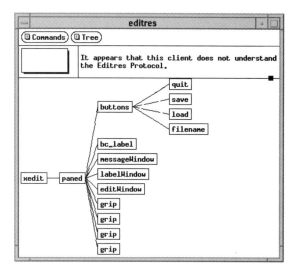

Figure 6.1 The Editres program in action.

Editres certainly isn't perfect, but it is a sign of what's to come with X. Future users can expect much better and easier methods to edit X resources. We hope, for example, that users never have to bother with resource files at all, nor worry about a host of X environment variables.

Resource Quick Reference

! starts a comment.

. (a period) separates widget names or classes, if you are specifying the widget hierarchy exactly.

* is a wildcard. The wildcard can separate widget names or classes, without specifying the widget hierarchy exactly. We recommend using wildcards. But be careful, because you easily set the resources of too many widgets.

A resource-setting command looks like:

```
name_what_we_want_to_set : value_to_set
```

Some examples:

```
*label:      This is a new label
xterm*font:  *courier-bold-r-normal—*-140-*-*-*
```

Summary

To really figure out resources, you're going to want to play around with all the examples above. This stuff is complex.

There are five main ways to set values into application resources:

1. In a user-resource file.
2. In a class-resource file, also called an application-defaults file.
3. In the **RESOURCE_MANAGER** property on the root window. This property is created by the standard X Window program called **xrdb**.
4. In command-line parameters passed to the program.
5. Hard-coding resource values inside a program. Programmers can do this, but users can't without access to the program's source code.

Set the **StringConversionWarnings** resource to *on* for useful debugging messages if you experience problems getting resource files to work.

Motif applications use the resource **fontList** to set font names, while Athena widget programs (which include the standard X programs like **xterm** and **xclipboard**) use the resource **font**.

Most class-resource files reside in the directory **/usr/lib/X11/app-defaults**. This is typically where system-wide application-default files (that is, class-resource files) are stored.

Each widget, such as a scrollbar or pushbutton, has an internal translation table that defines how that widget handles input events like keystrokes and mouse clicks. The translation table maps input events to internal functions. These internal functions are often called "actions," especially as references in a program's online manual entry.

You can use a program named **appres** to list the resources that an application is set up to load. This program won't tell you all the resources available, but it will tell you how an application is customized. **Appres** looks in all the standard places for resource files, as well as at the **RESOURCE_MANAGER** and **SCREEN_RESOURCES** properties, and then it prints out what resources have been set in all those places.

The **RESOURCE_MANAGER** property is stored on the root window (of the first screen) of a display and contains, in text format, resource-setting commands that apply to all X clients on that display.

With X11 Release 5, a new program named **editres** allows you to edit resource files with a graphical front end. **Editres** queries an existing application for the set of resources and widgets it supports. It can also change an application's resources on the fly, but only if the application was compiled with support for **editres**.

Chapter 7

Font Basics

The old days of line printers with dot-matrix characters are long gone. Today, adequate output means laser printers and fonts. Unfortunately, this is another area where the X Window System can be confusing to everyone involved.

A complete set of characters of one size of one typeface—including upper- and lowercase letters, punctuation marks, and numerals—is called a **font**. All fonts in X are **bitmaps**; each character has a specific bitpattern within the font. Each face, style, and size corresponds to at least one font: Times at 25 pixels high and Times at 12 pixels high are two different fonts. This is different from Adobe's Postscript-defined Type 1 and 3 fonts: Postscript describes fonts by outline, which can be resized depending on the dimensions defined by the application.

You gain access to these different typefaces by loading fonts into the X server, if you're using X11 Release 5. The X11 Release 5 font server offers the ability to scale fonts, and it serves fonts to the X server. Your X applications, though, still treat these fonts as bitmaps, once scaled to the proper size. (Sun's OpenWindows and other proprietary X servers also scale fonts.)

Different fonts and typefaces have different characteristics:

- *Fonts are either serif or sans serif.* **Serif** characters have a smaller line that finishes off a large stroke, such as the strokes at the top and bottom of the letter *I*. **Sans serif** fonts do not have these finishing strokes.

- *A font can be proportional-spaced or fixed-width.* A **fixed-width font** allows the same width for each character: For instance, an *m* takes up as much space as an *i*. A fixed-width font emulates a typewriter. A **proportional-spaced font** emulates typeset material, such as the letters on this page, where the proportions between letters are not equal.

Table 7.1 Some typical fonts.

Times Roman

Helvetica

`Courier`

Times Roman Italic

Helvetica Italic

`Courier Italic`

Times Roman Bold

Helvetica Bold

`Courier Bold`

- *A font has another set of attributes: single-byte (8-bit) fonts and two-byte (16-bit) fonts.* The **single-byte fonts** can handle up to 256 characters, while the **two-byte fonts** can handle up to 65,536 characters. Text in Japanese, Chinese, or Korean, for example, require many more than 256 characters. Unless you're a programmer creating an application intended for Asian users, you won't need to worry about multibyte fonts.

The fact that X uses a plethora of conflicting font formats only adds to the problem. In addition, most printers use completely different fonts than X, which makes hardcopy output all that more difficult.

Font File Formats

X includes a number of special font formats:

- **PCF (Portable Compiled Font)**, an enhanced version of the SNF font introduced in Release 5. These fonts are **portable**, which means they can be shared among machines of disparate types. This is especially useful if you have a UNIX host supporting a number of X terminals (probably an entirely different processor architecture than your UNIX host). Note that a number of vendors have used the PCF moniker in the past for proprietary font formats.

  If your X11 R5 vendor supports a font server, the vendor should also include a compiler to generate fonts for your particular system. If you're lucky, the vendor will also supply a few precompiled fonts to get you up and running immediately.

- **BDF (Bitmap Distribution Format)**, a portable format based on the ASCII bitmap format. A font file in this format must usually be converted to another (binary) format for use by X, but this is the format you use to exchange fonts between systems, since the files are ASCII text.

- **SNF (Server Normal Format)**, a BDF font compiled into the format best suited for your particular X server. Inherently nonportable, these fonts must be converted back to the BDF format to exchange fonts with other architectures and systems.

  The SNF format was replaced by PCF in Release 5.

- **Speedo**. Bitstream donated a number of Speedo scalable fonts with X11 Release 5. These fonts use the font server, described below.

- **Folio** (also called F3 or OpenFonts) fonts, a scalable format used under Open Windows. A program called **convertfont** converts to and from this format.

Managing these different font formats represents some work for the system administrator, who should maintain a separate directory on a network for every type of server on a network. Not every type of server needs a separate format; for instance, in the past, NCD X terminals and Sun workstations used the same font format.

Prior to Release 5, most X implementations included a program called **bdftosnf** to convert ASCII BDF font files to binary SNF files. Release 5 replaces **bdftosnf** with **bdftopcf**, which converts BDF files to the portable binary PCF format.

The contributed software with X often includes a **snftobdf** to reverse the process and create an ASCII bitmap BDF file from a binary X font. This is useful for exchanging fonts between systems.

What Fonts Do You Have?

A standard X application program called **xlsfonts** lists the available fonts on a workstation. Running **xlsfonts** on a Release 4 or higher X server will result in pages and pages of text output.

Here's some sample output:

```
-adobe-courier-medium-o-normal—8-80-75-75-m-50-iso8859-1
-adobe-courier-medium-r-normal—10-100-75-75-m-60-iso8859-1
-adobe-courier-medium-r-normal—11-80-100-100-m-60-iso8859-1
-adobe-courier-medium-r-normal—12-120-75-75-m-70-iso8859-1
-adobe-courier-medium-r-normal—14-100-100-100-m-90-iso8859-1
-adobe-times-medium-r-normal—24-240-75-75-p-124-iso8859-1
-bitstream-charter-medium-r-normal—14-100-100-100-p-78-iso8859-1
9x15
8x13
fixed
cursor
variable
olglyph-10
```

The long font names are based on an X standard called the *X Logical Font Description Conventions*, or XLFD. A document describing the XLFD is included with the X Window System from the MIT X Consortium. (The above list should look familiar; we covered fonts initially in Chapter 3.)

Some common fonts that seem to be universal are **fixed**, **8x13** (a fixed-width font where each character fits an 8-by-13 pixel cell), **9x15**, and **variable** (a proportional-width font that looks vaguely like Helvetica).

The names *fixed* and *variable* are called **aliases**. Instead of entering font names in the long format, applications can enter aliases that reference the real font name. Font aliases must be handled with care, though. System administrators must make sure that aliases are set up correctly and consistently. The variable font, for example, is normally an alias for another (usually Helvetica) font.

These aliases are normally stored in files named **fonts.alias**. Each font directory, like **/usr/lib/X11/fonts/100dpi**, should have such a file if you want to use aliases for font names. If you are having problems with font aliases, the **fonts.alias** files may very well be set up incorrectly.

In addition, each font contains a **fonts.dir** file, which maps font file names to the long XLFD-formatted font names. A standard program called **mkfontdir** generates these files. If you add a font to your system, you'll need to run **mkfontdir**.

A similar problem arises with versions of OpenWindows on SPARC machines. The X11/NeWS server provides scalable fonts, but it requires a **Families.List** file in font directories, usually **/usr/openwin/lib/fonts**. When installing new programs, such as Sun's Answer Book, the default **Families.List** file may get trashed as the new font families wipe out all the old font family entries in the file. In the case of the Answer Book installation, this can prevent OpenWindows from running. The fix, which Sun does document (if obscurely), is to run the **bldfamily** program to regenerate the **Families.List** file. **Bldfamily** is usually located in **/usr/openwin/bin**.

Decoding Long Font Names

When you run a program like **xlsfonts**, you'll see that most of the X font names are extremely long and complex:

-adobe-courier-bold-r-normal—11-80-100-100-m-60-iso8859-1

The actual format of these names makes sense and is described in the XLFD, mentioned above. Most names begin with a leading hyphen and then a font company name, such as **adobe**:

-*adobe*-courier-bold-r-normal—11-80-100-100-m-60-iso8859-1

These names must be registered with the X Consortium, so you know there will be some consistency within company names. A number of font vendors, such as Adobe and Bitstream, have donated fonts for X. Next comes the font family name field, such as **courier**:

-adobe-*courier*-bold-r-normal—11-80-100-100-m-60-iso8859-1

The weight follows, usually **bold** or **medium**:

-adobe-courier-*bold*-r-normal—11-80-100-100-m-60-iso8859-1

Then comes the slant field. The slant is one of the following codes:

Table 7.2 The font slant field.

Code	Meaning
i	italic
o	oblique
r	roman
ri	reverse italic
ro	reverse oblique
ot	other

`-adobe-courier-bold-r-normal—11-80-100-100-m-60-iso8859-1`

The set-width name describes how wide the letters are. Some examples are **condensed**, **semicondensed**, **narrow**, **normal**, and **double wide**:

`-adobe-courier-bold-r-normal—11-80-100-100-m-60-iso8859-1`

After the set-width name comes space for any extra information necessary to identify the font, such as **sans** (for sans serif). This space is not used in our example, nor for most fonts—hence the double dashes.

The pixel-size field indicates the size in dots on the screen, in our case, **11**. Zero indicates a scalable font (which we'll cover later).

`-adobe-courier-bold-r-normal—11-80-100-100-m-60-iso8859-1`

The point-size field describes the size in terms of points ($^1/_{72}$ of an inch). This field is ten times the point size. So, the 80 means our font is an 8-point font:

`-adobe-courier-bold-r-normal—11-80-100-100-m-60-iso8859-1`

After the point size follows the dots-per-inch in the X and Y directions. Our example is 100x100 dots per inch. Most are either 75 or 100 dpi:

`-adobe-courier-bold-r-normal—11-80-100-100-m-60-iso8859-1`

The spacing field determines whether a font is **monospaced** or **proportional**.

Table 7.3 The font spacing field.

Spacing	Meaning
p	proportional
m	monospaced
c	char cell/monospaced; suitable for using with **xterm**, for example

-adobe-courier-bold-r-normal—11-80-100-100-*m*-60-iso8859-1

The average width field provides an average size in tenths of pixels, or **6** pixels in our example:

-adobe-courier-bold-r-normal—11-80-100-100-m-*60*-iso8859-1

Finally, the **charset** registry and encoding fields tell what kind of character set we have. Most are **ISO 8859-1** (Latin-1, a superset of ASCII):

-adobe-courier-bold-r-normal—11-80-100-100-m-60-*iso8859-1*

The next step is to see what the fonts look like.

Viewing and Choosing Fonts

A program called **xfontsel** can help you choose fonts using the long font-name format.

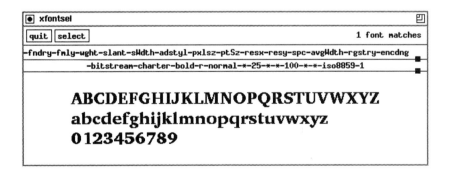

Figure 7.1 XFontsel at work.

Another X application called **xfd** (X font displayer) will display the characters in a font. Normally, if **xfd** cannot find the font, then your program will not, either. The command below will create a window and display the characters in the font-named **variable**:

```
xfd -fn variable
```

Once you know what a font looks like, you can decide whether the font is appropriate. You can choose a font through a common command-line argument:

```
-font fontname (or -fn fontname)
```

where **fontname** is the actual name of an X font. There's also a font editor named **xfed**, which you can find on the X contributed sources tapes or CD-ROM.

Choosing your own font when launching an application is especially useful, because X runs on very differing hardware. A color Sun SPARC workstation, for example, comes with either a sixteen-inch or nineteen-inch color monitor, both at the same pixel resolution. This means that the dots are much smaller on the sixteen-inch monitor. The standard X default font, **8x13**, looks tiny on a sixteen-inch monitor and more acceptable on the nineteen-inch screen. Users with the smaller screen may opt to use a larger font, such as **9x15**, just to be able to read the text. An Apple Macintosh IIx, on the other hand, has a standard 640-by-480 pixel resolution. On this screen, users typically want to use the smallest fonts available, due to the smaller screen resolution.

Adding a Font To Your System

If you get a new set of BDF fonts and want to add them to your system, there's a number of steps you must take.

Start by choosing the directory where the font should go. A good general choice is **/usr/lib/X11/fonts/misc**, a sort of catch-all font directory available on most systems. You can also make your own font directory, especially if you don't have permissions to change **/usr/lib/X11/fonts/misc**.

The next step is to convert your font to the PCF format required by the X server, or to the SNF format used by older X servers. The programs **bdftopcf** and **bdftosnf** take care of this:

```
bdftopcf fontfile.bdf > fontfile.pcf
```

or

```
bdftosnf fontfile.bdf > fontfile.snf
```

Place the resulting file in your font directory, and run **mkfontdir** on that directory. Then your new font will be in the **fonts.dir** file. (This file maps between file names and XLFD long font names.) Change to the font directory and run **mkfontdir**:

mkfontdir

If you're using your own font directory, you need to inform the X server about this directory, using the **xset** program, where *mydirectory* is the name of your font directory:

xset +fp *mydirectory*

Finally, tell the X server to rebuild its internal list of available fonts, also with **xset**:

xset fp rehash

Your new font should now be available. Run **xlsfonts** to check.

Introducing the Font Server

With X11 Release 5, the X Consortium introduced a new **font server**, promising a modern world of scalable fonts and greatly improved text options. Structurally, the font server is an add-on to the X server. If you need to change the text size, you merely ask for a new font in the desired size. The font server provides fonts to the X server.

Unfortunately, the true goal of scalable text is only partially met. The font server serves up bitmap fonts to the X server, scaling these bitmaps to the desired sizes. Your application cannot use the font server to output dynamically scaled text. Instead, it asks the X server for a particular font in a particular size. The font server is included in the general release of X11 Release 5, and it contains a number of scalable fonts provided by Bitstream, using the Speedo font format. As Release 5 proliferates, you'll no doubt be able to get scalable fonts from a number of vendors. We also expect to see a good number of public-domain fonts.

The font server causes problems in a number of environments, especially where users run X under another windowing system, such as NextStep, Microsoft Windows, or the Macintosh. Users on those systems may well want to use their native fonts with X, since supporting fonts in such an environment have proven difficult to execute.

Release 5 sorely needs a font-server overview document, because nothing really describes how to put all the parts together and actually use the font server. We've found that the following five steps work on our system:

1. Configure the font server using a configuration file.
2. Choose a TCP/IP port number for the font server.
3. Start the font server.
4. Configure the X server to recognize the font server.
5. Verify that scalable fonts are available and start using the fonts.

Configuring the Font Server

The font server requires a rigidly formatted configuration file. Any deviations result in program death. The only correct, or nearly correct, example configuration file is in the font server (**fs**) man page. All other example configuration files, including an example file that came with the X11 R5 sources, cause system crashes. Skip the doc directories in the X11 R5 source tree. They're all wrong.

Here is one proper **config** file, or at least one that works for us:

```
clone-self = on
use-syslog = off
catalogue = /usr/local/X11R5/lib/X11/fonts/Speedo
error-file = FSERRORS
default-point-size = 120
default-resolutions = 75,75,100,100
```

The catalogue path is where your scalable fonts are located. In our case, we stored the Speedo fonts in the directory **/usr/local/X11R5/lib/X11/fonts/Speedo**.

The **Speedo** directory contains some example scalable fonts. Usually, these will be in **/usr/lib/X11/fonts/Speedo**. Note that many example catalogues use *speedo* with a lowercase *s*. Our directory had an uppercase *S*. (Remember that in UNIX the case of the directory name makes a difference.)

The font server communicates to the X server using a TCP/IP port, for which you have to choose a port number. Use that same number consistently. All examples use port 7000, and we suggest sticking with 7000 unless you have a compelling reason to change.

Starting the Font Server

Once you get a good configuration file and choose a port number, you can start the font server. Start it in the background.

The **fs** program is the actual font server. You can start it with the following command:

```
fs -config ./config -port 7000 &
```

This tells the font server (**fs**) to use the configuration file named **config** in the current directory and the TCP/IP port number of **7000**. If the font server detects any problems, especially with your configuration file, it will crash—as it did several times for us, as we relied perhaps too heavily on the documentation. In fact, every piece of documentation describing the configuration file, in particular, contradicted other documents. For example, the catalogue command, above, does not have a leading name for the type of fonts. One example used:

```
catalogue = pcf:/usr/lib/X11/fonts/misc,speedo:/usr/lib/fonts/speedo
```

This fails. Not only does the **Speedo** directory start with an uppercase name, the leading **pcf:** or **speedo:** caused the font server to die a flaming death.

After starting the font server, you now need to configure the X server to recognize the font server and use the scalable fonts.

Configuring the X Server

To configure the X server for the font server, tell the X server to include the font server in its font path. This requires an X server from Release 5.

Using the font path is a clever way to extend the X server without breaking X application software. Since the font server communicates only with the X server, the programmer can essentially ignore it. The font server provides more fonts, so it fits naturally as part of the X server's font path—just another path for more fonts. This is probably the best part of the font-server design.

To configure the X server, we use a syntax much like that for current font paths. Use the **xset** command to add (extend) the font path:

```
xset +fp tcp/hostname:7000
```

The **+fp** tells **xset** to add to the font path, and the new font path is **tcp/host-name:7000**, where **hostname** is the computer-network name where the font server computes. The **7000** is the TCP/IP port number, used in the **fs** command line above.

If you don't replace the word ***hostname*** above with the proper hostname where the font server computes, you'll get a very strange X error from **xset**:

```
X Error of failed request: BadValue (integer parameter out of range
        for operation)
  Major opcode of failed request: 51 (X_SetFontPath)
  Value in failed request: 0x0
  Serial number of failed request: 4
  Current serial number in output stream: 6
```

A proper command for a computer with a hostname of **nicollet** is:

```
xset +fp tcp/nicollet:7000
```

Working with Scalable Fonts

Once you get the font server running and the X server to recognize the font server as part of its font path, you can try using some scalable fonts. First, try the **xlsfonts** command to see the available fonts. Look for fonts with zeros in the size fields.

xlsfonts

You'll see a lot of fonts with something like:

```
-adobe-courier-bold-r-normal—0-0-75-75-m-0-iso8859-1
-adobe-courier-medium-o-normal—0-0-75-75-m-0-iso8859-1
-adobe-helvetica-bold-r-normal—0-0-75-75-p-0-iso8859-1
-adobe-times-medium-i-normal—0-0-75-75-p-0-iso8859-1
-bitstream-charter-bold-i-normal—0-0-0-0-p-0-iso8859-1
-bitstream-charter-bold-i-normal—0-0-75-75-p-0-iso8859-1
-daewoo-mincho-medium-r-normal—0-0-100-100-c-0-ksc5601.1987-0
-dec-terminal-bold-r-normal—0-0-75-75-c-0-dec-dectech
```

These are fonts that are explicitly scalable by the font server.

The font server itself comes with a number of utility programs, including **fsinfo**, which provides information about the font server. We use **fsinfo** to help verify that the font server is actually running:

```
fsinfo -server hostname:7000
```

Again, replace **hostname** with the name of the machine containing the font server. Here's some sample output of **fsinfo**:

```
name of server: nicollet:7000
version number: 1
vendor string: MIT X Consortium
vendor release number: 5000
maximum request size: 16384 longwords (65536 bytes)
number of catalogues: 1
        all
Number of alternate servers: 0
number of extensions: 0
```

You can replace **-server hostname:7000** if you properly set up the **FONTSERVER** environment variable. Set **FONTSERVER** to the hostname and TCP/IP port number used for the font server, such as **hostname:7000**. For a hostname of **nicollet** and a TCP/IP port of **7000**, use:

setenv FONTSERVER nicollet:7000

Using a description of the long font names (from the X Logical Font Description, mentioned above), you can try the X font displayer program, **xfd**, with a rather large font. First, we take an XLFD name with zeros:

-bitstream-courier-medium-r-normal—0-0-0-0-m-0-iso8859-1

Then we build a proper name in the size we want, in this case, 39 point:

-bitstream-courier-bold-r-normal—39-390-75-75-m-39-iso8859-1

We have found that 39 point seems to be the largest-sized font. Trying a 40-point font, such as the font below, fails:

-bitstream-courier-bold-r-normal—40-400-75-75-m-40-iso8859-1

With the same font, 39 point works. You may want to play with the configurations to get around this limitation.

Typing in these long XLFD font names is a real chore, but the cut and paste offered in **xterm** windows really helps here. Beware of making a mistake, though. You must build a proper name or you'll get an error, and the X font server is not forgiving. You can try the **xfd**, or X font displayer, program to display a scaled font. The following command displays a 37-point scalable font.

```
xfd -fn "-bitstream-courier-bold-r-normal—37-370-75-75-m-37-
        iso8859-1"
```

Another program that comes with the font server is **fslsfonts**, which lists the fonts supported by the font server:

```
fslsfonts -server hostname:7000
```

Note that the outputted list is much smaller than the list of scalable fonts reported by **xlsfonts**.

```
-bitstream-charter-bold-i-normal—0-0-0-0-p-0-iso8859-1
-bitstream-charter-bold-r-normal—0-0-0-0-p-0-iso8859-1
-bitstream-charter-medium-i-normal—0-0-0-0-p-0-iso8859-1
-bitstream-charter-medium-r-normal—0-0-0-0-p-0-iso8859-1
-bitstream-courier-bold-i-normal—0-0-0-0-m-0-iso8859-1
-bitstream-courier-bold-r-normal—0-0-0-0-m-0-iso8859-1
-bitstream-courier-medium-i-normal—0-0-0-0-m-0-iso8859-1
-bitstream-courier-medium-r-normal—0-0-0-0-m-0-iso8859-1
```

The program **showfont** outputs a text description of a whole font. These text descriptions tend to be long. Here's just one letter, the right bracket, }, from the following command:

```
showfont -fn "-bitstream-charter-bold-i-normal—0-0-0-0-p-0-
          iso8859-1"
char #125 ('}')
Right: 6   Left: 1   Descent: 3   Ascent: 8   Width: 6
##--
-##-
-##-
-##-
-##-
--##
-##-
-##-
-##-
-##-
##--
```

Programming and X Fonts

The release of the font server in X11 R5 may be a boon for users, but it adds some problems for programmers and system administrators. Users can incorrectly configure their system—and they probably will never know about it. That's why programmers must, to an extent, protect users from themselves.

First of all, programmers must learn that their applications cannot depend on any X fonts. Applications require some form of fallback strategy in case needed fonts aren't available. Programmers must also limit the number of fonts they use, purely for pragmatic reasons. Some servers, especially for X terminals, simply won't have the resources to load a lot of different fonts. (Remember that each point size is a different font in X.) Due to cost constraints, though, most X terminals have a limited amount of RAM. Fonts, like any other X resource, use up RAM. In an X terminal environment, using the least amount of resources is a good idea, because there's not many resources to share.

For More Information

For more information on the X font server, look for a number of documents in the X11 Release 5 source tree:

- "The X Font Service Protocol," by Jim Fulton (Network Computing Devices), in **mit/doc/FSProtocol/protocol.ms**.
- "Font server implementation overview," by Dave Lemke (also of Network Computing Devices), in **mit/doc/fontserver/design.ms**. If you read this, ignore the configuration section at the end. It didn't work.
- Font-server manual page, in **mit/fonts/server/fs.man**. Ignore the sample config file, **config.cpp**. It doesn't work, either.

Summary

As with any graphical software, using X means using fonts. A complete set of characters of one size of one typeface—including upper- and lowercase letters, punctuation marks, and numerals—is called a font. All fonts in X are bitmaps; each character has a specific bitpattern within the font. We discuss the characteristics that distinguish fonts.

X includes a number of special font formats: PCF (Portable Compiled Font), BDF (Bitmap Distribution Format), and SNF (Server Normal Format). You'll need to create your own fonts from these formats. Prior to Release 5, most X implementations included a program called **bdftosnf** to convert ASCII BDF font files to SNF files. Release 5 replaces **bdftosnf** with **bdftopcf**, which converts BDF files to the portable binary PCF format. **Snftobdf** reverses the process and creates an ASCII bitmap BDF file from a binary X font.

A standard X application program called **xlsfonts** lists the available fonts on a workstation. Running **xlsfonts** on a Release 4 or higher X server will result in pages and pages of text output. When you run a program like **xlsfonts**, you'll see that most of the X font names are extremely long and complex. The actual format of these names, however, makes sense and is described in the XLFD, mentioned above. Most names begin with a leading hyphen and then a font company name, such as **adobe**.

Most systems will include fonts with the names of fixed and variable, which are called aliases. Instead of entering font names in the long format, applications can enter aliases that reference the real font name.

A program called **xfontsel** can help you choose fonts using the long font name format. Another X application called **xfd** (X font displayer) will display the characters in a font. Normally, if **xfd** cannot find the font, then your program will not, either.

With X11 Release 5, the X Consortium introduced a new font server, promising a modern world of scalable fonts and greatly improved text options. Structurally, the font server is an add-on to the X server. If you need to change the text size, you merely ask for a new font in the desired size. The font server provides fonts to the X Server.

The font server requires a rigidly formatted configuration file, as any deviations result in program death. The only correct, or nearly correct, example configuration file is in the font server (**fs**) man page. All other example configuration files, including an example file that came with the X11 R5 sources, cause system crashes. We provide a **config** file that actually works.

To configure the X server for the font server, tell the X server to include the font server in its font path. This requires an X server from Release 5.

Once you get the font server running and the X server to recognize the font server as part of its font path, you can try using some scalable fonts. First, try the **xlsfonts** command to see the available fonts. Look for fonts with zeros in the size fields.

The release of the font server in X11 R5 may be a boon for users, but it adds some problems for programmers and system administrators. Users can incorrectly configure their system and never know it. That's why programmers must, to an extent, protect users from themselves.

III

Window Managers

This section concentrates on working smarter with window managers, programs that control how you interact with X Window System applications. In this section we:

- Introduce the concept of window managers and how to change the system defaults;
- Cover in-depth the major window managers—Motif, Open Look, and Tab window managers—and how to customize each.

Chapter 8

Using Window Managers

Unlike most other graphical windowing systems, such as Microsoft Windows or the Macintosh, X allows you to change the entire look and feel of your environment. One way to change this look and feel is through the choice of window managers. A **window manager** is a special X application that controls the layout of windows on the screen. A window manager controls how much of the screen's real estate any application can have. It also allows you to resize, iconify, and move windows. You can run only one window manager per screen, and usually only one per X display.

In this chapter, we'll cover the basic concepts of window managers. In the next three, we'll cover the three main window managers in depth.

Window Manager Title Bars

Most window managers place a **title bar** and other **decorations** around applications' main windows. This title bar helps enhance the look and feel (or detract, depending on your perspective), and the decorations present a number of controls that allow users to manipulate the window.

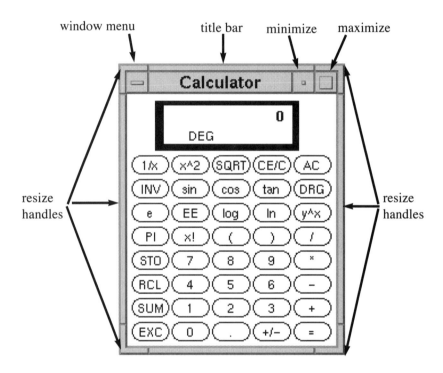

Figure 8.1 The Motif window manager controls.

You can use the mouse to drag a corner of the window, thereby changing the window's size. You can click the left mouse button in the minimize button and turn the window into an icon. You can click in the maximize button and enlarge the window to its full size. And you can click on the window menu icon and get a window manager menu to control that window.

The above example is from the **Motif window manager**, or **mwm**. With **mwm**, and most other window managers, you can press the left mouse button over the title bar and then drag the window to a new location. You can also choose the Move choice from the window menu.

The title bar is placed by the window manager and is not part of your application. The same application used above, **xcalc**, looks different under the **Tab Window Manager**, or **twm**:

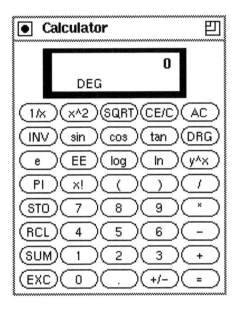

Figure 8.2 The Tab window manager running xcalc.

The **xcalc** application itself—the area inside the title bar—looks the same in both examples, but the window frame is different. This frame is what the window manager provides. (This frame is actually made up of a number of windows.)

One thing always to remember is that the window manager is in control of the screen. This means that the window manager may, or may not, do what you want. The window manager controls the layout of all the windows and may not allow you to change the size of a window, or it may not provide a title bar or allow you to iconify a window. In such cases, your only recourse is to change window managers. This is not always an option, however, since few good window managers exist, and your organization may have already made one window manager standard.

The concept of window managers controlling the screen helps make window managers one of the least-understood features provided by the X Window System. On one hand, it's nice that you can define any interface that you want. On the other hand, ultimate freedom can be dizzying and confusing. The same application, **xcalc**, looks different under a variety of window managers, including the **Open Look window manager**, **olwm**:

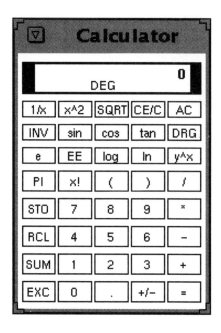

Figure 8.3 The Open Look window manager running xcalc.

Which Interface Am I Running?

If you run **xcalc** under the Open Look window manager, are you an Open Look user? **Xcalc** isn't an Open Look program, since it doesn't follow the Open Look style. You can also run **xcalc** under **mwm**, the Motif window manager. Does this then mean you're a Motif user? In our judgment, the question doesn't really matter, but it does confuse a lot of people and make for a lot of polemical discussions on on-line services like CompuServe or Usenet.

Bottom line: **xcalc** is an X application. It doesn't matter what window manager you run the program under. You, the user, are free to choose the window manager you prefer (or the one that bothers you the least).

The window managers listed above (**mwm**, **twm**, and **olwm**) are the most widely used window managers. There are others, though, as, the following list shows:

Table 8.1 Common Window Managers.

Program	Description
mwm	Motif Window Manager
dxwm	DECwindows Window Manager
olwm	Open Look Window Manager
olvwm	Open Look *Virtual* Window Manager (provides a virtual desktop)
4Dwm	Silicon Graphics version of **mwm**
NCDwm	local window manager on NCD X terminals
XDSwm	local window manager on Visual X terminals
twm	Tab Window Manager (formerly Tom's, as in Tom LaStrange, author of the original **twm**)
vtwm	Virtual Tab Window Manager (provides a virtual desktop)
tvtwm	Tom's Virtual Tab Window Manager (provides a virtual desktop)
vuewm	Hewlett-Packard Visual User Environment Window Manager (provides a virtual desktop)
swm	Solbourne Window Manager (also provides a virtual desktop)
uwm	Universal or Ultrix Window Manager (this old program doesn't provide title bars)

Most of these window managers are variations on **mwm**, **twm**, or **olwm**. Hewlett-Packard's **vuewm** and Silicon Graphics' **4Dwm** look and act essentially like the Motif window manager, **mwm**, for example.

Virtual-Root Window Managers

Virtual-root window managers place a *very* large window between the root window, the screen background, and your applications, providing a number of virtual screens. Application windows are then placed on this very large canvas, and the user can pan between virtual screens.

You can, for example, divide a large virtual screen into areas, based on your current projects or however you like to divide up your work. Window managers such as **swm**, **olvwm**, **vtwm**, **tvtwm**, and **vuewm** all present variations on this concept. Some of these window managers also allow for **sticky** windows; applications like **xclock** can remain in the same position on every virtual screen. When you change from one virtual screen to another, the **xclock** window remains stuck to its position.

Title-Bar Geometry

Window managers place title bars on application windows by a process called **reparenting**. When an application creates a top-level window, the window manager intercedes by adding its own window around the application's window, as shown in the diagram below.

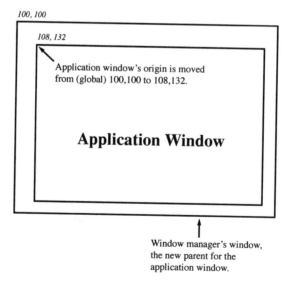

Figure 8.4 Reparenting windows.

This new window, owned and placed by the window manager, is slightly larger than your application's window. The extra space is used for the frame surrounding the application's window, including space for the title bar.

When this new window appears, it changes your application's layout. Most window managers move your window down and slightly to the right. For example, if you start an application at 100,100, the window itself won't appear at 100,100. The window manager's title bar will, at least with most window managers.

For example, if we start an **xcalc** with the following, we find that the **xcalc** window has moved:

```
xcalc -geometry +100+100 &
```

Using the **xwininfo** command, we discover the new location. Under **twm**, the location shown by **xwininfo** is:

```
xwininfo      ==> Window id: 0x2000011 (Calculator)
              ==> Absolute upper-left X:   102
              ==> Absolute upper-left Y:   123
              ==> Relative upper-left X:   0
              ==> Relative upper-left Y:   21
```

In this case, the **xcalc** window is at position 0, 21 in the new window-manager window, using the local origin, or 102, 123 on the screen. The extra space is used by the window manager.

With the Motif window manager, though, we discover a new position:

```
xwininfo      ==> Window id: 0x1c00011 (Calculator)
              ==> Absolute upper-left X:   101
              ==> Absolute upper-left Y:   101
              ==> Relative upper-left X:   0
              ==> Relative upper-left Y:   0
```

This window is one pixel down from where we wanted it, meaning that the window manager frame is above and to the left of our window. (Note that you can customize this position with the **positionIsFrame** resource, as we describe in the next chapter.)

Xwininfo, mentioned above, is a program that prints out window information. You run this program from an **xterm** or another terminal window, and it prompts you to choose a window using the mouse. Once chosen, **xwininfo** prints out more information than you care to know concerning the given window. If you use the **-tree** command-line parameter, **xwininfo** prints out the window tree from the chosen window on downward. (Choose the root window to get a list of all windows on your display.)

The Motif window manager, as one example, creates more than one larger window encompassing your application as part of this reparenting process. Each control, shown in figure 8.1, above, such as the iconify button, has its own window. Using the **oclock** application as an example, here's a listing of all the 10 windows **mwm** creates, again using **xwininfo** to generate the data:

```
0x1400053 (has no name): ()   96x113+893+0   +893+0
   10 children:
   0x140005d (has no name): ()   80x80+8+25   +901+25
      1 child:
      0x1800007 "oclock": ("oclock" "Clock")   80x80+0+0   +901+25
         1 child:
         0x1800008 (has no name): ()   80x80+0+0   +901+25
   0x140005c (has no name): ()   82x18+7+7   +900+7
   0x140005b (has no name): ()   8x63+0+25   +893+25
   0x140005a (has no name): ()   25x25+0+88   +893+88
   0x1400059 (has no name): ()   46x8+25+105   +918+105
   0x1400058 (has no name): ()   25x25+71+88   +964+88
   0x1400057 (has no name): ()   8x63+88+25   +981+25
   0x1400056 (has no name): ()   25x25+71+0   +964+0
   0x1400055 (has no name): ()   46x7+25+0   +918+0
   0x1400054 (has no name): ()   25x25+0+0   +893+0
```

The window with ID **0x1400053** is the window that encompasses the **oclock** window, with ID **0x1800007**. All of the windows starting with **0x14** were created by **mwm**.

Window Menus

Most window managers provide some sort of menu for each window. Most window managers also provide at least one menu over the background, a **root window**. These menus are also configurable, both from configuration files and from within application programs.

This menu is used to control the application window. The Close menu choice tells the application to get rid of the window, which normally causes the program to quit. This menu is also used to launch applications, raise or lower windows (a necessary operation when your screen gets cluttered with large windows), and quit the window manager.

Turning Windows Into Icons

ᵔre small pictures that represent windows. When you iconify a window, you ₊y exchange the window for the small picture—the icon. This removes clutter from your screen. Windows you aren't interested in at the moment are those you might want to inconify.

Most, but not all, window managers support icons. Again, the window manager is in charge, so if you want to iconify your application windows, you must run a window manager that supports this. Normally, you can click the first mouse button once or twice in the icon for the window to reappear.

Typing Into Windows

With X, you can type into only one window at a time. The process of choosing which window gets the keyboard input (called the **keyboard focus**) is called **focus management**. Window managers usually display one window as the active window—the window with the keyboard focus. This active window often displays different colors in the title bar to show you that it "owns" the keyboard. When you type, your keystrokes will go into that active window.

Window managers are free to use any policy for focusing the keyboard. Most, though, present two models: click to type and focus follows mouse.

In the **click-to-type mode**, you must first move the mouse pointer into a window and click on a mouse button (normally the left button, called Button 1), making that window the active window. The Macintosh under System 7 and Microsoft Windows 3.x both use this model.

In the **focus-follows-mouse mode**, the keyboard focus travels with the mouse. If you merely move the mouse pointer into a window, that window becomes the active window. As you move the mouse about the screen, you can watch as windows become active while the mouse is in a window.

In the next three chapters we'll show you how to change the keyboard focus to the click-to-type or focus-follows-mouse policies for the three most-used window managers, **mwm**, **olwm**, and **twm**.

Summary

X allows you to change the entire look and feel of your environment through window managers. A window manager is a special X application that controls the layout of windows on the screen. A window manager controls how much of the screen's real estate any application can have. It also allows you to resize, iconify, and move windows.

Most window managers place a title bar and other decorations around the applications' main windows. This title bar helps enhance the look and feel (or detract, depending on your perspective) of the environment, and the decorations present a number of controls that allow users to manipulate the window.

One thing always to remember is that the window manager is in control of the screen. This means that the window manager may, or may not, do what you want. The window manager controls the layout of all the windows and may not allow you to change the size of a window, or it may not provide a title bar or allow you to iconify a window. In such cases, your only recourse is to change window managers.

Virtual-root window managers place a *very* large window between the root window, the screen background, and your applications, providing a number of virtual screens. Application windows are then placed on this very large canvas, and the user can pan between virtual screens.

Window managers place title bars on application windows by a process called reparenting. When an application creates a top-level window, the window manager intercedes by adding its own window around the application's window.

Most window managers provide some sort of menu for each window. Most window managers also provide at least one menu over the background, the **root window**. These menus are also configurable, both from configuration files and from within application programs.

Icons are small pictures that represent a window. When you iconify a window, you essentially exchange the window for the small picture, the icon. This frees cluttered space on your screen, especially for windows you aren't interested in at the moment.

With X, you can type into only one window at a time. The process of choosing which window gets the keyboard input is called focus management. Window managers are free to use any policy for focusing the keyboard. Most, though, present two models: click to type and focus follows mouse.

In the next few chapters, we'll cover the three main window managers, **mwm**, **olwm**, and **twm** in depth, showing you how to configure each and also how to get around the strange quirks offered by the programs.

## Chapter 9

Customizing the Motif Window Manager

The Motif window manager and close variants come as the default window manager on a number of systems, including those from IBM, Hewlett-Packard, Silicon Graphics, SCO, and Data General. In this chapter we'll cover the Motif window manager in depth and show you how to get the most out of this common window manager.

The Motif window manager's program name is **mwm**, and you can run it from the command line. Usually, though, you'll run **mwm** as the last item in a **.xinitrc** or **.xsession** file.

You won't need any command-line parameters unless you need the standard **display** parameter. If you have multiple screens on your X display, you'll want to use the **-multiscreen** parameter, which tells **mwm** to manage windows on all screens for your display. By default, **mwm** manages windows on just one screen. Most workstations have just one screen anyway, so this normally isn't an issue.

We'll run through some basic actions under the **mwm** window manager. We've already introduced the basic Motif window manager controls in the last chapter; this chapter builds on those controls.

Changing Window Sizes

To change the size of a window under **mwm**, move the mouse cursor over any resize area on the window frame. Hold down the left mouse button and use the mouse to move the ghosted window to the desired size.

Various resize areas in the window frame allow you to change the window's size in different directions. The top area, for example, allows you to change only the window's height, not its width. This is useful for **xterm** windows, where you want to keep 80 columns in width but want to change the number of rows. Conversely, the side areas change only the window's width. The corners allow changes in both width and height. Just look at how the cursor changes over the sizing areas and you will know how you can change the window's size.

Moving Windows

To move a window, move the mouse pointer over the title bar and hold down the left mouse button while moving the mouse. A ghosted outline of the window should follow the mouse pointer position. Release the mouse button when the window is in the proper position. You can also move a window by using the window menu. Move the mouse to the window menu button and hold down the left or right mouse button. To select a choice, release the mouse button over the choice you want.

The default window manager menu allows you to control a window's placement and size. The Move choice allows you to move the window.

Table 9.1 The default Mwm window menu.

Menu Choice	Shortcut	Mnemonic
Restore	Alt-F5	R
Move	Alt-F7	M
Size	Alt-F8	S
Minimize	Alt-F9	n
Maximize	Alt-F10	x
Raise	Alt-F1	a
Lower	Alt-F3	L
Close	Alt-F4	C

In Motif terminology, **minimize** means to turn the window into an icon, or iconify. **Maximize** means to make the window as large as it can be (a setting that the application can control); this process is also called **zooming** the window to its full size.

You can minimize a window by clicking the first mouse button over the minimize icon on the window frame. You can also or use the window menu.

To restore a window back from an icon, you can double-click over the icon.

Table 9.2 Actions with icons.

Button	Action	Meaning
1	click	Selects icon
1	double-click	Opens (restores) window from icon
1	drag	Moves icon
3	press and hold	Displays window menu

You can also use the icon's window menu, which appears if you click the mouse button once over the icon. The Restore choice brings back the window.

These menu choices are configurable, both on a displaywide basis or specific to just one application, by editing the Motif configuration files.

Mwm Configuration Files

You can customize **mwm** using standard resource files as described in Chapter 6. **Mwm** uses a resource name of *mwm* and a class name of *Mwm*, so a class resource file will also be named **Mwm**. You can place **mwm** resource commands in your **.Xdefaults** or **.Xresources** files, too.

In addition to the resource files, **mwm** uses a special configuration file named **.mwmrc**. Your **.mwmrc** file is normally located in your home directory, but as with most aspects of X, you can configure it to a different location.

Mwm starts looking for the **.mwmrc** file in the **$HOME/$LANG/.mwmrc** file, where **HOME** is your home directory and **LANG** specifies your local language. If you don't have the **LANG** environment variable set, then **mwm** looks for **$HOME/.mwmrc**. **Mwm** has a system-wide configuration file, too, in **/usr/lib/X11/$LANG/system.mwmrc** or **/usr/lib/X11/system.mwmrc**.

Of course, you can change these settings by changing the **configFile** resource in a **mwm** resource file to a different file name, such as:

Mwm*configFile: /users/erc/mwm/my_mwmrc

The resource files follow the standard resource-file precedence we described in Chapter 6. The normal place for a systemwide default class-resource file is in **/usr/lib/X11/app-defaults/Mwm**. This is where system administrators will set up installationwide defaults. The normal place for your **mwm** resource commands is in your home directory, **$HOME/Mwm**. The **.mwmrc** file normally controls **mwm**'s menus and keyboard bindings. The resource files control everything else.

For the rest of this chapter, we'll show you how to use and change various features of **mwm**. We won't go over every single option. The on-line manual pages for **mwm** should help you once you've finished this chapter.

When we mention the **.mwmrc** file in our examples we mean whatever file you chose for your **mwm** configuration file, which is normally **$HOME/.mwmrc**. If you don't have a **.mwmrc** file already, start out by making a copy of the system **.mwmrc** file, normally in **/usr/lib/X11/system.mwmrc**. Copy this file into **.mwmrc** in your home directory. You can start out by taking advantage of any customizations your system administrator set up.

When we mention the **Mwm** resource file, this is the class resource file for **mwm**, again in whatever location you chose.

The first thing we'll show, though, is how to quit **mwm**, because for some stupid reason **mwm** starts up by default with a no-quit option. We really don't consider this to be user-friendly behavior. Most users, though, quickly customize the **mwm** root menu to add a quit choice.

Mwm Root Window Menu

Look in the **.mwmrc** file for the default root menu, which should look like the one below.

```
Menu RootMenu
{
        "Root Menu"         f.title
        "New Window"        f.exec "xterm &"
        "Shuffle Up"        f.circle_up
        "Shuffle Down"      f.circle_down
        "Refresh"           f.refresh
        no-label            f.separator
        "Restart..."        f.restart
}
```

In the above menu, the menu name is **RootMenu** and the menu contents appear between the curly braces. Some of the commands supported by **mwm** include the following:

Table 9.3 Mwm commands.

Mwm Command	Meaning
f.exec	Execute the string following with **/bin/sh**.
f.kill	Send a kill message to the application window.
f.menu	Call up another menu, by name.
f.quit_mwm	Quit **mwm**.
f.refresh	Cause every application to redraw their windows, which cleans up a corrupted display.
f.restart	Cause **mwm** to reread in its configuration files and restart.
f.separator	Places a line separating menu choices.
f.title	Places a title for the menu.

Each menu entry uses the following format:

"label" [mnemonic] [accelerator]   function

The optional mnemonic is a character in the label that can be used as a keyboard shortcut to execute the menu choice. The format is **_character**, such as **_R** for a label of "Resize." The optional accelerator is in the format of a key event (much like the translation tables introduced in Chapter 6), such as **Alt<Key>F5** for Alt-F5.

Customizing the Root Menu

To add a Quit choice to the **mwm** root menu, add the following line inside the curly braces in your **.mwmrc** file:

"Quit mwm"   f.quit_mwm

The root menu in **.mwmrc** should then look something like this:

```
        Menu RootMenu
{
        "Root Menu"     f.title
        "New Window"    f.exec "xterm &"
        "Shuffle Up"    f.circle_up
        "Shuffle Down"  f.circle_down
        "Refresh"       f.refresh
        no-label        f.separator
        "Restart..."    f.restart
        "Quit mwm"      f.quit_mwm
}
```

The **f.restart** command makes **mwm** read in its configuration files again. Whenever you change the **.mwmrc** file, you'll need to execute the Restart choice on the root menu. If you don't have a Restart choice, we suggest you add one now. Before you do, you'll have to quit **mwm**, which probably includes logging out and then starting X over again. The next time you run **mwm**, it should use the new root menu. If you add the Restart choice right away, this should save you time later on, as you can just execute that choice to get **mwm** to reread the **.mwmrc** file.

After going through that rigamarole, you should be able to quit **mwm** in an easier fashion. Since most users set up their window manager as the terminating X application, quitting **mwm** most likely means quitting X. In that case, you may want to have the Quit menu choice text read "Quit X session" rather than "Quit mwm."

When you quit **mwm**, you get a second chance to cancel the operation. You'll see a Quit dialog in the center of the screen. You can choose OK to quit **mwm** and Cancel to stop the operation.

Mwm uses the **f.quit_mwm** command to quit, while **twm** uses **f.quit**.

Now that we've customized the root menu, we find that this menu is a great place from which to launch frequently used X applications.

Launching Programs from the Root Menu

In a network environment, you often log in to other computers on the network using **xterm**'s **-e** command-line parameter. Typing in these long commands, though, quickly becomes tedious. We want to place these long commands as menu choices, so we can avoid retyping the commands.

Using the **f.exec** command from above as an example, you can add the following command to the **mwm** root menu to log in remotely to a machine named **nokomis**:

"Nokomis"   f.exec "xterm -name nokomis -geom 80x46 -e rlogin nokomis &"

The programs you launch with the **f.exec** command should execute in the background, hence the trailing ampersand, **&**.

Cascading Menus

You're not limited to one **mwm** root menu. You can create submenus that cascade off the main root menu. Doing this is simple: Just add a menu choice that uses the **f.menu** command:

"Clocks"   f.menu ClockMenu

Then create the new menu:

```
Menu ClockMenu
{
        "Round Clock"          f.exec "oclock &"
        "Square Clock"         f.exec "xclock &"
        "Digital Clock"        f.exec "xclock -digital &"
}
```

After changing the root menu, you can customize the default window menu the same way.

Customizing the Default Window Menu

To change this menu, look in your **.mwmrc** file for the **DefaultWindowMenu**. It should look something like this:

```
Menu DefaultWindowMenu
{
        Restore   _R    Alt<Key>F5    f.normalize
        Move      _M    Alt<Key>F7    f.move
        Size      _S    Alt<Key>F8    f.resize
        Minimize  _n    Alt<Key>F9    f.minimize
        Maximize  _x    Alt<Key>F10   f.maximize
        Lower     _L    Alt<Key>F3    f.lower
        no-label                      f.separator
        Close     _C    Alt<Key>F4    f.kill
}
```

You can customize this menu the same way you changed the root menu. Normally, though, most X users don't change the window menu.

Typing Into Windows

After changing the **.mwmrc** file, the next step is to change the **Mwm** resource file. By default, **mwm** enforces a keyboard scheme called **click-to-type**. This means you must click the first mouse button in a window before **mwm** will allow you to type into that window. This mode is called **explicit** keyboard focus. (We covered these concepts in Chapter 8.)

In the explicit-focus mode, you can use Alt-Tab to move the keyboard focus to the next window (allowing for mouseless operation). Alt-Shift-Tab moves the focus back to the previous window. You can change the keyboard-focus policy to a mode in which the keyboard focus follows the mouse. Then, when you move the mouse cursor into a window, you can start typing right away. You can watch **mwm** make the window under the mouse active as you move the mouse about the screen. We greatly prefer this mode.

Add the following resource command to your **Mwm** file to use the focus-follows-mouse policy:

Mwm*keyboardFocusPolicy: **pointer**

If you like the click-to-type mode, use the following resource command:

Mwm*keyboardFocusPolicy: **explicit**

Changing Mwm Colors

Users have a high degree of control over **mwm**'s choice of colors. This is very useful on sixteen-color systems, because the 3-D window frame borders take up four colors: foreground, background, top shadow and bottom shadow. Add in four more colors for highlighting the active window and half your colors are defined on a sixteen-color VGA system. On systems with 256 or more colors, this isn't so much an issue, but it's still nice to be able to control the colors used.

Table 9.4 Motif window frame resources.

Resource	Value
activeBackground	name of color for the background
activeBackgroundPixmap	image name
activeBottomShadowColor	color name, usually generated by **mwm**
activeBottomShadowPixmap	image name
activeForeground	name of color to set foreground to
activeTopShadowColor	color name, usually generated by **mwm**
activeTopShadowPixmap	image name
background	name of color to set background to
backgroundPixmap	image name
bottomShadowColor	color name, usually generated by **mwm**
bottomShadowPixmap	image name
foreground	name of color to set foreground to
topShadowColor	color name, usually generated by **mwm**
topShadowPixmap	image name

We suggest that you change only the **foreground**, **background**, **activeForeground**, and **activeBackground** resources, unless you have a low-color system. Motif's algorithm for choosing the 3-D shadow colors has improved markedly since early versions, and you generally can't beat Motif for making the right shades for the best 3-D effects.

Unless you have a monochrome system, don't set any of the pixmap resources. These resources allow you to use a pixmap, such as a 50 percent gray bitmap in place of a color. This is how you can get still get 3-D effects on monochrome systems. The image name can be a built-in image, such as **50_foreground** or the name of a pixmap file.

Customizing Applications Under Mwm

In addition to changing the colors, you can change the way **mwm** treats each class of application. A common reason to do this is to remove the title bar over clock windows. For the **xclock** program, you can turn off the window frame and all decorations with the following resource command:

Mwm*XClock.clientDecoration: none

You can mix and match the decoration values below. If you use **none** or **all**, though, don't expect to include other decorations also. You can remove decorations by using the minus sign (-) before the option, such as **–maximize** to remove the maximize button.

Table 9.5 Mwm client decorations.

Value	Meaning
all	Use all decorations
border	Place a window border
maximize	Place maximize button
minimize	Place minimize button
none	Place no decorations
resizeh	Place resize "handles"
menu	Place window menu button
title	Place title bar

The **clientDecoration** resource controls the look of the window frame, not really how the user can interact with it. Remember, the user can perform the functions from the window menu. Because of this, there's also a **clientFunctions** resource, which controls the actual functions of minimizing, maximizing, and resizing. The **clientFunctions** resource acts much like **clientDecoration**, but the available values are: **all**, **none**, **resize**, **move**, **minimize**, **maximize**, and **close**. The resource name for **clientFunctions** is plural, while **clientDecoration** is singular.

Strangely enough, the most-used X application, **xterm**, doesn't set an icon. In such cases, **mwm** sets up its own icon, normally dull icon.

You can change this to something more vibrant and "upscale" using the **iconImage** resource:

```
Mwm*XTerm.iconImage:   mryuk.xbm
```

This tells **mwm** to use the bitmap file **mryuk.xbm** as the icon for **xterm**. (This is a Mr. Yuck icon, and not every system will have a Mr. Yuck icon, obviously. You can substitute whatever xbm-formatted file you want.) Since **xterm** doesn't set its own icon, there's no potential conflict with the application's icon. In the case of **xclock**, for example, there would be a conflict. In that case, the **useClientIcon** resource resolves the conflict. If set to **True**, the application's icon wins. If set to **False**, the icon you configured wins.

You can also change the colors used for individual client window frames, such as the following, which changes the background color for the window title area on the **xcalc** application:

```
Mwm*XCalc*title*background: bisque2
```

Mwm Resources

Here are the resources you can set:

Table 9.6 Common mwm resources.

Name	Value
clientAutoPlace	If True, windows are placed automatically by **mwm**.
focusAutoRaise	If True, raises window if it has keyboard focus.
fontList	Names font to use.
frameBorderWidth	Sets width of frame without counting the resize handles; defaults to 5 pixels.
interactivePlacement	If True, the user places new windows; defaults to False.
moveOpaque	If True, then move whole window, `a la` NeXT, not just frame; defaults to False.
positionIsFrame	If True, layout is position of window frame, if False, position is client area; defaults to False.
resizeBorderWidth:	Sets the pixel width of the resize handles. We prefer pixels.

The **positionIsFrame** resource seems confusing. Using the example from the last chapter, we'll run the command below with **positionIsFrame** set to **True**, then to **False** to see the differences:

```
xcalc -geom +100+100 &
```

If set to **True**, **positionIsFrame** places the **xcalc** window at the location below, as reported by **xwininfo**:

```
xwininfo      ==> Window id: 0x3400044 (Calculator)
              ==> Absolute upper-left X:   108
              ==> Absolute upper-left Y:   132
              ==> Relative upper-left X:   0
              ==> Relative upper-left Y:   0
```

If set to **False**, we get this position:

```
xwininfo      ==> Window id: 0x3400044 (Calculator)
              ==> Absolute upper-left X:   101
              ==> Absolute upper-left Y:   101
              ==> Relative upper-left X:   0
              ==> Relative upper-left Y:   0
```

Icons

Mwm provides a host of resources to control icons. If you want, **mwm** places icons in an icon box instead of on the screen. The icon box helps because it presents a scrolled-list window of icons, which saves on-screen space if you have a lot of icons. To get the icon box, set the **useIconBox** resource to **True** (it defaults to **False**). You can set the title of the icon box with the **iconBoxTitle** resource, and its size and location with the **iconBoxGeometry** resource.

The **iconBoxGeometry** resource takes a geometry specification, just as we described in Chapter 5, only the width is represented by the number of icon columns to display and the height by the number of icon rows. A geometry of **4x2+0+0** would make an icon box that is wide enough for four icons and high enough for two, placed at the origin, 0,0, the upper left corner.

Icon Placement

If you don't use the icon box, you can control where **mwm** places icons by using the **iconPlacement** resource. Set this resource with two strings. The first tells the primary way to place icons, such as **left**, which means from left to right. The second string tells the secondary order for placing icons, such as **bottom**, which means from the bottom to the top. Combine the two, as in the following command:

```
Mwm*iconPlacement: left bottom
```

This places icons going left to right across the bottom of the screen. You can also use **top** and **right**, in any combination.

Resetting Mwm

If you really mess things up, you can use a special trick to reset **mwm**. If you hold down the Alt, Shift, Control, and ! keys, **mwm** will toggle its behavior back to the built-in defaults. Use this option only if you have misconfigured **mwm** so badly that you cannot seem to recover.

A Sample Mwm Configuration File

The following is an example **.mwmrc** file, showing how we customize **mwm** for our use. You no doubt have a different set-up, but we wanted to show a real **.mwmrc** file. Use this as a base for customization. Notice that we really didn't change much of this file from the system defaults, except for adding to the menus.

```
#
#  Mwm configuration file. Customized from the system .mwmrc file.
#


#
# menu pane descriptions
#

# Root Menu Description
Menu RootMenu
{
        "Root Menu"         f.title
        "New Window"        f.exec "xterm -geom 80x42 &"
        "Nokomis"           f.exec "xterm -geom 80x42 -name
           nokomis -e rlogin nokomis &"
        "Shuffle Up"        f.circle_up
```

```
        "Shuffle Down"      f.circle_down
        "Refresh"           f.refresh
        no-label            f.separator
        "Applications"      f.menu AppMenu
        no-label            f.separator
        "Restart..."        f.restart
        no-label            f.separator
        "Quit"              f.quit_mwm
}


#
#       This menu can be used to launch a number of applications.
#
Menu AppMenu
{
        "Debugger"          f.exec "xdbx &"
        "Clipboard"         f.exec "xclipboard &"
        "Calculator"        f.exec "xcalc &"
        "Select Font"       f.exec "xfontsel &"
        "CPU Load"          f.exec "xload &"
        no-label            f.separator
        "Mahjongg"          f.exec "xmj &"
        no-label            f.separator
        "Edit Resources"    f.exec "editres &"
        "Screen Magnifier"  f.exec "xmag &"
        no-label            f.separator
        "Round Clock"       f.exec "oclock &"
        "Square Clock"      f.exec "xclock &"
        "Digital Clock"     f.exec "xclock -digital &"
}


# Default Window Menu Description

Menu DefaultWindowMenu
{
        Restore     _R Alt<Key>F5  f.normalize
        Move        _M Alt<Key>F7  f.move
        Size        _S Alt<Key>F8  f.resize
        Minimize    _n Alt<Key>F9  f.minimize
        Maximize    _x Alt<Key>F10 f.maximize
        Lower       _L Alt<Key>F3  f.lower
        no-label                   f.separator
        Close       _C Alt<Key>F4  f.kill
}
```

```
#
# key binding descriptions
#

Keys DefaultKeyBindings
{
    Shift<Key>Escape           window|icon        f.post_wmenu
    Meta<Key>space             window|icon        f.post_wmenu
    Meta<Key>Tab               root|icon|window   f.next_key
    Meta Shift<Key>Tab         root|icon|window   f.prev_key
    Meta<Key>Escape            root|icon|window   f.next_key
    Meta Shift<Key>Escape      root|icon|window   f.prev_key
    Meta Shift Ctrl<Key>exclam root|icon|window   f.set_behavior
    Meta<Key>F6                window             f.next_key transient
    Meta Shift<Key>F6          window             f.prev_key transient
        <Key>F4                icon               f.post_wmenu
}


#
# button binding descriptions
#

Buttons DefaultButtonBindings
{
    <Btn1Down>                 icon|frame         f.raise
    <Btn3Down>                 icon               f.post_wmenu
    <Btn1Down>                 root               f.menu
RootMenu
}

Buttons ExplicitButtonBindings
{
    <Btn1Down>                 frame|icon         f.raise
    <Btn3Down>                 frame|icon         f.post_wmenu
    <Btn1Down>                 root               f.menu
RootMenu
    Meta<Btn1Down>             window|icon        f.lower
!   Meta<Btn2Down>             window|icon        f.resize
!   Meta<Btn3Down>             window|icon        f.move
}
```

```
Buttons PointerButtonBindings
{
        <Btn1Down>        frame|icon        f.raise
        <Btn3Down>        frame|icon        f.post_wmenu
        <Btn1Down>        root              f.menu    RootMenu
        <Btn1Down>        window            f.raise
        Meta<Btn1Down>    window|icon       f.lower
!       Meta<Btn2Down>    window|icon       f.resize
!       Meta<Btn3Down>    window|icon       f.move
}

#
#   end of .mwmrc file
#
```

A Sample Mwm Resource File

We've also included our **Mwm** resource file below, showing the colors, client decorations, icons, and modes we use with **mwm**:

```
!
!   Mwm application defaults resource file.
!
Mwm*moveThreshold:        3
Mwm*buttonBindings:       DefaultButtonBindings
Mwm*resizeBorderWidth:    7


!
! Set up fonts. We use a nice helvetica
! font for the title bars.
!
Mwm*fontList: -adobe-helvetica-bold-r-normal-14-140-75-75-p-82-iso8859-1
Mwm*icon*fontList:        9x15


!
! Set up colors
!
Mwm*activeBackground:     CadetBlue
Mwm*background:           LightGray
```

```
!
! Place icons along the lower edge,
! starting from the left.
!
Mwm*iconPlacement:            left bottom

Mwm*clientAutoPlace:          false
Mwm*positionIsFrame:          false
Mwm*interactivePlacement:     false


!
! Use a special icon for xterm
!
Mwm*xterm.iconImage:       /u/erc/bitmaps/mryuk.xbm


!
! We want the keyboard focus to follow the mouse
!
Mwm*keyboardFocusPolicy: pointer


!
! Change the deocrations on oclock
!
Mwm*Clock*clientDecoration:    title menu resizeh
!
!   end of Mwm resource file
!
```

Summary

This chapters covers the basics of working with and modifying the Motif window manager and its variants.

Basics covered include moving windows, resizing windows, and minimizing (sometimes called iconifying) windows.

Configuration options include editing **mwm** resources (found in any number of configuration files), changing menu choices, and placing icons. We provide our own configuration files for your use.

## Chapter 10

Customizing the Open Look Window Manager

The **Open Look window manager**, or **olwm**, comes configured with every Sun Microsystems SPARC workstation, along with AT&T UNIX and a host of SPARC-compatible systems.

For the past few years, Sun sold more UNIX workstations than any other workstation vendor, so there are many OpenWindows users running **olwm**. Unfortunately, **olwm** seems limited to OpenWindows sites and a few other systems, such as UNIX System V Release 4 on some 386 platforms. If you work in a multi-vendor environment, **olwm** probably will not be available on all your platforms. If you're working in a Sun-oriented environment, you are probably running **olwm**.

Olwm follows the Open Look style guide, which defines a look and feel much differently than what most X users are used to.

Launch **olwm** with the following:

olwm -3

or the newer

olwm -3d

Both of these commands launch **olwm** with the 3-D mode. This mode looks the best, but it requires a color system. The 3-D mode uses color shades to simulate a 3-D effect, much like **mwm** does. On a monochrome system the 2-D parameter, **-2d**, is in effect.

If you have multiple screens on your X display and want **olwm** to manage windows on all these screens, use the **-multi** command-line parameter. This acts like **mwm**'s **-multiscreen**.

Like most window managers, **olwm** places a title bar above application windows. Small resize handles appear at the corners of the window, which you can use to resize the window. A small downward-pointing arrow contains a window menu, which you can call up with the right mouse button.

Olwm shows the active window by drawing two lines in the active window's title bar.

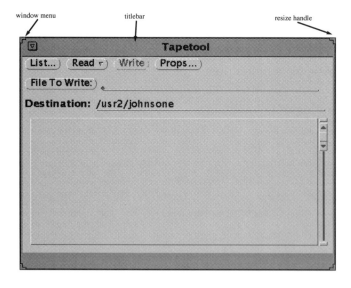

Figure 10.1 Olwm controls.

Open Look uses the mouse buttons in a nontraditional manner, which may require some adjustments on your part. It certainly did for us.

Table 10.1 Open Look mouse buttons.

Button	Usage
1	SELECT, selects item or executes default menu choice.
2	ADJUST.
3	MENU, calls up a menu.

The trickiest part is that the right mouse button, Menu, calls up menus, while the left mouse button, Select, executes the default choice in that menu. This can lead to great problems. Since most other X style guides (like Motif) use the left button to pull down a menu, new Open Look users may accidentally press Select (the left mouse button) instead of Menu (the right mouse button). This action, of course, executes the default menu choice.

If this default menu choice is something serious (or time-consuming) you may experience problems. At the very least, you'll get unexpected behavior.

This notion is enforced with the **olwm** title bar. If you press the left mouse button, Select, over the downward-pointing arrow icon, then **olwm** iconifies the window, which is the default choice in the menu that really sits beneath this icon. This encourages users to forget there is a menu under this icon. In addition, the icon's menu really does nothing, as you can press the right mouse button, Menu, anywhere on the title bar and get the same menu.

In addition to this unorthodox paradigm, Open Look also uses odd terminology:

Table 10.2 Terminology translations.

Open Look	Motif	Meaning
Close	Minimize	Iconify
Full Size	Maximize	Zoom to full size
Quit	Close	Sends delete message to window
Back	Lower	Sends window back behind other windows

These same terms take on radically different meanings depending on your window manager, especially the term *Close*. If you work in a multivendor environment, you must stress the differences.

Configuring Olwm

Olwm uses a **.openwin-menu** file in your home directory to configure the root, or **Workspace** menu. Other configuration options come from X resource files, such as **.Xdefaults**.

In looking for the **.openwin-menu** file, **olwm** first checks the **OLWMMENU** environment variable, which can name any file you want. Then **olwm** looks for **$HOME/.openwin-menu.localename**, if you've set up a locale, which is used for internationalization. If your locale is *japanese*, then **olwm** looks for **.openwin-menu.japanese**. Finally, **olwm** checks **$HOME/.openwin-menu** if you haven't set up a locale.

If all these fail, **olwm** uses the system files stored in **$OPENWINHOME/lib/openwin-menu.localename** if you have set up a locale, and **$OPENWIN-HOME/lib/openwin-menu** if you haven't.

When we mention the **.openwin-menu** file in our examples below, we mean the file you've configured your system to use.

A **$HOME/.openwin-init** file is generated when you save the Workspace. This is used by the **openwin** script that starts X under OpenWindows, and not **olwm**, even though this file is normally associated with Open Look users.

Changing the Olwm Menus

You can change the root menu, which **olwm** calls the **Workspace** menu, by editing the **.openwin-menu** file. In a nice touch, **olwm** automatically reads in this file when it has been changed, which can save you a lot of hassle restarting the window manager. (This also uses up CPU cycles. If this is important to you, you can turn it off with the **AutoReReadMenuFile** resource.)

The default Workspace menu includes the following choices:

Table 10.3 Olwm Workspace Menu.

Choice	Action
Xterm	Launch an xterm
Cmdtool	Launch a cmdtool, the Open Look equivalent of xterm
Refresh	Redraw all windows on the display
Restart WM	Restart olwm
Reread Menu File	Regenerate menus from .openwin-menu
Exit WM	Exit olwm only
Exit	Exit olwm and kill all X applications

Each menu choice executes a built-in **olwm** command or a UNIX program. These commands don't work with **mwm** and **twm**, which use commands like **f.exec** and **f.restart**.

Table 10.4 Olwm menu commands.

Commands	Meaning
BACK_SELN	Lower selected windows.
DEFAULT	Makes menu choice the default choice. Button 1 (Select) executes the default choice.
END	Ends a submenu.
EXIT	Kills all X applications, then exits olwm.
EXIT_NO_CONFIRM	Exits without asking user to confirm.
FULL_RESTORE_SIZE_SELN	Toggle the full size/normal size of the selected windows.
MENU	Starts a submenu.
NOP	Does nothing. Must use a name of " " (note the space) with NOP or you'll generate an error. Used as a separator.
OPEN_CLOSE_SELN	Toggles opened/closed states of selected windows.
PIN	After an END statement, sets a pushpin on the submenu.

Table 10.4 continued...

Commands	Meaning
`QUIT_SELN`	Sends delete message to selected windows.
`REFRESH`	Sends redraw message to all windows.
`REREAD_MENU_FILE`	Rereads the .openwin-menu file.
`RESTART`	Restarts olwm.
`SAVE_WORKSPACE`	Saves the configuration of your current set of running X programs, using the owplaces program.
`WMEXIT`	Exits olwm, but does not kill all other X applications.
`#`	Starts a comment, which extends for the rest of the line.

Here's an example menu we set up:

```
"Workspace Menu"    TITLE
Applications        MENU
      "Xterm"       DEFAULT xterm -geom 80x44
      "Nokomis"     xterm -geom 80x42 -name nokomis -e rlogin nokomis
      "Calculator"xcalc
Applications END PIN
" "                 NOP
"Refresh Screen"    DEFAULT REFRESH
" "                 NOP
"Restart"           RESTART
"Reread Menu File"  REREAD_MENU_FILE
" "                 NOP
"Exit Olwm"         WMEXIT
"Exit and Quit X"   EXIT
```

NOTE

Note how we defined a submenu and set up a pushpin for it. The **Workspace** menu, by default, also gets a pushpin. (See below for more on pushpins.) We don't run the X programs in the background (with an ampersand, **&**) nor do we enclose the commands in quotation marks.

Pushpins

A neat feature of Open Look is the ability to "pin" menus and dialog windows. Once pinned, the menu or dialog remains on the screen, where you use it as a regular menu or dialog at all times, until you "unpin" it. This is one of the best features of Open Look and is emulated in Motif with tear-off menus.

You can use the left mouse button to pin and unpin Open Look pushpins. We added a pushpin, with the **PIN** command in the menu above, so you can practice using pushpins.

The Window Menu

Olwm also provides a menu for each window, which you cannot modify without access to program source code.

Table 10.5 The Olwm window menu.

```
Close
Full Size
Move
Resize
Properties
Back
Refresh
Quit
```

This menu allows you to quit an application, iconify the window (close it), move it, and resize it.

Olwm Resources

In addition to the **Workspace** menu, you can also configure a number of **olwm** resources. **Olwm** uses the resource name of **olwm**, unless you pass the **-name** command-line parameter to change this name. Many resources also support the older resource name of **OpenWindows**. We advise you to use the newer **olwm** format, though.

Olwm provides a number of font resources, including **ButtonFont** for menus and buttons, **TitleFont** for window title bars, and **GlyphFont**, used to draw the Open Look glyphs, like the downward-pointing arrow icon. The text fonts default to the Lucida family, like **Lucida-Sans** or **Lucida-Sans-Bold**.

The **GlyphFont** defaults to **-sun-open look glyph-*-*-*-*-*-120-*-*-*-*-*-*-***, which you shouldn't change unless you really know what you are doing.

Other **olwm** resources include the **ServerGrabs**, **RunSlaveProcess**, and **MinimalDecor** resources. The **ServerGrabs** resource, if set to **true**, allows **olwm** to grab the server when you use menus. This often speeds performance, but if any problems develop, your system can get locked up, since **olwm** has grabbed the X server from all other X applications.

The **RunSlaveProcess**, if set to **true**, runs a program called **olwmslave**, which provides on-the-fly help (called **spot help**) on various aspects of the window frame. If you set **RunSlaveProcess** to **false**, you won't get any spot help.

The **MinimalDecor** resource tells **olwm** to place only minimal decoration on certain windows, such as the following:

```
olwm.MinimalDecor: calctool clock
```

Typing Into Windows

Olwm and **mwm** both define a click-to-type mode where you must first select a window (with the left mouse button) before you can type into that window. This also follows the Microsoft Windows and Macintosh models. This click-to-type mode is the default for **olwm**.

You can change this mode to focus-follows-mouse, where the keyboard focus goes to whatever window the mouse pointer is over. There are two ways to change the keyboard-focus mode: through a command-line parameter or in a resource file. The **-c** command-line parameter installs click-to-type mode, the default. The **-f** command-line parameter initiates focus-follows-mouse mode. The **SetInput** resource also controls this mode. You can set this resource to **select**, which sets the click-to-type mode, or **followmouse**, which sets the focus-follows-mouse mode.

You can also set the active window to raise to the top automatically, using the **AutoRaise** resource. Set this resource to **true** to raise the active window automatically.

Older programs may have trouble with keyboard input under **olwm**. We cover this problem in Chapter 16, but if your applications aren't getting any keyboard input under **olwm**, set the **FocusLenience** resource to **true**. As more and more applications follow the X rules for well-behaved programs, this is becoming less and less of a problem.

Setting Olwm Colors

Olwm provides a number of color-changing resources, so you can control the look of your display. The **Background**, **Foreground**, and **BorderColor** resources set colors like you'd expect. The **WindowColor** resource sets the background color of the title bar and decorations. The **ReverseVideo** resource, if set to **true**, reverses the **Foreground** and **Background** colors.

The **WorkspaceColor** resource sets the color of the screen background. **Olwm**, by default, sets the screen background to a variant of light blue. You can change this color with the **WorkspaceColor** resource. And, if you don't want **olwm** changing the root window's background color at all, you can set the **PaintWorkspace** resource to **false** (it defaults to **true**), and use programs like **xsetroot** to change your root-window background color.

Olwm Icons

Olwm allows you to change a few parameters associated with icons, but generally with less freedom than is allowed by **mwm** and **twm**.

The **IconFont** resource sets the font name for icons, which, as usual, defaults to **Lucida-Sans**. The **IconLocation** resource allows you to tell **olwm** where to put program icons, or at least along what edge of the screen to place the icons. The **IconLocation** resource can take one of the following values:

Table 10.6 IconLocation values.

Value	Meaning
top-lr	Top, from left to right
top-rl	Top, from right to left
bottom-lr	Bottom, from left to right
bottom-rl	Bottom, from right to left

Table 10.6 continued...

Value	Meaning
left-tb	Left, from top to bottom
left-tb	Left, from bottom to top
right-tb	Right, from top to bottom
right-tb	Right, from bottom to top

```
olwm.IconLocation:        bottom-lr
```

The **DefaultIconImage** sets the file name for an X bitmap image to use for applications, such as **xterm**, that don't provide their own icon.

```
olwm.DefaultIconImage:   /u/erc/bitmaps/mryuk.xbm
```

Olwm Files

We place the following resource-setting commands in our **.Xdefaults** file, to customize **olwm**:

```
!
!        Set up for olwm, Open Look Window Manager
!
olwm.SetInput:           followmouse
olwm.FocusLenience:      true
olwm.WorkspaceColor:     bisque2
olwm.IconLocation:       bottom-lr
olwm.DefaultIconImage:   /u/erc/bitmaps/mryuk.xbm
olwm.MinimalDecor:       xcalc xclock oclock mailbox
olwm.WindowColor:        burlywood
```

The **.openwin-menu** file contains a Workspace menu definition:

```
#
#        Eric and Kevin's menu file for olwm, the
#        Open Look Window Manager.
#
"Workspace Menu"    TITLE
Applications        MENU
```

```
        "Xterm"        DEFAULT xterm -geom 80x44
        "Nokomis"      xterm -geom 80x42 -name nokomis -e rlogin nokomis
        "Calculator"   xcalc
Applications END PIN
" "                    NOP
"Refresh Screen"       DEFAULT REFRESH
" "                    NOP
"Restart"              RESTART
"Reread Menu File"     REREAD_MENU_FILE
" "                    NOP
"Save Workspace"       SAVE_WORKSPACE
" "                    NOP
"Exit Olwm"            WMEXIT
"Exit and Quit X"      EXIT


#
#       end of .openwin-menu
#
```

Summary

The Open Look window manager, or **olwm**, comes configured with every Sun Microsystems SPARC workstation, along with AT&T UNIX and a host of SPARC-compatible systems. **Olwm** follows the Open Look style guide, which defines a look and feel much different from what most X users are used to.

Open Look uses the mouse buttons in a nontraditional manner, which may require some adjustments on your part; it certainly did for us. The trickiest part is that the right mouse button, Menu, calls up menus, while the left mouse button, Select, executes the default choice in that menu. Since most other X style guides (like Motif) use the left button to pull down a menu, new Open Look users may accidentally press Select (the left mouse button) instead of Menu (the right mouse button). This action, of course, executes the default menu choice.

Olwm uses a **.openwin-menu** file in your home directory to configure the root, or **Workspace** menu. Other configuration options come from X resource files, such as **.Xdefaults**.

You can change the root menu, which **olwm** calls the **Workspace** menu, by editing the **.openwin-menu** file. **Olwm** automatically reads in this file when it has been changed, which can save you a lot of hassle restarting the window manager.

A neat feature of Open Look is the ability to "pin" menus and dialog windows. Once pinned, the menu or dialog remains on the screen, where you use it as a regular menu or dialog at all times, until you "unpin" it.

Olwm and **mwm** both define a click-to-type mode where you must first select a window (with the left mouse button) before you can type into that window. You can change this mode to focus follows mouse, where the keyboard focus goes to whatever window the mouse pointer is in. There are two ways to change the keyboard focus mode: through a command-line parameter or in a resource.

## Chapter 11

Customizing the Tab Window Manager

The **Tab window manager**, or **twm**, comes with the default X Window System from the X Consortium. Many vendors include **twm** as part of their X platform, although some delete **twm** in favor of **mwm**, the Motif window manager.

Since X is free—or nearly free—**twm** has become one of the most popular window managers. Originally written by Tom LaStrange of Solbourne, when it was called "Tom's window manager," **twm** is now controlled by the X Consortium, which added the "tab" (or squeeze) title feature and renamed it the Tab window manager.

Like most window managers, **twm** places a title bar above application windows. The left button turns the window into an icon, and the right button allows you to resize the window.

Twm makes it tougher to resize windows than do other window managers, like **mwm** or **olwm**, because there is only one place, the upper-right corner, from which you can resize windows. If you choose the resize choice from the **twm** root menu, though, you can then resize in other directions.

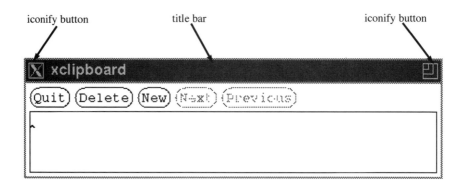

iconify button   title bar   iconify button

Figure 11.1 Twm controls.

Twm Configuration Files

Unlike most other window managers, **twm** doesn't use a class-resource file. **Twm** is controlled with a configuration file in your home directory named **.twmrc**. (When we mention the **.twmrc** file in this chapter, we mean whichever configuration file you've set up, which will normally be **$HOME/.twmrc**.) If that file doesn't exist, **twm** uses a system file normally located at **/usr/lib/X11/twm/system.twmrc**.

You can override this default configuration by using the **-f** (for **filename**) command-line parameter to **twm**. For example, to use a configuration file named **my_twmrc**, you would use the following command:

```
twm -f my_twmrc
```

Inside the configuration file there are **variable values**, **key bindings**, and **menu definitions**.

Twm Root Menu

Like **mwm** and **olwm**, **twm** places a menu on the root window by default.

The syntax for this menu is much like that for **mwm**. You'll notice menu commands, like **f.exec** and **f.restart**, that work much like their counterparts in **mwm**, even though their menus look slightly different.

Unlike **mwm** and **olwm**, **twm** doesn't provide a window menu.

Table 11.1 Common twm menu commands.

Twm Command	Meaning
f.destroy	Destroy X connection for selected window—much like mwm's f.kill.
f.delete	Send a delete-window message to the application.
f.exec	Execute the string following with /bin/sh.
f.nop	Does nothing. Used as a separator, like mwm's f.separator.
f.quit	Quit twm—much like mwm's f.quit_mwm.
f.restart	Cause twm to reread configuration files and restart.
f.title	Make text string the menu title.

The extra **f.delete** sends a delete message to an application's window. Most modern X applications will then take this message and delete the window in question, often quitting the application if that was its only window. Older applications, though, don't support this protocol, and so you must kill the windows separately. The best idea is to try **f.delete** first and **f.destroy** only if the delete attempt failed.

Changing the Root Menu

You can change the **twm** root menu, or add menus of your own, by editing the end of the **.twmrc** file. The end of the file is important, since menu definitions must go after the variable values and the key bindings.

The default **twm** root menu appears below:

```
menu "defops"
{
"Twm"              f.title
"Iconify"          f.iconify
"Resize"           f.resize
"Move"             f.move
"Raise"            f.raise
"Lower"            f.lower
""                 f.nop
""Focus"           f.focus
"Unfocus"          f.unfocus
"Show Iconmgr"     f.showiconmgr
"Hide Iconmgr"     f.hideiconmgr
""                 f.nop
"Kill"             f.destroy
"Delete"           f.delete
""                 f.nop
"Restart"          f.restart
"Exit"             f.quit
}
```

You can add choices to this menu or remove the choices you don't like or don't use.

Since there's no confirmation on the Exit choice, we edit the file to place a separator between the Exit and the Restart choices, because it's too easy to choose Exit by accident when you mean Restart. We also remove the Iconify, Move, Focus, and Unfocus choices, since we never use the **twm** menu for these tasks; using the mouse is easier.

The **twm** syntax for menus follows the model of :

```
menu "menu name" { menu definitions }
```

Twm places most multipart items between curly braces.

Here's a modified root menu:

```
menu "defops"
{
"Modified Twm Menu"        f.title
"Xterm"           f.exec "xterm -geom 80x42 &"
"Nokomis"         f.exec "xterm -geom 80x42 -name nokomis -e rlogin nokomis &"
"Calculator"      f.exec "xcalc &"
"Magnifier"       f.exec "xmag &"
" "               f.nop
"Resize"          f.resize
" "               f.nop
"Raise"           f.raise
"Lower"           f.lower
" "               f.nop
"Show Iconmgr"    f.showiconmgr
"Hide Iconmgr"    f.hideiconmgr
" "               f.nop
"Kill"            f.destroy
"Delete"          f.delete
" "               f.nop
"Restart"         f.restart
" "               f.nop
"Exit"            f.quit
}
```

Typing into Windows

Twm follows the keyboard-focus-follows-the-mouse-pointer model. Whatever window in which the pointer resides gets the keys typed at the keyboard. You don't have to change the configuration, but you can use the **f.focus** and **f.unfocus** menu commands.

Changing Twm Colors

You can change the colors **twm** uses for most everything, although this can get tedious. **Twm** seems to have a separate color variable for everything, but we usually use just two colors (see below): one for the foreground and another for the background.

Like menus, colors are set between curly braces, after the **Color** command. Here's a set of colors that we use:

```
Color
{
        BorderColor "black"
        DefaultBackground "burlywood"
        DefaultForeground "black"
        TitleBackground "burlywood"
        TitleForeground "black"
        MenuBackground "burlywood"
        MenuForeground "black"
        MenuTitleBackground "black"
        MenuTitleForeground "burlywood"
        IconBackground "burlywood"
        IconForeground "black"
        IconBorderColor "black"
        IconManagerBackground "burlywood"
        IconManagerForeground "black"
}
```

Changing Colors on Monochrome Systems

The **Monochrome** variable acts the same as the **Color** variable, but it is engaged on monochrome systems. You can specify colors for both color and monochrome systems in one **.twmrc** file.

Remember to set the colors to **black** or **white** for the **Monochrome** variable.

```
Monochrome
{
        BorderColor             "black"
        BorderTitleBackground   "white"
        BorderTitleForeground   "black"
        IconBorderColor         "white"
        IconManagerBackground   "white"
        IconManagerForeground   "black"
        IconManagerHighlight    "white"
        IconBackground          "white"
        IconForeground          "black"
        MenuBackground          "white"
        MenuForeground          "black"
```

```
        TitleBackground              "white"
        TitleForeground              "black"
}
```

Twm Cursors

Twm allows you to control cursors. These cursors are from the font named **cursor**, which you can display with the following command:

```
xfd -fn cursor
```

Each cursor in this font has a name. In its true programmer tradition, these names are given in a C language include file, normally in **/usr/include/X11/cursorfont.h**The names in this file begin with **XC_**, as the following excerpt shows:

```
#define XC_draped_box 48
#define XC_exchange 50
#define XC_fleur 52
#define XC_gobbler 54
#define XC_gumby 56
#define XC_hand1 58
#define XC_hand2 60
#define XC_heart 62
```

The name used by twm is that same name, with the **XC_** part removed. Thus **XC_gumby** becomes **"gumby"** if you want to use this cursor. Here's how we change the default **twm** cursors:

```
Cursors
{
        Frame           "top_left_arrow"
        Title           "top_left_arrow"
        Icon            "top_left_arrow"
        IconMgr         "top_left_arrow"
        Move            "fleur"
        Resize          "fleur"
        Menu            "left_ptr"
        Button          "left_ptr"
        Wait            "watch"
        Select          "dot"
        Destroy         "pirate"
}
```

We kept most of the cursors the same, but changed the **hand2** and **sb_left_arrow** cursors to the better-looking **left_ptr**.

Twm Variables

Twm also provides a number of variables to control how the window manager treats applications, as the table below shows.

Table 11.2 Common Twm variables.

Variable	Meaning
DecorateTransients	Put a title bar on dialog windows. Default is no title bar.
DontMoveOff	If set, windows won't be able to move off screen.
OpaqueMove	Move whole windows, rather than just a frame—like mwm's **moveOpaque** resource.
TitleFont	Sets title-bar font to given fontname.

The **TitleFont** is the only one of these variables that needs a value, which in this case is the font name enclosed in quotation marks.

You can also customize how **twm** treats individual applications. The **NoTitle** variable names a set of applications that should not have title bars. Common applications to place here include clocks:

NoTitle { "xclock" "oclock" "xload" }

The **AutoRaise** variable makes certain application windows rise to the top if you move the mouse into their windows. There is a bit of a delay; just moving the mouse about the screen doesn't result in every window rising to the top.

AutoRaise { "XTerm" "xmail" }

We don't recommend using the **AutoRaise** variable, because it seems confusing when some windows rise up and others don't.

Twm Tabs

The most interesting feature of **twm**, and what sets it apart from other window managers, is the **SqueezeTitle** option. As mentioned earlier, the "Tab" part of the name **twm** comes from this **SqueezeTitle** option. With it, the window title bar is kept from stretching across the top of the whole window. Instead you get a "tab" that covers only part of the window's top edge. The width of the title bar provides only the space needed for the window's title.

The **SqueezeTitle** variable controls this.

```
SqueezeTitle
{
    "XTerm"  left     0  0
    "oclock" center   0  0
}
```

The name is quotes in the application name, or application class name. The word following is the justification (where the smaller title bar should appear) and can be **center**, **left**, or **right**.

The numbers are the numerator and denominator that give a relative position for placing the title bar. The ratio of numerator/denominator determines the relative position of the title bar. It is measured from left to right if the numerator is positive; otherwise, it is measured right-to-left. There are complex rules for handling zeros, but we find that 0/0 for center justification places the title bar in the center and 0/0 for left justification places the title bar on the left. We generally don't mess with the numerator or denominator.

The **SqueezeTitle** option requires the **SHAPE extension** to X, an extension that allows for odd-shaped, nonrectangular windows. Not all systems support the SHAPE extension, though. You can check if your system does with the **xdpyinfo** program. Run **xdpyinfo** from a command line and look for SHAPE under the list of extensions:

```
number of extensions:    4
    SHAPE
    MIT-SHM
    Multi-Buffering
    MIT-SUNDRY-NONSTANDARD
```

We find that the **SqueezeTitle** option is better in concept than execution. It looks neat on an **xterm** window, as the picture below shows. But you soon find out that the shorter window title bars get constantly buried by other windows.

Thus you'll have to use the root window menu to raise windows. Using this menu takes a lot longer than the normal action of clicking the left mouse button over the title bar. We usually end up skipping the **SqueezeTitle** option.

```
┌────────────────────────────────────────────────────────────────────────┐
│ ◉  nicollet   /u/erc/usingx      ⊟                                        │
│ athena*        chap4*        connect.c     fontname.c    startupx.c       │
│ athena.c       chap4.c       da_draw.c     gc.c          test.xbm         │
│ bitmap.c       chap4cms.c    da_edit.c     geometry.c    toolkit.c        │
│ chap1*         chap5*        da_file.c     icon.c        topwind.c        │
│ chap1.c        chap5.c       da_meta.c     icon.xbm      tranwind.c       │
│ chap10*        chap6*        da_pix.c      key.c         usage.c          │
│ chap10.c       chap6.c       da_undo.c     label.c       visual.c         │
│ chap11*        chap7*        dialog.c      loadfont.c    window.c         │
│ chap11.c       chap7.c       display.c     makefile      wmhints.c        │
│ chap12*        chap8*        drawapp*      motif*        wmname.c         │
│ chap12.c       chap8.c       drawapp.c     motif.c       xor.c            │
│ chap13*        chap9*        drawapp.h     oval.c                         │
│ chap13.c       chap9.c       drawapp.xbm   pixmap.c                       │
│ chap2*         classhnt.c    drawstr.c     pushb.c                        │
│ chap2.c        color.c       entry.c       query.c                        │
│ nicollet|3|112>□                                                          │
└────────────────────────────────────────────────────────────────────────┘
```

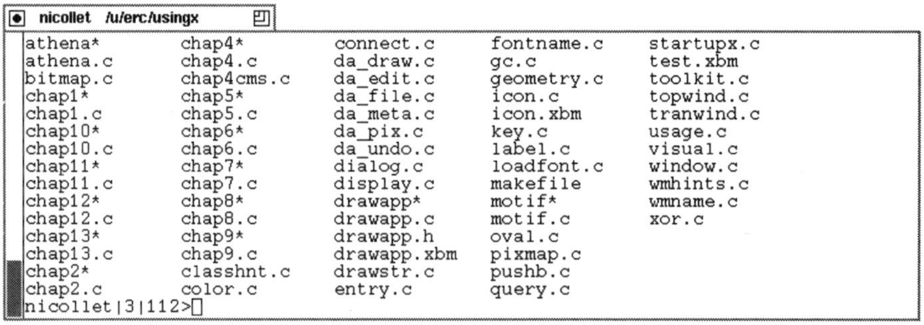

Figure 11.2 Xterm with a squeezed title.

You can turn off the **SqueezeTitle** option by using the **DontSqueezeTitle** variable or just commenting out the **SqueezeTitle** variable.

Icons

Twm provides a lot of control over icons, although the default mode acts strangely. When you iconify a window, the icon by default appears where the cursor is. We find that **mwm**, which places icons together, works much more conveniently. In addition, **twm** doesn't create a default icon for those applications (particularly **xterm**) that don't set their own icon.

Twm provides a number of variables for managing icons, including the following.

Table 11.3 Twm icon variables.

Variable	Meaning
IconFont	Sets font for icons. The font name should be enclosed in quotes.
IconManagerGeometry	Sets the geometry of the icon manager window. The geometry must also be in quotes.
NoIconManagers	Turns off all icon managers.
ShowIconManager	Shows the icon manager.

Changing Icons for Applications

As we noted in the last chapter, **xterm** doesn't provide its own icon. As with **mwm**, we can configure **twm** to use our icon for **xterm**. This is especially important with **twm**, since the window manager just uses the icon name and places a box around it, instead of using a default icon, as **mwm** does. This leads to very small **xterm** icons.

To change this, we use the **Icons** command in the **.twmrc** file:

```
Icons
{
        "XTerm"    "/u/erc/bitmaps/peace.xbm"
}
```

The first part lists the name of the application;—in this case, the resource class name. The second part is the name of an X bitmap file.

The Twm Icon Manager

Twm provides an icon manager much like **mwm's** icon box. This icon manager lists the windows on the screen, with a small button indicating iconified windows. This saves on screen real estate for users who have many icons. Clicking on an entry in the icon manager iconifies the named window—or un-iconifies it, if the window was already iconified.

You can show the icon manager with the **f.showiconmgr** menu command and hide it with the **f.hideiconmgr** command.

The **ShowIconManager** variable, if set, turns on the icon manager at startup.

You can control the location of the icon manager box with the **IconManager Geometry** command. But watch out: Although the **IconManagerGeometry** command takes a standard X geometry specification, that geometry must be enclosed in quotes. The following puts the geometry manager in the lower-left portion of the screen:

```
IconManagerGeometry "+0+650"
```

If you forget the quotes, **twm** silently ignores the error and your geometry.

Tvtwm, the Virtual Desktop Twm

Since the source code to **twm** is freely available, many people take this window manager as a start and then create their own custom versions. One of the best of these is called **tvtwm**, which presents a virtual desktop. This virtual desktop is a very large window that sits between your applications and the root window. **Tvtwm** then allows you to pan across this virtual desktop. Except for its virtual desktop, **tvtwm** acts in most respects like **twm**. This desktop includes a small panner window, which displays a view—in miniature—of the windows on the virtual desktop.

Configuring Tvtwm

The **tvtwm** configuration file is named **.tvtwmrc** and should be located in your home directory. If **.tvtwmrc** can't be found, **tvtwm** looks for a **.twmrc** file, also in your home directory. The system default configuration file is the same as **twm**'s, **/usr/lib/X11/twm/system.twmrc**.

Table 11.4 New tvtwm variables.

Variable	Meaning
PannerBackgroundPixmap	Names a pixmap to use as the panner background.
PannerOpaqueScroll	Scrolls the virtual desktop opaquely, like **OpaqueMove**.
ShowVirtualNames	Displays window titles in the miniature panner window.
Sticky	Lists "sticky" applications, which remain in the same position no matter how the user pans the desktop.
StickyAbove	Makes sticky windows sit above nonsticky windows.
VirtualDesktop	Turns on the virtual desktop. Must be followed with a string in quotes that specifies the virtual desktop size.

The **Sticky** variable names those applications that should remain in the same position no matter how the user pans the virtual desktop. It is called by:

Sticky { "oclock" }

The **Sticky** variable is often used for clock programs and **xload**, which presents a picture of CPU usage.

The **VirtualDesktop** variable turns on the virtual desktop feature and sets the size of the desktop. This size can be the traditional width and height, such as **"16000x16000,"** or a multiple of the current screen size. For example:

VirtualDesktop "3x3"

This makes the virtual desktop three times the size of the screen, in each direction.

Most of the virtual desktop window managers act much like **tvtwm**.

A Sample Twm Configuration File

We've placed our **.twmrc** file below, which you can use as a base for your customizations. Note that you should always start with a copy of the system file, **/usr/lib/X11/twm/system.twmrc**. This way, you can take advantage of any customizations set up by your system administrator.

The **.twmrc** file follows:

```
#
#        .twmrc, as modified by Eric and Kevin.
#
# $XConsortium: system.twmrc,v 1.8 91/04/23 21:10:58 gildea Exp $
#
# Default twm configuration file; needs to be kept small to
#         conserve string
# space in systems whose compilers don't handle medium-sized
#         strings.
#
# Sites should tailor this file, providing any extra title
#         buttons, menus, etc.
# that may be appropriate for their environment.  For example,
#         if most of the
# users were accustomed to uwm, the defaults could be set up
#         not to decorate
# any windows and to use meta-keys.
#


# NoGrabServer means twm won't grab the server for menus.
NoGrabServer

RestartPreviousState
DecorateTransients
#ClientBorderWidth

#
# Set up fonts.
#
TitleFont "-adobe-helvetica-bold-r-normal-*-120-*-*-*-*-*-*"
ResizeFont "-adobe-helvetica-bold-r-normal-*-120-*-*-*-*-*-*"
MenuFont "-adobe-helvetica-bold-r-normal-*-120-*-*-*-*-*-*"
IconFont "-adobe-helvetica-bold-r-normal-*-100-*-*-*-*-*-*"
IconManagerFont "-adobe-helvetica-bold-r-normal-*-100-*-*-*"
```

```
#
# ShowIconManager turns on the icon manager
# when twm starts up.
#ShowIconManager


#
# Set up the icon manager's initial geometry
# to the lower left corner.
IconManagerGeometry "+0+650"


# Moving whole windows instead of just an outline runs
# far too slow on our systems, so we comment this out.
# Comment the following line in to move the whole window.
#OpaqueMove

Color
{
        BorderColor "black"
        DefaultBackground "burlywood"
        DefaultForeground "black"
        TitleBackground "burlywood"
        TitleForeground "black"
        MenuBackground "burlywood"
        MenuForeground "black"
        MenuTitleBackground "black"
        MenuTitleForeground "burlywood"
        IconBackground "burlywood"
        IconForeground "black"
        IconBorderColor "black"
        IconManagerBackground "burlywood"
        IconManagerForeground "black"
}


#
#       Change the default cursors.
#
Cursors
{
        Frame     "top_left_arrow"
        Title     "top_left_arrow"
        Icon      "top_left_arrow"
        IconMgr   "top_left_arrow"
        Move      "fleur"
```

```
        Resize       "fleur"
        Menu         "left_ptr"
        Button       "left_ptr"
        Wait         "watch"
        Select       "question_arrow"
        Destroy      "pirate"
}


#
# The "Tab" part of twm comes from the SqueezeTitle option.
#
#SqueezeTitle
#{
#       "XTerm" left    0       0
#       "oclock" center         0       0
#}


#
# Xterm doesn't provide its own icon, so we set one.
#
Icons
{
        "XTerm"      "/u/erc/bitmaps/peace.xbm"
}


#
# Name the windows that shouldn't have a
# title bar.
NoTitle { "xclock" "oclock" "xload" }


#
# Name those applications you wish to raise to
# the top if the mouse is in their windows.
# We don't recommend this option.
AutoRaise { "XTerm" "xmail" }


#
# Define some useful functions for motion-based actions.
#
MoveDelta 3
Function "move-or-lower" { f.move f.deltastop f.lower }
Function "move-or-raise" { f.move f.deltastop f.raise }
Function "move-or-iconify" { f.move f.deltastop f.iconify }
```

```
#
# Set some useful bindings.  Sort of uwm-ish, sort of simple-
          button-ish
#
Button1 = : root : f.menu "defops"

Button1 = m : window|icon : f.function "move-or-lower"
Button2 = m : window|icon : f.iconify
Button3 = m : window|icon : f.function "move-or-raise"

Button1 = : title : f.function "move-or-raise"
Button2 = : title : f.raiselower

Button1 = : icon : f.function "move-or-iconify"
Button2 = : icon : f.iconify

Button1 = : iconmgr : f.iconify
Button2 = : iconmgr : f.iconify


#
# And a menus with the usual things
#
menu "defops"
{
"Modified Twm Menu"    f.title
"Xterm"                f.exec "xterm -geom 80x42 &"
"Nokomis"              f.exec "xterm -geom 80x42 -name nokomis
          -e rlogin nokomis &"
"Calculator"           f.exec "xcalc &"
"Magnifier"            f.exec "xmag &"
""                     f.nop
"Resize"               f.resize
""                     f.nop
"Raise"                f.raise
"Lower"                f.lower
""                     f.nop
"Show Iconmgr"         f.showiconmgr
"Hide Iconmgr"         f.hideiconmgr
""                     f.nop
"Kill"                 f.destroy
```

```
"Delete"            f.delete
" "                 f.nop
"Restart"           f.restart
" "                 f.nop
"Exit"              f.quit
}
```

Summary

The Tab window manager, or **twm**, comes with the default X Window System from the X Consortium. Many vendors include **twm** as part of their X platform, although some delete **twm** in favor of **mwm**, the Motif window manager. Since X is free—or nearly free—**twm** has become one of the most popular window managers.

Unlike most other window managers, **twm** doesn't use a class-resource file. **Twm** is controlled with a configuration file in your home directory named **.twmrc**.

You can change the **twm** root menu, or add menus of your own, by editing the end of the **.twmrc** file.

The most interesting feature of **twm**, and what sets it apart from other window managers, is the **SqueezeTitle** option. With it, the window title bar is kept from stretching across the top of the whole window to a "tab" that only covers part of the window's top edge. The width of the title bar provides only the space needed for the window's title.

Much like **mwm's** icon box, **twm** provides an icon manager. This icon manager lists the windows on the screen; a small button indicates iconified windows. This saves on-screen real estate for users who have many icons.

IV

Using X

This section concentrates on working smarter with X Window System applications. In this section we:

- Describe how to work with colors and customize to your hearts' content; and
- Cover the main applications that ship with the generic X Window System.

Chapter 12

Changing Colors

X defines colors using the RGB—Red, Green, and Blue—model. Most users, though, don't think in terms of numeric RGB triples. Instead, they think in terms of colors like red, blue, green, and variants thereof. To aid users, X provides a database of color names, along with their corresponding RGB values. For most applications, you can request colors like rose, honeydew, and chocolate, using English names and not worrying about the RGB triples for those colors.

This color database, in a readable version, is located in **/usr/lib/X11/rgb.txt**. The actual database used by the X server is in **/usr/lib/X11/rgb.dir**, but it is not readable. You can display all the colors in this file by using the X program **showrgb** from the UNIX command line:

```
showrgb | more
```

Since this is a simple text file, you can also use the **more** program directly, if the **rgb.txt** file is in the standard location:

```
more /usr/lib/X11/rgb.txt
```

You'll find hundreds of colors, including the following:

```
 64 224 208      turquoise
 50 205  50      limegreen
255 160 122      light salmon
230 230 250      lavender
 32 178 170      light sea green
208  32 144      violet red
```

Color names can be in uppercase or lowercase. You'll also notice that color names can have spaces between words, or be cramped together, as in the following:

```
245 255 250      mintcream
245 255 250      mint cream
255 250 205      lemonchiffon
255 250 205      lemon chiffon
```

You can then use the color names for **foreground** and **background** resources for X programs, as well as on the command line. We've already shown how to change colors for applications, both from the command line with the **-fg** (foreground) and **-bg** (background) parameters (see Chapter 5), as well as through resource-setting commands using the **foreground** and **background** resources (see Chapter 6).

A word of warning: Don't use a space in color names in resource files. That is, use **limegreen** rather than **lime green**.

Setting Color Values Directly

If the color-name format doesn't appeal to you, you can use RGB values directly, with the following syntax:

#rgb

where **r**, **g**, and **b** are hexadecimal numbers for the amount of each color. For example, in this format the color *magenta* is:

#FFFF0000FFFF

Use four hexadecimal digits for red, green, and blue. You can use fewer digits, but the values are padded to four digits anyway. **FFFF** is full-on and **0000** is full-off for a color. This format is valid through X11 Release 5.

Release 5 supersedes this **#rgb** format with the newer format below, which again shows magenta:

rgb:FFFF/0/FFFF

The old format is still supported in R5. This is again one place where you need to know which version of X you are running. In most cases, you'll run a vendor-supplied version of X, not the code direct from the X Consortium. You need to find which X Consortium version your vendors used to create their versions of X.

Release 5 Device-Independent Color Values

In Release 5 you can also use a number of other methods for providing color values—like the RGB format above—including standard CIE color formats. These CIE formats require you to calibrate your monitor to achieve the best results.

Due to screen differences, the same RGB numeric values look different on different monitors. To address this, Release 5 added the **X Color Management System**, or **Xcms**, to allow you to specify colors more exactly and achieve the goal of device-independent color.

Table 12.1 Release 5 color value schemes.

Format	Color Scheme
rgb:red/green/blue	Red, green, blue value
rgbi:*red/green/blue*	Red, green, blue *intensity*, with values from 0 to 1
CIEXYZ:*X/Y/Z*	CIE XYZ
CIEuvY:*u/v/Y*	CIE uvY
CIExyY:*x/y/Y*	CIE xyY
CIELab:*L/a/b*	CIE Lab
CIELuv:*L/u/v*	CIE Luv
TekHVC:*H/V/C*	Tektronix HVC

Most of the more complex color schemes are needed only if you do prepress work or exacting scientific visualization where you need *exact* colors.

Most of the rest of us can work with plain old *red, bisque,* and *maroon.* If you don't need exact colors, avoid these formats, since they entail a high overhead.

Setting the Screen Background

To practice using X color names, we can use the **xsetroot** program to change the root window background. Most users want to customize the background of their display, and **xsetroot** is one way to do this. **Xsetroot** also helps by showing how a given color looks on your monitor. To set the root window to use the color *bisque2* (which we find to be a good background), use the following command:

```
xsetroot -solid bisque2
```

The **-solid** parameter tells **xsetroot** to use a solid color rather than a bitmap. The **-bitmap** parameter uses a bitmap file. You can also then pass the **-fg** and **-bg** parameters to color the bitmap.

```
xsetroot -bitmap /u/erc/bitmaps/mryuk.xbm -bg green -fg black
```

Color Limitations

Many systems based on 386 or 486 hardware sport a severely limited set of colors; Super VGA systems, for example, have only sixteen colors. On these systems you'll soon run out of colors unless you're careful, especially if you run Motif or Open Look programs that use extra colors to provide 3-D effects. Every 3-D widget uses up to four colors, so it's best to try to limit the colors.

Summary

X defines colors using the RGB—Red, Green, and Blue—model. Most users, though, don't think in terms of numeric RGB triples. Instead, they think in terms of colors like red, blue, green, and variants thereof To aid users, X provides a database of color names, along with their corresponding RGB values.

In Release 5, you can also use a number of other methods for providing color values—like the RGB format above—including standard CIE color formats. These CIE formats require you to calibrate your monitor to achieve the best results.

Most users want to customize the background of their display, and **xsetroot** is one way to do this. **Xsetroot** also helps by showing how a given color looks on your monitor.

Chapter 13

Running X Applications

When it comes down to it, people don't spend a lot of time working directly with the operating system or an add-on environment like the X Window System. Instead, users use applications. We find that most users don't adopt an operating system because of the wonderfulness and elegance of its structure but because the operating system runs a needed application.

The X Consortium, to its credit, ships X with a large set of programs, some primitive demo programs and some full-fledged, useful applications. We've mentioned some of these X applications through the first twelve chapters of this book, and we'll mention many more before we're through. This chapter introduces additional, standard X programs. The basic concepts behind these programs are also found in most other X software, so this is a good place to learn the basics. You'll discover some neat features that the designers of X provided in the latest releases of X.

To start, you need to locate these programs. If you're already running X—and we certainly hope you are by now—you should have accomplished this, especially if you have an **xterm** window on your screen.

X applications normally reside in **/usr/bin/X11**. On OpenWindows platforms, such as Sun workstations, this is **$OPENWINHOME/bin**, or **/usr/open-win/bin** by default. The relevant directories should be in the path searched by **csh** (or the shell you use).

X Applications

Standard X applications fall into three categories: necessary applications, such as the X server, **X**, **twm**, and **xterm**; utility programs, such as **xlsfonts** and **xdpyinfo**; and demos, such as **xeyes** or **xcalc**. Most of these demos are working programs in their own right, but they are far from commercial-grade applications. Among these demonstration programs, X provides the **xedit** text editor and **xeyes**, a program that follows the mouse pointer with two eyes. It also eats CPU cycles.

Run **xeyes** in the background, as you should do with most X programs:

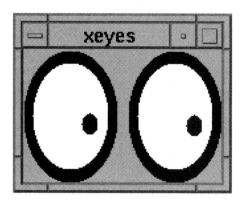

Figure 13.1. Xeyes in action.

This is a frivolous demo, but X also provides very useful demo programs, like **bitmap**, a bitmap editor.

Creating Icons with the Bitmap Program

The **bitmap** program allows you to create the monochrome bitmap files used as icons by many programs, such as **xterm**. **Bitmap** presents an enlarged image to help you edit small icons or cursors. This **bitmap** program has been dramatically improved in X11 Release 5, so use that version if you have it.

Figure 13.2 The bitmap program.

Bitmap accepts a **-size** command-line parameter, with a width and a height (**widthxheight**). The **-dashed** options turns on (the default) dashed lines between cells in the enlarged bitmap; **+dashed** turns them off. This is very useful for slower machines, which can take a long time to draw dashed lines.

```
bitmap -size 45x32 +dashed foo.xbm &
```

In older versions of X, the **+dashed** option was **-nodashed** instead. If **+dashed** doesn't work, use **-nodashed**.

In the Release 5 **bitmap**, you select a shape, like a line or circle, and then draw by holding down the left mouse button. If you're drawing a line, you'll see a rubber-band line to help you choose the position of the line. If you're drawing a circle, you select the center first. Holding down the right mouse button allows you to draw in white instead of black.

You can select an area to copy by holding down the Shift key and the leftmost mouse button. While holding these down, stretch a rectangle on the bitmap. This area should highlight. You can also use the Mark palette choice. Paste this area into another area in the bitmap, or into another X application, although few X applications accept pasted bitmap data. X applications copy and paste text well (see Chapter 3 on **xterm**), but they don't do well with bitmaps or images.

Meta-I brings up a window that shows the bitmap in its real, as opposed to magnified, size.

The files created by **bitmap** can then be used for icons in your programs and for standard X programs, like **xterm**, that don't set their own icons. These files are in the **xbm** format. You must configure your window manager to use **xbm** files as icons, however; we covered such configurations in previous chapters.

Xman

Xman is a useful online manual page browser, especially since it lists the available manual page files. **Xman** presents a window, shown below, that displays an online manual page. Unlike the traditional UNIX **man** program, though, **xman** easily allows you to call up other manual files from a directory listing.

Press the Manual Page button to get a man page browser. The menu choices allow you to check various sections of the online manual. One drawback is that you are browsing file names, not topic names, and many X routines use very long names, like **XmCreateFileSelectionBox**, which will be heavily abbreviated for the manual file name.

The problem with xman isn't an X problem, but a common UNIX one: Many systems don't have all their manual pages configured properly, especially for programs compiled locally and stored in nonstandard places.

You can set your **MANPATH** environment variable to add your local directories, as with the following command:

```
setenv MANPATH /u/erc/man:/usr/local/man:/usr/man
```

Another problem, especially in regard to 386/486 UNIX systems: Some programs won't work with manual pages. In these cases (we've experienced problems when working with **neqn** and **tbl**, for example), you end up with garbage in the **xman** manual window.

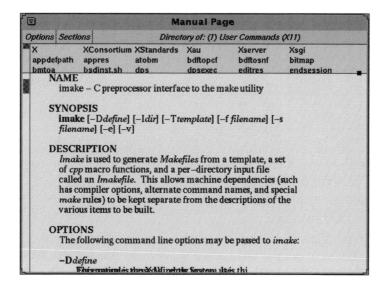

Figure 13.3 The Xman online manual browser.

Xedit

X provides a text editor called **xedit**. **Xedit** is highly configurable through resource files, but you'll find it rather primitive. If you want a simple type-as-you-go editor that avoids the nefarious modes of **vi** or **emacs**, then **xedit** may help.

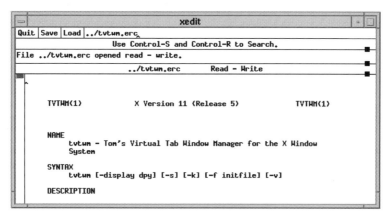

Figure 13.4 The Xedit text editor.

The confusing part of **xedit** is setting the file name. If you're used to the old SunView environment, you'll feel right at home, but for users used to more modern systems, **xedit** tends to confuse. Type in the desired file name next to the Load button.

Xload

Xload provides a histogram that shows the approximate system load. This requires the ability to read **/dev/kmem**, as well as the existence of this special device file, so **xload** won't work on all systems. If it does work, you can use **xload** to help identify what causes heavy system loads and adjust accordingly. Of course, **xload** causes a load itself.

The **-highlight** command-line parameter sets the color for the histogram. The **-update** parameter sets how many seconds **xload** should wait between updates to the graph. The **-label** option sets up a string to label the graph (the default is your **hostname**).

```
xload -update 5 -label "My Label" -highlight tan &
```

Xbiff

Xbiff is an X Window version of the venerable UNIX **biff** program. **Xbiff** beeps and displays a full mailbox icon if you have unread incoming electronic mail. The normal icon denoting a lack of mail is an empty mailbox.

```
xbiff &
```

Xbiff isn't a very interesting program, but it is useful if you get a lot of electronic mail.

Clocks

The two main clock programs provided by X are **xclock** and **oclock**, a rounded clock. **Oclock** requires the **SHAPE** extension, just like the Tab option for **twm** that we discussed in Chapter 11.

By default, **xclock** uses the current time-zone information. However, you can set **xclock** to display a clock calibrated to a different time zone. You can change this, as the following example shows:

```
setenv TZ EST5EDT ; xclock -name "New York" &
setenv TZ CST6CDT ; xclock -name "Minneapolis" &
setenv TZ PST8PDT ; xclock -name "Seattle" &
```

Other useful X programs include **xrefresh**, which causes every X program to redraw its windows, and **xkill**, which allows you to kill errant X applications.

Summary

None of us really work that often with the operating system; instead, our work is done with applications. This chapter reviews the major applications that ship free of charge with the X Window System.

V

Troubleshooting X

Just about every X user we've ever met has dealt with untold hassles when they started to use X. This section aims at solving common problems and helping you to discover what went wrong and find a way to do something about it.

Much of this section will be presented in a problem/solution format. That is, we state the symptoms, discuss what went wrong, and then describe how to get around the problem. Among the topics to be covered:

- Exploring the X environment, finding your X files, and providing techniques for determining what went wrong;

- Trying to get what you see on the screen onto the printed page;

- Solving an especially annoying problem: when applications don't get any keystrokes at all. If this has hit you, you'll know how annoying this can be;

- Finally, Chapter 17 covers a set of common problems in problem/solution format.

Chapter 14

Exploring Your X System

Many X problems result from misguided assumptions and configuration rules that seem arbitrary or haphazard. Before you can track down problems, however, you need to know how your system is set up. Often your current set-up—or what's missing from your current set-up—will provide necessary clues for solving X problems.

In a full installation, the X sources and executables together total more than one-hundred megabytes of disk space, although you can get by with as few as twenty megabytes for a runtime-only system. With X eating up one-hundred megabytes of disk space, there must be a lot of flexibility in an X configuration. There are few hard-and-fast rules regarding X configurations, with vendors slipping in their own customizations, so it's sometimes hard to tell whether your X system has been properly configured.

X, by default, expects that executable programs reside in **/usr/bin/X11**. This rule, obviously, was meant to be broken. For example, you might find these files in **/usr/opt/X11/bin** on Data General Aviions. With OpenWindows, particularly on SPARC systems, the default is **$OPENWINHOME/bin**, which is normally **/usr/openwin/bin**. But OpenWindows throws us another curve by placing **xterm** in the demo directory, normally **/usr/openwin/demo**, which is an illogical place to put a frequently used application. OpenWindows also uses dynamic libraries by default, which reside in **$OPENWINHOME/lib**, or **/usr/openwin/lib** by default. Thus, to run X programs under OpenWindows, you'll need to set your **LD_LIBRARY_PATH** environment variable to **$OPENWINHOME/lib**. Make sure the **OPENWINHOME** environment variable is set to your OpenWindows directory, such as **/usr/openwin**. Other versions of X place the X libraries in **/usr/lib**, along with the rest of your system libraries, both static and dynamic.

The **/usr/lib/X11** directory contains system default class application files, configuration files for **xdm**, **twm**, and **mwm**, as well as X font files.

X Font Files

X font files appear in **/usr/lib/X11/fonts**, normally in up to five subdirectories:

/usr/lib/X11/fonts/100dpi	for 100-dpi monitors.
/usr/lib/X11/fonts/75dpi	for 75-dpi monitors.
/usr/lib/X11/fonts/misc	for miscellaneous fonts like the cursor font.
/usr/lib/X11/fonts/Speedo	for scalable Bitstream Speedo fonts.
/usr/lib/X11/fonts/PEX	for PEX (PHIGS Extension to X) fonts.

Application default files (class-resource files) normally go into **/usr/lib/X11/app-defaults**, and include files such as:

Bitmap	**XCalc-color**	**XLogo**	**Xgc**
Bitmap-color	**XClipboard**	**XLogo-color**	**Xmag**
Clock-color	**XClock**	**XTerm**	**Xman**
Editres	**XConsole**	**Xditview**	**Xmh**
Editres-color	**XFontSel**	**Xditview-chrtr**	
Viewres	**XGas**	**Xedit**	
XCalc	**XLoad**	**Xfd**	

Missing Files

Some files are more equal than others; their absence will cause you major problems. The X error explanation file (**/usr/lib/X11/XErrorDB**) and the keyboard file (**/usr/lib/X11/XKeysymDB**) are prime examples. The keyboard file is necessary for Motif applications and can cause literally thousands of X toolkit translation errors if the Motif set of virtual keysyms is not in this file. This problem is especially acute on OpenWindows systems, since the directory **/usr/lib/X11** normally doesn't exist. Instead, OpenWindows uses **/usr/openwin/lib**.

For application developers, X requires a large number of include files. These files go in **/usr/include/X11**. With X11 Release 4, many of these files migrated to **/usr/include/X11/Xaw**. This can cause problems when compiling older X programs.

Motif include files go in **/usr/include/Xm**, although some appear in **/usr/include/X11**.

As you can tell, there's a large number of places where standard X files go. Add to this the ability to put the files elsewhere in custom installations, and you get a recipe for many problems. In addition, the same files have changed over releases of X. If you're migrating your system to X11 Release 5, you may have the older Release 4 files in the standard X locations. To ease the transition, you place the Release 5 files in a custom location, such as **/usr/local/X11R5**. This, of course, complicates the way you set up your command paths and configure X programs.

What Kind of Display Is Running X?

The **xdpyinfo** program provides much information about your X server. Some of this information won't make any sense at all, but much is useful for figuring out what kind of system you have. **Xdpyinfo** starts by providing general information about the version of the X protocol, the name of the display, and the byte ordering. In this case, we're running on a 486 UNIX platform, hence the **LSBFirst** byte ordering shown in the highly edited output below:

```
name of display:      :0.0
bitmap unit, bit order, padding:     32, LSBFirst, 32
image byte order:     LSBFirst
default screen number:    0
```

You'll see information on the graphics resolution, starting with the number of screens:

```
number of screens:     1
screen #0:
  dimensions:     1152x900 pixels (390x304 millimeters)
  resolution:     75x75 dots per inch
  depths (2):     1, 8
  default number of colormap cells:     256
  preallocated pixels:     black 1, white 0
  options:     backing-store YES, save-unders YES
  number of visuals:     6
  visual:
    class:     PseudoColor
    depth:     8 planes
    size of colormap:     256 entries
```

The above information tells us that we have a screen resolution of 1152x900 pixels and eight color planes for a total of 256 colors. The screen resolution is odd, since the monitor in this case only supports resolutions of up to 1024x768.

With this, we see something that **X386**, an implementation of X on 386 and 486 systems, offers. **X386** allows us to have a virtual screen larger than the whole display area. The X server can pan the display when the mouse gets near the edges. We can also run a virtual-root window manager (like **tvtwm**, as introduced in Chapter 11), but here we just use the features of the X server.

Xdpyinfo also tells us that the default visual is PseudoColor, which means we have a color system and that applications can allocate their own color cells. This can be important, since many X programs assume a color system has writable color cells. (This isn't a valid assumption and violates the rules for well-behaved X programs, but as a user you have to deal with the results, not the rules.) **Xdpyinfo** also tells us that the X server supports a total of six visuals, including **DirectColor**, **GrayScale**, **StaticGray**, **StaticColor**, and **TrueColor** (all the available visuals X supports). This means our X server can simulate a number of other systems, such as a read-only gray-scale system (**StaticGray**). The important part is that the **PseudoColor** visual is the default, as 99 percent of all color X systems have this default.

Backing store and save unders are means to save the area underneath windows, such as pop-up menus, to speed processing. The Yes answer to both is heartening.

Determining X Extensions

X was designed in a way to allow for the addition of extensions. Users can thus add functionality to X on demand—and also remove functionality when functionality is not needed. Look in the output of **xdpyinfo** for the listing of extensions. The list below is the default list for MIT X11 Release 5.

```
number of extensions:      6
    XTestExtension1
    SHAPE
    MIT-SHM
    X3D-PEX
    Multi-Buffering
    MIT-SUNDRY-NONSTANDARD
```

The **X3D-PEX** shows that this X server supports the PEX extension (or PHIGS Extension to X), which supports 3D PHIGS programs. The **SHAPE** extension shows that odd-shaped windows will be allowed, such as the one used by **oclock**. (Even if your system supports the **SHAPE** extension, you must make sure your window manager also supports **SHAPE**-based programs.)

The **MIT-SHM** is a means to use shared memory for transporting the X protocol requests. This can often lead to dramatic speed improvement, especially for large images.

What Version of X Are You Running?

Xdpyinfo also gives us information about which version of X we're running:

```
version number:      11.0
vendor string:       MIT X Consortium
vendor release number:      5000
```

Most vendor strings will pertain to specific computer manufacturers, like "Apple Computer, Inc." The MIT vendor here means that we're using the X source code from the MIT X Consortium and built our own version of X (see Chapter 20 for more on how to do this). The release number of 5000 means that we're running X11 Release 5, the latest version of X as of this writing. (Note that most vendors will place *their* release number here, not the generic X release number.) The version number of 11.0 indicates that the low-level X network protocol hasn't changed since it was introduced with the first version of X11. This fact is relatively meaningless.

There are some very specific circumstances in which you should know what version of X you're running, and we've tried to highlight those circumstances throughout this book. For instance, we've already mentioned a number of features new in X11 Release 5. To take advantage of these features, you obviously have to be running Release 5. For everyday usage, you really don't need to know which version you have.

And in other cases, the actual version number may be difficult to determine. Most vendors take a version of X and customize it for their hardware. The best bet in this case is to look in the manual. The online manual page for **x** often lists the release number, and many vendors list the compatibility in printed manuals; they will say "compatible with X11R4," for instance.

What Windows Are on the Display?

The **xlswins** and **xwininfo** programs provide information about all the windows created on a screen. Note that most applications create a host of windows—often one for each pushbutton or text label. Scroll bars often use a total of six windows each, so expect to see a lot of windows listed on the display.

The **xwininfo -tree** option replaces **xlswins** with X11 Release 5. Running **xwininfo -tree** provides a lot of information. To give you the flavor of this, some sample output follows:

```
xwininfo: Window id: 0x2a (the root window) (has no name)

   Root window id: 0x2a (the root window) (has no name)
   Parent window id: 0x0 (none)
      8 children:
      0x140003f (has no name): ()   739x585+300+270   +300+270
         2 children:
         0x100000d " nicollet    /u/erc/usingx": ("xterm"
            "XTerm")   739x564+0+21   +302+293
            1 child:
            0x1000011 (has no name): ()   739x564+0+0   +302+293
               1 child:
               0x1000012 (has no name): ()   14x564+-1+-1   +301+292
         0x1400040 (has no name): ()   739x19+-2+-2   +300+270
            3 children:
            0x1400047 (has no name): ()   549x15+166+2   +468+274
            0x1400044 (has no name): ()   11x11+723+3   +1025+275
            0x1400043 (has no name): ()   11x11+3+3   +305+275
      0x1400034 (has no name): ()   739x585+1+1   +1+1
         2 children:
```

```
    0xc0000d " nicollet   /u/erc/usingx": ("xterm"
       "XTerm")  739x564+0+21  +3+24
  0x140002f (has no name): ()  120x120+900+10  +900+10
     1 child:
     0x1800007 "oclock": ("oclock" "Clock")  120x120+0+0
       +902+12
     0x1400020 "TWM Icon Manager": ()  150x66+0+21  +2+673
Outer window is 0x1c00001, inner window is 0x1c00002
```

Xwininfo can often help you discover what happened to a window and also how to get a window ID, if needed. Capturing a screen dump of a pulldown menu, for example, may require you to discover the window ID for the menu (see the next chapter for details).

Xprop lists the properties placed on a window. Properties in X are named and typed data associated with a window. Most often these properties are used by well-behaved X applications to tell the window manager about their needs, such as window size and title, as the following output for **xterm** shows:

```
WM_STATE(WM_STATE):
          window state: Normal
          icon window: 0x0
WM_PROTOCOLS(ATOM): protocols  WM_DELETE_WINDOW
WM_CLASS(STRING) = "xterm", "XTerm"
WM_HINTS(WM_HINTS):
          Client accepts input or input focus: True
          Initial state is Normal State.
WM_NORMAL_HINTS(WM_SIZE_HINTS):
          user specified location: 300, 270
          user specified size: 739 by 564
          program specified minimum size: 28 by 18
          program specified resize increment: 9 by 14
          program specified base size: 19 by 4
          window gravity: NorthWest
WM_CLIENT_MACHINE(STRING) = "nicollet"
WM_COMMAND(STRING) = { "/usr/local/X11R5/bin/xterm", "-geom",
          "80x40+300+270" }
WM_ICON_NAME(STRING) = "xterm"
WM_NAME(STRING) = " nicollet   /u/erc/usingx"
```

In the above output, the input focus hint shows **True**, which is necessary for applications to receive keyboard input (see Chapter 16). The **WM_CLIENT_MACHINE** is the hostname for the machine running **xterm**.

What X Applications Are Running?

The **xlsclients** program lists the X applications (also known as clients) that have registered their presence in the well-behaved manner. **Xlsclients** detects X applications that follow the rules, as most—but not all—X applications do. **Xlsclients** also lists the hostname where these programs are computing. A simple X configuration is shown below by **xlsclients**.

```
nicollet  /usr/local/X11R5/bin/oclock -geom 120x120+900+10
nicollet  /usr/local/X11R5/bin/xterm -geom 80x40+1+1
nicollet  /usr/local/X11R5/bin/xterm -geom 80x40+300+270
```

Note that **xlsclients** doesn't detect the window manager (**twm** in this case).

Decoding the Keyboards

Since the X Window System has to deal with just about any style of keyboard, the designers of X came up with the concept of a **KeySym**, a logical key, to hide the differences in proprietary keyboards from X users and programmers. The idea is quite logical: Not every keyboard is the same. X needs a mechanism to make sure that what is labelled a Shift key on one keyboard will work the same way as a Shift key from the keyboard of another manufacturer. For instance, the X server maps between the eighty-second key code and the Page Up key, which X calls the *Prior* KeySym. X provides KeySyms for Escape, Return, function keys such as F3, and all the keys on the keypad. The Up Arrow key, for example, may have any odd number for its key code, but the X server translates that to the Up KeySym. (X programs then determine how to use the up arrow.)

There are KeySyms for more keys than you'd ever have on your keyboard; so, your keyboard might not have all the right keys. In addition, you might not like your keyboard layout. Since all keys in X are mapped to logical KeySyms, there's the potential to change things. The first problem, though, is figuring out your current keyboard layout—from X's perspective.

The **xev** application (technically it's a demo, so you know where to find it) creates a window and then prints out voluminous output for every event that happens in the **xev** window. This is a lot more output than you will ever want to deal with. The best use of **xev** is to type every key on your keyboard that doesn't seem to do what you think it should. **Xev** will then tell you what X thinks a given key is. Sometimes the key choices make no sense, especially with the keypad on Sun Type 4 keyboards.

Try using **xev** and typing on these keys. Then hold down the shift key and try typing the same keys again. You'll note the difference.

Another common problem with X keyboards is handling the Num Lock key. To those with a PC background, the Num Lock key should toggle behavior of the keypad, from arrows to numbers and vice versa. Generic X, however, doesn't support the Num Lock key as a toggle (or modifier). X recognizes the Num Lock key just fine—it just doesn't do anything about it. Some vendors have implemented routines to handle the Num Lock toggle, but, unfortunately, all have chosen different ways to implement the same functionality.

Here's some sample output of **xev**, after the user typed the *f*, *Enter*, *F5*, and *Num Lock* keys.

```
KeyPress event, serial 15, synthetic NO, window 0x1c00001,
        root 0x2a, subw 0x0, time 1258265166, (84,142), root:(158,691),
        state 0x0, keycode 41 (keysym 0x66, f), same_screen YES,
        LookupString gives 1 characters:  "f"

KeyPress event, serial 15, synthetic NO, window 0x1c00001,
        root 0x2a, subw 0x0, time 1258266366, (84,144), root:(158,693),
        state 0x0, keycode 36 (keysym 0xff0d, Return), same_screen YES,
        XLookupString gives 1 characters:  ""

KeyPress event, serial 15, synthetic NO, window 0x1c00001,
        root 0x2a, subw 0x0, time 1258270946, (84,144), root:(158,693),
        state 0x0, keycode 71 (keysym 0xffc2, F5), same_screen YES,
        XLookupString gives 0 characters:  ""

KeyPress event, serial 15, synthetic NO, window 0x1c00001,
        root 0x2a, subw 0x0, time 1258582886, (130,103), root:(243,684),
        state 0x0, keycode 77 (keysym 0xff7f, Num_Lock), same_screen YES,
        XLookupString gives 0 characters:  ""
```

For each **KeyPress** event there's a corresponding **KeyRelease** event, which we've edited out for space. If a key doesn't act the way you expect it to, try **xev** to determine what key X thinks it is.

The Meta Key

Xev is also useful in determining the **Meta key**. Many windowing systems use an Alt key or a Command key combination to perform certain operations; an **Alt-F**

can pull down the file menu in both Microsoft Windows and Motif, for instance. The user holds down the Alt key and presses another key to complete the command.

Under X, though, the Alt key is named Meta. Why? Again, because X must support a wide variety of keyboards. The X designers invented the generic term Meta for this key. On 386 PCs, SGI Iris workstations, and Data General Aviions, the Meta key *is* labeled **Alt**. On Hewlett-Packard keyboards, Meta is the **Extend Char** key. And, to show how devious X can be, the Meta key is *not* the key labeled Alt on a Sun Type 4 keyboard, but the diamond-shaped key right next to the Alt key. We know of no keyboard that uses a key actually named Meta.

If you type what you think is the Meta key and X doesn't seem to respond, try using **xev** to discover the Meta key your particular X uses. Many keyboards supply a number of Meta keys, usually right and left Meta keys (X supports up to five Meta keys). Below, we pressed the left Meta key on an SGI Iris:

```
KeyPress event, serial 13, synthetic NO, window 0x3400001,
        root 0x29, subw 0x0, time 1133486580, (103,58), root:(295,250),
        state 0x0, keycode 91 (keysym 0xffe9, Alt_L), same_screen YES,
        XLookupString gives 0 characters:  ""
```

If you have problems with the keyboard layout, you can change things with an X program called **xmodmap**. **Xmodmap** changes the keyboard layout and it is mainly intend to change modifier keys (Shift, Control, Caps Lock, and Meta, or mod 1 to 5, but not Num Lock), although you can use it to change any key as well as the mouse buttons.

Typing **xmodmap** without any parameters presents the current list of modifier keys:

```
xmodmap:  up to 2 keys per modifier, (keycodes in parentheses):

shift     Shift_R (0xc),  Shift_L (0xd)
lock      Caps_Lock (0xb)
control   Control_L (0xa),  Control_R (0x5d)
mod1      Alt_L (0x5b),  Alt_R (0x5c)
mod2      Num_Lock (0x72)
mod3      Scroll_Lock (0x6b)
mod4
mod5
```

This list includes a customized Num Lock key, not part of the X standard (not yet, anyway—we're still hoping). This shows us the current layout. From that layout, with **xev** to determine keysyms, we can change the way X treats the keyboard.

For example, many PC AT-style keyboards place the Control and Caps Lock keys in an odd order. Many users prefer to place the Control key *above* the Shift key and the Caps Lock key *below* the Shift key—in reverse order from the default. To do this, we first need to find the X logical key, or KeySym, for both the Control key and the Caps Lock key. Normally these KeySyms will be **Control_L** (left Control key, as some keyboards have a right Control key as well) and **Caps_Lock**. To swap these two keys, edit a temporary file for use by **xmodmap** and add the following lines:

```
remove lock = Caps_Lock
remove control = Control_L
add lock = Control_L
add control = Caps_Lock
```

The two remove lines remove the logical modifiers for **lock** and **control**. The next two lines add keys for **lock** and **control**. The syntax is rather simple for modifier keys.

Then run **xmodmap** using the file you just created.

xmodmap filename

where **filename** is the name of the file you created above. After executing this command, try **xmodmap** again, without any command-line parameters. This should output the new set of modifier mappings:

```
xmodmap:  up to 2 keys per modifier, (keycodes in parentheses):

shift        Shift_R (0xc),   Shift_L (0xd)
lock         Control_L (0xa)
control      Caps_Lock (0xb),   Control_R (0x5d)
mod1         Alt_L (0x5b),   Alt_R (0x5c)
mod2         Num_Lock (0x72)
mod3         Scroll_Lock (0x6b)
mod4
mod5
```

Caps Lock (**lock**) and Control (**control**) are swapped. This, of course, may mess up the LED display for Caps Lock, but a good X server will light the proper LED.

Look at the on-line manual page for **xmodmap** for more information on mapping keys.

Summary

These X programs probably provide more information than you ever wanted to know about your X configuration. Normally, you won't run these programs unless you are trying to track down some strange behavior or other problems. We review:

- Where to find standard X files and determine whether any are missing;
- How to determine what server you're running;
- How to determine which extensions are installed and running;
- Finding out what version of X you're running;
- How to determine which windows are on the screen; and
- Configuring your keyboard set-up.

## Chapter 15

Trying to Get What You See on the Screen

With all the industry interest in What-You-See-Is-What-You-Get (WYSI-WYG) interfaces and high-resolution printers, it's amazing that something as graphical as the X Window System doesn't provide many tools when it comes to printing out graphics from the screen.

X concerns itself, at least in part, with the drawing of dots on raster monitors, which we happen to think is *somewhat* akin to drawing dots on the printed page. Other graphics-based systems, like the Macintosh and Next systems, spend a lot more effort than X on printing out graphics. Next, in particular, uses Display PostScript to approximate the ability to print all displayable graphics in a manner that matches what you view on the monitor.

Possible uses for screen dumps include documentation and electronic publishing. Most X users will (at some point) want to combine images on the printed page with text, be it an academic paper, a software manual, or, in our case, a book. Generally, most people also want to capture a screen image to a file and then further process that file: touching it up, scaling it, or cropping the image to fit better on a page.

In our books, for example, we needed to capture the output of our sample programs into image files, so we can provide pictures that show how the programs work (or should work, as the case may be). Our problem was further compounded by the need to import those image files into an electronic-publishing package, usually a package that didn't run on UNIX. If you create any form of documentation—whether it's a guide for your fellow computer users or a manual for your company's product—you're in the same boat we are.

X really doesn't have a lot to offer in this regard, at least not with the generic X from the MIT X Consortium. Even so, having written three X-related books, we know it is possible to capture X screen images and transfer them to the printed page. It hasn't been easy, but a number of methods work.

Capturing Screen Images of Menus

The first step, obviously, is capturing screen images. The biggest problem we've encountered is in capturing images of pulldown menus.

To get good interactive performance, especially over a network (remember that X is network-oriented), many menus grab keyboard and mouse events while the menu is pulled down. This means that no other applications will get input while you are making a menu choice. The problem is selecting the window to capture with the mouse when the menu grabs all the mouse events.

The answer is: You don't. Instead, you must determine the window ID for the pop-up menu, and then pass that ID on the command line to **xwd** or **xgrabsc** (both of which we'll cover a little later). Or, if you want to show a whole application with a menu pulled down, then you want to figure out the window ID of the application's main window. Use **xlswins** or **xwininfo -tree**, both standard X programs, to list the window IDs that are in use on a given screen. Then you need to figure out which window ID corresponds to your application's main window. Both programs print out window titles (for those windows that have titles), so you can usually get a good idea of which window ID you want.

Here's part of the output of **xlswins** while running a Motif program named **foo**:

```
0x8006d   ()
  0x50009d   ()
    0x50009e   ()
    0x50009f   ()
    0x5000a0   ()
    0x5000a1   ()
    0x5000a2   ()
      0x5000a3   ()
    0x800012   (foo)
      0x800013   ()
        0x800015   ()
        0x800016   ()
        0x800017   ()
          0x800018   ()
          0x80001b   ()
          0x80001c   ()
        0x80001d   ()
          0x80001e   ()
        0x800021   ()
        0x800022   ()
        0x800023   ()
        0x800024   ()
```

0x8006d is the root window, and **0x800012** is the window that has a name of **foo**. The windows **0x50009d** to **0x5000a3** are probably put there by the window manager (in this case, **olwm**) and include our **foo** application's title bar. Note the different major number **0x5** for the window-manager windows, as opposed to **0x8** for the **foo** application's windows.

Once you get the window ID, you must start the screen-capture program, such as **xgrabsc**, with a delay of a few seconds. During this delay, you move the mouse over to your application and pull down the desired menu. **Xgrabsc** provides a sleep option (**-s** on the command line) just for this purpose.

The following command grabs the contents of window **0x50009d** after waiting five seconds (**-s5**), placing the Encapsulated PostScript (**-Pe**) output in the file **screenfile.eps**:

```
xgrabsc -Pe -s5 -i 0x50009d > screenfile.eps
```

Xgrabsc

We've used **xgrabsc** in our example, but unfortunately it's not a part of the standard X Window distribution; we grabbed it when it came across the **comp.sources.x** newsgroup on Usenet. **Xgrabsc** is the handiest screen-capture program we've seen. **Xgrabsc** is an image-capture program that outputs images into X bitmap, PostScript, and Encapsulated PostScript (EPS) formats. We've had the best luck with the EPS format, since many more publishing and image packages import EPS files than they do PostScript (or **xwd**) files.

Xgrabsc also lets you grab an arbitrary rectangular area on a screen, which means you can capture more than one window at a time without having to grab the entire contents of the root window. This is especially useful for capturing multiwindow programs in action. **Xgrabsc**, version 1.6, was written by Bruce Schuchardt and also includes a graphical front end called **xgrab**.

Xwd, an X Window "Dumper"

If you don't have **xgrabsc**, you'll have to fall back on **xwd**, which forms the basic X screen-capture program. Primitive at best, **xwd** dumps the contents of a window to an **xwd**-formatted image file. You can specify the window ID, using a technique similar to the one described above, from the command line, or you can choose the window interactively with the mouse.

With **xwd**, you choose the window to dump with the mouse or pass the **-id** command-line parameter, along with a window ID, such as

```
xwd -id 0x50009d
```

You can select the root window using the **-root** command-line parameter.

The other key command-line parameters include **-frame**, which includes the window frame or border, and **-nobdrs**, which doesn't include the window border.

The **-out** filename parameter specifies the name of the output file (instead of standard output). The standard output option can be used if you want to pipe the output of **xwd** to another program, such as **xpr**.

```
xwd -frame -out screendump.xwd
```

The image format used by **xwd** is rather obtuse and is used by very few X programs. **Xwud** (X Window Un-Dumper) displays an **xwd** image file. **Xpr** prints an **xwd** image file. **Xdpr** acts as a combination of **xwd** and **xpr**, capturing and printing an image.

xpr requires a number of command-line parameters and normally sends its output to standard output, which you can pipe to **lp** or **lpr** or whatever you use for your system's printers.

Table 15.1 Xpr command-line parameters.

Parameter	Meaning
-device device	Specifies output device, such as "ps" for PostScript.
-gray number	Uses a number of 2, 3, or 4 for dithering.
-header string	Sends *string* as the image header.
-landscape	Specifies landscape mode for the paper. (Default.)
-output filename	Sends output to *filename* rather than standard output.
-portrait	Specifies portrait mode for the paper.
-scale value	Scales each pixel to *Valuex Value* pixel grids.

Here's an example of **xpr** in use:

```
xpr -device ps -gray 3 -portrait -header "My Header" screen-
       dump.xwd | lp
```

With **xpr**, which prints **xwd** image files, you can format for PostScript and then print the PostScript image to a file. Unfortunately, while many software packages will *export* PostScript images, few will actually *import* PostScript. Thus we need to convert an **xwd** or PostScript file to something your publishing or word-processing package can use.

Some Other Potential Problems

You may also have a problem with a lack of printer support. **Xpr** supports Digital LN03, LA100, Hewlett-Packard LaserJet, ThinkJet, QuietJet and color PaintJet, generic PostScript, and IBM PP3812 page-printer formats. If you don't have a PostScript printer, check your manual for the names of those devices your printer can use.

Xwd also doesn't work very well with **tvtwm** and other virtual-root window managers. These window managers create a very large virtual-root window, one much bigger than your screen. On this very large virtual-root window, you can place a number of application programs and somehow navigate around, displaying only as much of the virtual root as your screen's resolution allows.

If you use these types of window managers, try to pin your target window first.

Also, we have never had very good luck converting color-program output into black-and-white images on the printed page. We strongly advise you to use gray-scale or monochrome output for your programs when capturing screen images. If you have a monochrome system available, such as a Sun ELC, try that. After all, the printed page is usually in plain old black-and-white. Another technique is to change the default blue Motif background color to a light gray, which makes the images a lot more readable. The key here is that gray colors typically translate better to black-and-white than do other colors.

Magnifying Images

We've found that magnifying an image can often make it look better on the printed page. **Xpr** offers the **-scale** parameter, but you can also magnify an image with the X program **xmag**.

Xmag creates a window that shows a magnified picture of another area of the screen. (Note that this picture does not update itself when the original area changes.) When you run **xmag**, the program prompts for an area to magnify. The **-source** parameter allows you to change the default 64x64 geometry for the size of the area to be magnified. The following command magnifies a 100-by-100 pixel area of the screen.

```
xmag -source 100x100 &
```

This command calls up a window like the one illustrated below.

A Graphics-File Primer

There are two main types of graphics files: **raster** (sometimes called **bitmapped**) and **vector**. A raster file contains a physical description of an image, bit by bit; as a result, without some sort of compression raster files can be extremely large. (Both the GIF and TIFF file types include compression of some sort.) Still, even with the compression, raster files can be large and inconvenient to transport and use.

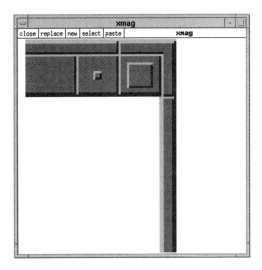

Figure 15.1 Xmag in action.

Vector files are much smaller; instead of including a bit-by-bit description of a file, a vector file contains a mathematical description of an image. (For instance, a line that is three inches long is described in a single statement; with a raster file, each of the dots within the line would be described.) Generally, when you transfer between file types, you end up losing something in the description. That's why it's best to make sure you perform as few conversions as possible; also, if you have a choice in the matter, make sure you use vector files instead of raster files.

As we discussed earlier, one of the biggest problems with **xwd** or PostScript files is converting them to something your publishing or word-processing package can use. There are two solutions we've found to work, with various degrees of efficiency.

Pbmplus

The first is the Portable BitMap package, now called **pbmplus**, by Jef Poskanzer. **Pbmplus** is a set of programs that convert images in many different formats to and from a PBM neutral format. Thus, with **pbmplus**, you can convert an **xwd** image file into a MacPaint file, for example. The nice thing about **pbmplus** is that versions are on the X11R4 and X11R5 release tapes from MIT (in the contributed section). You may already have this package.

The hardest task with **pbmplus** is converting an **xwd** image file into the proper PBM neutral format (there are color, gray-scale, and monochrome PBM neutral formats). Then, from this neutral format, you can use other PBM programs to convert the image to your desired format. We often pipe together these programs at the UNIX prompt to form a fairly long command. It works, but you'll have fun teaching this to your documentation folks.

Table 15.2 Image formats supported by pbmplus (Oct. 5, 1991 version, as on the X11 R5 contrib tapes).

X Formats	*Reading/Writing?*
X10 and X11 bitmap (**xbm**)	reading/writing
X11 window dump, **xwd**, including color	reading/writing
X10 window dump, including color	reading
Motif UIL icon	writing
XPM color pixmaps	reading/writing
Common Formats	*Reading/Writing?*
GIF	reading/writing
Group 3 FAX	reading/writing
HP LaserJet format	writing
MacPaint	reading/writing
Macintosh PICT	reading/writing
PostScript "image" data	reading
Encapsulated (including color) PostScript	writing
Epson printer	writing
HP PaintJet	reading/writing
PC Paintbrush (.PCX) format	reading/writing
Sun raster, including color	reading/writing
Tagged Interchange File Format (TIFF)	reading/writing
Amiga IFF ILBM	reading/writing
Andrew Toolkit raster object	reading/writing

Table 15.2 continued...

Other Formats	Reading/Writing?
ASCII graphics	writing
Atari Degas .pi1, .pi3	reading/writing
Atari Spectrum	reading
BBN BitGraph graphics	writing
CMU window manager format	reading/writing
FITS	reading/writing
GEM .IMG	reading/writing
GraphOn graphics	writing
HIPS	reading
MGR format	reading/writing
MTV/PRT ray-tracer output	reading
Printronix format	writing
Portable BitMap (PBM)	reading/writing
QRT ray-tracer output	reading
Sun icon file	reading/writing
TrueVision Targa file	reading/writing
Unix plot(5)	writing
Usenix FaceSaver file	reading/writing
Xerox doodle brushes	reading
Xim	reading

Image Alchemy

The second solution is Image Alchemy. Available in DOS and Sun SPARCstation versions, Image Alchemy is an amazing software package that converts between many types of raster and vector file formats. Image Alchemy is geared toward the advanced, high-end user who is already familiar with file formats. The program is command-line driven, which means there's no interface of any sort, and the commands are entered directly at the DOS **c:>** or UNIX **%** prompts. This may present some problems for the beginning user, who could benefit from a little guidance when dealing with arcane file formats.

With Image Alchemy, you can dump a screen in the **xwd** format and then output it to a format commonly used in the publishing world—EPS or TIFF work very well, in our experience.

Table 15.3 Image formats supported by Image Alchemy 1.5.

X Formats	Reading/Writing?
X10 and X11 bitmap (**xbm**)	reading/writing
X11 window dump, **xwd**, including color	reading/writing

Common Formats	Reading/Writing?
GIF	reading/writing
HP Printer Command Language (PCL)	raster images only
Macintosh PICT/PICT2	reading/writing
Encapsulated (including color) PostScript	writing
PC Paintbrush (.PCX)	reading/writing
Sun raster, including color	reading/writing
Tagged Interchange File Format (TIFF)	reading/writing
WordPerfect Graphic file (.WPG)	reading/writing

Other Formats	Reading/Writing?
ADEX	reading/writing
Amiga IFF ILBM	reading/writing
Autologic	reading/writing
Binary Information Files (BIF)	reading/writing
Erdas LAN/GIS	reading/writing
Freedom of the Press	writing
GEM .IMG	reading

Table 15.3 continued...

Other Formats	Reading/Writing?
HP Raster Transfer Language (RTL)	writing
HSI JPEG	reading/writing
HSI Palette	reading/writing
HSI Raw	reading/writing
JPEG/JFIF	reading/writing
Jovian VI	reading/writing
MTV ray-tracer output	reading/writing
PC Paint/Pictor (.PIC)	reading/writing
Portable BitMap (PBM)	reading/writing
QO	reading/writing
QDV	reading/writing
QRT ray-tracer output	reading/writing
Scodl	writing
Silicon Graphics Image	reading/writing
Stork	reading/writing
TrueVision Targa file	reading/writing
Utah Raster Toolkit (RLE)	reading/writing
Vivid	reading/writing
Windows Bitmap (BMP)	reading/writing

How to Get These Software Packages

First, you may already have **pbmplus**, so check your X sources. Then ask around for local archive sites. Both **pbmplus** and **xgrabsc** have appeared in **comp.sources.x** on the Usenet. Please don't bother the authors with electronic mail; if you're desperate for information, post a general note in **comp.windows.x** on the Usenet. Some kind soul will surely take pity on you.

Image Alchemy is available from Handmade Software (15951 Los Gatos Blvd., Suite 17, Los Gatos, CA 95032; 408/358-1292); you can also reach the company via the Internet (**hsi@netcom.com**) or Compuserve (user ID: 71330,3136). It requires MS-DOS 3.3 or better (5.0 recommended), 80286 or better PC, 380K of free memory (more than 420K recommended), and a hard drive. The DOS version costs $79.95, while SPARCstation and Sun-3 versions cost $199.95. It's also available from many leading BBSs and on-line services such as CompuServe and America Online.

Summary

Grabbing screen images from the X Window System should be a simple process, but it isn't. There are a great many uses for screen dumps, such as documentation and electronic publishing. Generally, most people also want to capture a screen image to a file and then further process that file: touching it up, scaling it, or cropping the image to fit better on a page.

You must use a utility like **xgrabsc** or **xwd** to grab a screen image. Grabbing the entire contents of a screen is no problem. However, grabbing a screen with a menu pulled down is more difficult: You must determine the window ID for the menu (using **xwininfo**, a standard X program) and then pass that ID on the command line to **xwd** or **xgrabsc**. Or, if you want to show a whole application with a menu pulled down, then you want to figure out the window ID of the application's main window. Once you get the window ID, you must start the screen-capture program, such as **xgrabsc**, with a delay of a few seconds.

Once you've grabbed the image, you must convert it into a format that other software can use. We recommend two widely available packages, **pbmplus** and Image Alchemy, to convert files between the proprietary **xwd** format and many other popular formats, like TIFF and EPS.

## Chapter 16

Help! I've Fallen and I Can't Type into My Program Window!

Y̶ou're rolling along within X, and you're ready to launch an application. You're dusting off some older software created with X11 Release 3, and you're ready to start it under the newest version of the Open Look window manager, **olwm**. But your application won't accept any input from your keyboard.

Sometimes what appears to be a deeply rooted problem within the X Window System can be solved with little effort. Such is the case of the X window that won't accept keyboard input—a too-common problem for X users and programmers.

In Chapter 9 we covered how the Motif window manager handles the issue of keyboard focus, and how you can change from click-to-type to focus-follows-mouse focus. Similarly, we discussed in chapters 10 and 11 how the Open Look and Tab window managers treat keyboard focus.

However, the situations we discussed previously represented shifts in window-manager policies and assumed that everything was working normally. What do you do when X stops working normally and refuses to accept keyboard input?

The window manager would be the *logical* starting point, since it controls interaction between the user and X, but not in this case. Instead, the problem can be traced to an application or the way it has been configured—or, perhaps, not been configured. (This configuring process is done through the editing of resource files, as we discussed earlier in Chapter 6.) To correct the problem, you must edit a class-resource file for the offending application, setting the **input** resource to **True**. This tells the window manager that your application really, really wants keyboard input. *You* knew that the application wanted keyboard input, but the window manager didn't get the hint.

To solve this problem with **xterm**, for instance, edit a class-resource file. (A file named **XTerm** in your home directory is one possibility; see Chapter 6 for a review of finding this file.) Add the following line:

```
xterm*input: True
```

This solves the problem. Taking a look at what actually causes the problem, however, will go a long way toward explaining how and why X does what it does.

Applications must let the window manager know whether they want keyboard input. This desire is conveyed in the form of **hints** sent from the application to the window manager. (Applications must send many types of hints; this is merely one of several.) Hints to the window manager don't guarantee that the window manager will obey your direction, but sometimes the window manager will accept a not-so-subtle hint. Most of the hinting is done by a toolkit, such as Motif, XView, or the Athena widget set. With older versions of these toolkits, however, the toolkit itself may not be setting all the proper hints that the window manager demands, so you have to take some action yourself.

How window managers peaceably coexist with applications is defined in the infamous *Inter-Client Communications Conventions Manual*—the ICCCM that contains the rules for well-behaved X programs. Older programs might not follow ICCCM rules to the letter. Moreover, these ICCCM rules have changed over the years, so when newer window managers become more fascistic about ICCCM rules, older software tends no longer to work the same way. Even programs created for Motif 1.0 will fail on X11 Release 4 servers if they use the paned window widget.

Who loses in all of this? The user. There are, however, some steps that programmers can take to cut down on the number of potential problems. Most of the rest of this chapter is more oriented toward programmers, so if you don't want to program X, skip ahead to the last section on Open Look.

Xt Intrinsics Hints: Input Resources

A good starting point is setting the input resource for the top-level shell widget from within an Athena- or other Xt Intrinsics-based program:

```
Widget       widget;
Arg          args[10];
int          n;

n = 0;
XtSetArg(args[n], XtNinput, True); n++;
XtSetValues(widget, args, n);
```

Or, from Motif:

```
Widget       widget;
Arg          args[10];
int          n;

n = 0;
XtSetArg(args[n], XmNinput, True); n++;
XtSetValues(widget, args, n);
```

In both cases, make sure that you're setting the values for the top-level shell widget, returned by **XtInitialize()** or **XtAppInitialize()**. The input resource is actually part of the WMShell widget, an ancestor class of the top-level shell that **XtInitialize()** or **XtAppInitialize()** return, but the shell widget inherits the input resource just fine. In Motif programs the input resource usually defaults to **True**, anyway, so normally you don't have to set this from within your programs.

You can usually set the input resource to **True**, but if you try to set it to **False**, other widgets can override it—particularly in **xterm**s and Motif programs. Normally you don't want to mess with this resource if you're writing Xt-based programs.

On the other hand, programmers using the low-level X library won't use the input resource. Instead, set the input hint in the window manager hints (necessary under ICCCM rules, anyway).

Xlib Hints: The XWMHints Structure

Programmers working with Xlib or a toolkit not based on the Xt Intrinsics must approach the situation a little differently by setting the input field of the **XWMHints** structure and pass this value onto the window manager via the **XSetWMHints()** function.

Most Xlib-based programs send a number of hints to the window manager, asking that the window manager treat the application properly, especially regarding such things as an application's window size, location, and icon bitmap. One set of these hints is stored in the **XWMHints** structure.

The **XWMHints** structure contains a number of fields, including information about the initial state of the program (iconic or not), the bitmap for an icon (if any), and whether the program wants the window manager to give it the keyboard focus.

As of X11 Release 5, the **XWMHints** structure looks like:

```
typedef struct {
        long        flags;
        Bool        input;
        int         initial_state;
        Pixmap      icon_pixmap;
        Window      icon_window;
        int         icon_x, icon_y;
        Pixmap      icon_mask;
        XID         window_group;
} XWMHints;
```

Using XAllocWMHints

With X11 Release 4, the X designers changed the older methods for using the **XWMHints** structure; they maintained the newest method in Release 5. Release 4 added a new function, **XAllocWMHints()**, which allocates the **XWMHints** structure.

If you don't have Releases 4 or 5, by all means update as soon as possible. You can emulate **XAllocWMHints()** with **malloc()**:

```
XWMHints        *wmhints

wmhints = (XWMHints *)
        malloc( sizeof(XWMHints) );
```

Be sure to free the memory for the structure when you're done with it.

The reason for the **XAllocWMHints()** function is that the size of the **XWMHints** structure can change. If your applications always call a special function to allocate the structure, you won't need to change code·to have it still work with newer versions of the X library. Here's how you set the input hint with a Release 4 or 5 version of the X library:

```
XWMHints        *wmhints;
wmhints = XAllocWMHints();

/* Set your other hints and OR together the bits in the */
/* flag field. Then, set the InputHint. */

wmhints->flags |-InputHint;
wmhints->input = True;

XSetWMHints( display, window, wmhints );

XFree( wmhints );
```

For Users of Open Look

If you're running OpenWindows and the Open Look window manager, **olwm**, particularly on a Sun workstation (or clone), there's one other solution if the tips above don't solve your problems. Try adding the following line to your **.Xdefaults** resource file:

```
OpenWindows.FocusLenience:   true
```

or the newer format:

```
olwm.FocusLenience:        `true
```

The **FocusLenience** resource allows you to relax the ICCCM-based input-hint requirements, especially for older X software that no longer follows the rules for well-behaved X programs (if it ever did). The default value for this resource is **false**, which means no lenience is given. Far too many aspects of X follow this philosophy.

Summary

Sometimes what appears to be a complex problem within X can be solved via simple means. Such is the case when an application refuses keyboard input, which can happen when older versions of software are run with newer window managers. This chapters solves that simple problem and tells programmers how to avoid the problem in the future.

## Chapter 17

Solving Common Problems

There's a dark side to the great flexibility offered by the X Window System. With so many options available to users and programmers, there's also a greater possibility that many, many things can go wrong. The three previous chapters covered a number of major problems in depth, but there remain many problems that plague users. No X installation is perfect, and we've found that X problems are usually baffling—to say the least. This chapter covers problems and solutions (or at least work-arounds) that we've faced.

Each section starts with a short description of the problem in **_bold italicized_** text. Then we briefly cover a number of potential solutions.

General Troubleshooting Techniques

The best troubleshooting technique we can offer is very simple: backtrack to where you weren't plagued by the problem. Did your system *ever* work? Go back to that point.

What changed since then? Something must have changed between then and now, or else you wouldn't have a problem. Chances are that whatever changed will point you to a solution. Of course, sometimes it's very hard to remember what changed.

Other questions you should ask yourself include the following:

- Check your command path. Does it include **/usr/bin/X11** or the directory in which you keep your X programs?
- Are any cables, such as the mouse line, unplugged? This hits 386 UNIX systems especially hard.
- Did you set up **xhost** or **xauth** to disable remote access to your X display? Or did the system do this for you?
- Is your **DISPLAY** environment variable set up incorrectly?

Authorization Problems

The most common X error is the following:

X Toolkit Error: Can't open display.

This often occurs when you are computing on a number of machines in a network environment. This can be a problem with your **DISPLAY** environment variable, covered in Chapter 4, or an authorization problem.

If **DISPLAY** is set up properly, then for some reason the program is not allowed to access the X server. Most likely you're facing a lack of authorization.

X allows for two main authorization schemes. The simplest, based on the program **xhost**, lists hosts that you are allowed to connect to your X server. Using **xhost**, any program, from any user, on accepted hosts can then connect to your X server.

To allow programs from a given machine to connect to your X server, use the **xhost** command:

```
xhost +hostname
```

where **hostname** is the name of the host allowing access. Once you execute this command, any program on the given host can connect to your display, which opens a very large potential security hole. Malicious users could watch each keystroke you make, in addition to engaging in all sorts of nastiness.

To turn off hosts and prevent programs on a given host from connecting to your X server, use the **-** option with **xhost**:

xhost -hostname

The file **/etc/X0.hosts** contains the default list of the hosts with access to display 0 on a given host. You can create one of these files for every X server on a given computer. The file name is **/etc/Xnumber.hosts** where *number* is the display (X server) number (starting at 0). **xhost** can override the entries in this file.

A more detailed authorization scheme is used with the program **xauth**. This scheme uses special protocols, by default **MIT-MAGIC-COOKIE-1**, to limit access to the X server. Under this scheme, client programs must send the proper "magic cookie" value to the X server for it to accept the connection. The X server then maintains a list of valid cookie values.

The **X Display Manager**, **xdm**, stores a cookie value in the **.Xauthority** file in your home directory, or in the file named by the **XAUTHORITY** environment variable. Once stored in your home directory, X programs must access this file to get the cookie value. If a program doesn't have access to your home directory's **.Xauthority** file, then that program cannot get the magic cookie value, and therefore cannot connect to your X server.

Neither of these schemes is foolproof. The real answer is to secure your full environment instead of trying to secure only X.

If you're using one of these magic-cookie protocols, you'll need to pass around your **.Xauthority** file or use **xauth** to add the cookies to other systems you want to connect to your X server.

See the **xauth** manual page for more details.

Problems Running X Applications

You may face a number of problems running X applications, including:

- not finding commands (programs);
- not finding shared libraries; or
- not finding the correct shared libraries and having X programs "die" if run overnight.

XIO: fatal IO error 32 (Broken pipe) on X server ":0.0" after 15 requests (15 known processed) with 0 events remaining. The connection was probably broken by a server shutdown or KillClient.

If you get an error like this, something terrible happened to the X program in question. Many times *you* did the terrible thing by choosing a kill command from the window manager's menu or using **xkill** to knock off an errant program.

The XIO message means that the problem is with the X program's connection to the X server. If you didn't explicitly kill the program, something is amiss with the network link between that program and the X server. Network problems are usually serious, so check to make sure your network links are still up and running.

Command not found.

If your UNIX shell cannot find your X programs, chances are your command path is not properly set up. Set **path** to include **/usr/bin/X11** or the location of X programs on your system. The following command works for the C shell:

```
set path = ( $path /usr/bin/X11 )
```

/usr/lib/libX11.so.4.2 not found.

This is a shared library problem. How do we know that? Because *lib* tells us "library" and *.so* tells us "shared." (Remember: normal static UNIX libraries end with *.a*.) If you get shared library problems, check your **LD_LIBRARY_PATH** environment variable on Sun and SPARC systems. It should be set to the location of the shared libraries you need. For example:

```
setenv LD_LIBRARY_PATH /usr/openwin/lib
```

Windows get lost behind other windows.

To solve this problem, you need to know what window manager you're running. Chapter 8 should help you if you don't know.

Once you determine your window manager, you must lower the windows in front until you find the window that "disappeared" under the pile of windows. Most window managers, like **twm** and **mwm**, offer a Lower or Shuffle Down menu choice from their root menu. **Mwm** also offers a Lower choice from the window menu. Start lowering the windows on top until you see the window that was buried.

If you can see part of the window, **twm** offers a keystroke combination to raise a window. Hold down the Meta (Alt) key while you press the right mouse button, when the mouse is over the window in question. This operation should raise the window if you use **twm**.

With **mwm** or **olwm**, click on any part of the window's border, and the window manager should raise the window.

ld.so: warning: /usr/lib/libX11.so.4.2 has older revision than expected 3.

This warning message appears a lot on SPARC-based systems using shared libraries. The message is fairly explanatory: The shared library version is out of sync with what the program expects.

On SunOS, for example, **/usr/lib/libX11.so.4.2** is the name of the shared library file. Normally, this could be a problem, but one so-called "fix" to the X sources included the wrong version number, which makes us treat this warning less seriously. Your applications might be using the proper version without knowing it.

If the X programs still run acceptably, don't worry about this warning. If you experience problems, however, you should look into your X installation and check the shared libraries.

X applications die if run overnight.

Running X overnight can lead to problems. If you use **unix:0** for a display name, the X server will create a special file for the UNIX domain socket off the **/tmp** directory. The UNIX program **cron** may then delete all files in **/tmp** every night, causing problems with your X environment. Check your **cron** setup if you experience these problems.

Motif programs crash when you adjust the size of window panes.

Older Motif programs crash when run on newer X servers if you adjust the panes on paned window widgets. The reason is simple: X servers have become more demanding about the rules over the years, and programs that skirted by less-restrictive X servers are nailed by newer servers. To allow for older Motif programs, use the **xset** command with the **bc**— or "bug compatibility"— mode:

```
xset bc
```

You may also have problems running Motif applications under X11 Release 5 X servers. Check to make sure your X server was compiled with the **MotifBC** directive set to yes (see Chapter 20 for more on this).

When the window manager quits, which should stop X, the window manager starts again.

In this instance, you probably edited your **.xinitrc** file while running X. Remember, **xinit** executes this file. If you change it (by adding characters, for example), you're essentially creating a self-modifying code. It's always best to stop X before editing the **.xinitrc** file.

Installing Sun's AnswerBook makes OpenWindows unusable.

In Chapter 7 we described installing X fonts, but many SPARC-based workstations run OpenWindows and use Sun fonts. Even though this problem is documented (albeit obscurely), Sun's AnswerBook can trash the key **Families.List** file used by OpenWindows, stored normally in **/usr/openwin/lib/fonts**.

Rebuild this file by using the OpenWindows **bldfamily** program. Change to the **/usr/openwin/lib/fonts** directory and run the **bldfamily** command, stored in **/usr/openwin/bin**.

Xterm Problems

Since **xterm** is the most-used X program, problems with **xterm** bedevil many users.

The delete or backspace key doesn't work.

If you hit the backspace key and see **^H** or **^?**, you probably have the wrong key set-up for editing the command line. This problem occurs most often when you log onto another machine with a different operating system over a network, such as logging onto a Sun SPARCstation from an HP 720 workstation.

This really isn't an X problem; it's a shell problem. The answer is to use the **stty** program to change what key the shell uses to erase characters. Type in the following command:

```
stty erase erase_key
```

where **erase_key** is the actual key on the keyboard you want for the erase function in the shell. For example, if you want your key labeled Backspace to act as the erase key, type in **stty erase** and then press the Backspace key. Hit return to end the command.

Vi doesn't work right in screen-editing mode.

If **vi** or other programs that use characteristics of your terminal don't work, your system probably doesn't have the **TERM** environment variable set up properly.

Set **TERM** to **xterm**. If that doesn't solve the problem, try setting TERM to vt100:

```
setenv TERM xterm
```

or

```
setenv TERM vt100
```

Both commands are in the **csh** format. Your system may not have **termcap** or **terminfo** entries under the name "**xterm**." If neither command works, or if you resized the **xterm** window, you need to run the **resize** command, as we described in Chapter 3. If you run the Bourne shell, **sh**, you can use the following commands:

```
resize -u  > /tmp/foo
. /tmp/foo
```

386/486 UNIX Problems

Due to the wide variety of hardware and installation set-ups, 386 and 486 versions of UNIX seem to suffer the most problems related to X. One factor that compounds these problems is that most 386 versions of UNIX software are sold on a piece-by-piece basis. Thus standard items (like networking) are sold as options in the 386 market. This, of course, dramatically increases the number of different configurations and adds to problems.

This next section covers a number of problems that we've seen only on Intel 80x86-based systems. Most deal with networking software implementations.

The X server won't start.

Don't restart the X server too quickly on 386 systems. Typically, the networking system requires about forty-five seconds to one minute to reset all the sockets that the X server uses. Wait at least forty-five seconds before trying to restart the X server.

If you start X when you log in, wait at least that long after logging out before trying to log in again. In fact, X works best on a 386 if you log out after stopping X. Some problems you'll see include the following error messages:

```
t_bind failed: Couldn't allocate address
X Tcp port for display 0 is busy, will try again...
```

You might also get a corrupted screen display. The worse problem is when your X server won't start and the text display is corrupted. Many times the only answer is to reboot—a drastic solution to what should be a simple problem.

Cannot connect to server "L."

This error, or a similar one, often pops up when you have a system like Interactive (SunSoft) UNIX System VR3.2 ver. 3.0 set up for a certain type of network link—say, streams—and you're running an X server set up for a different kind of link—TCP/IP sockets, for example. Many 386 implementations of UNIX make networking an add-on item, which is where this problem comes from. You won't face this error on most other systems.

Set the **DISPLAY** environment variable from **unix:0** to **:0**, using a command like:

```
setenv DISPLAY :0
```

Wildly out-of-sync monitor.

We find this problem a lot on SCO Open Desktop, especially with Paradise VGA graphics controllers. The only answers that seem to work include turning off the monitor, unplugging and replugging the monitor cable, and then turning the monitor back on. If this doesn't work, you can try cycling power to the monitor very rapidly, although this is not very nice to your monitor.

Otherwise, you can try to quit X and then restart your X session. This can be difficult with the wildly oscillating display. If you use a window manager like **mwm** to quit your X session, you often can move the mouse pointer over the root window. Then pull down the window-manager root menu and choose the last choice. This should be Quit, right? With Motif, you can also set up a keyboard mnemonic for the Quit choice, avoiding the need to move the mouse anymore.

Screen-Saver Problems

Most X servers include a screen-saving option, where the screen will go blank (or display an X) after a defined period during which the keyboard or mouse is not used. The screen saver helps you avoid monitor burn-in and extend the life of your monitor.

The screen suddenly goes black.

Having the screen suddenly go black can be disconcerting, especially for new X users. (This originally came up for us at a marketing presentation. Up to that time, we assumed everyone knew what a screen saver was.)

You can get the screen back by pressing a key on the keyboard or juggling the mouse back and forth. We recommend using the mouse, as typing a key may do something unexpected in the program with the current keyboard focus. In a marketing presentation, though, juggling the mouse every five minutes isn't really an option. In such a case, you probably want to turn the screen saver off entirely. Use the **xset** command to do this:

```
xset s off
```

You can also set the timeout for the screen saver with the **xset** command. First, check what settings you have with the **xset** program:

```
xset q
```

This command returns all the settings controlled by **xset**, including the screen saver:

```
Screen Saver:
  prefer blanking:  yes    allow exposures:  yes
  timeout:  600    cycle:  600
```

Table 17.1 Screen-saver commands.

Command	Meaning
xset s off	Turns off screen saver.
xset s on	Turns on screen saver.
xset s default	Turns on screen saver to default values.
xset s blank	Sets screen saver to blank video.
xset s noblank	Sets screen saver to display a background pattern.

To adjust the screen-saver timeouts, use the following command:

```
xset s value1 value2
```

where **value1** is the number of seconds after the last key or mouse event to wait before turning on the screen saver. The optional **value2** is the number of seconds between changes to the background pattern to avoid monitor burn-in. This last value only matters if you use the **noblank** screen-saver mode.

You can also use **xset** to control other aspects of your X server, including the volume of the bell, the key repeat rate (not supported by all X servers), the bc backwards (or "bug") compatibility mode mentioned above, the font paths (as shown in Chapter 7), and the mouse acceleration. See the on-line manual for **xset** for more details.

Using Imake to Compile Contributed X Sources

There are hundreds of free X programs. Unlike DOS and Macintosh counterparts, most free X programs are distributed with just the source code. You then compile these programs on your system. Most UNIX sources are written in the C programming language and use a program called **make** to control compiling and linking.

There is no Makefile, or the Makefile doesn't work.

X uses a program called **imake** to generate a **Makefile**. This **Makefile** is customized to your local configuration, using an **Imakefile** and a set of local rules normally stored in **/usr/lib/X11/config**. In that directory you should see files such as **Imake.rules**, **Imake.tmpl**, and **Project.tmpl**.

Imake builds the **Makefile** from the **Imakefile**. **Make** takes over and builds the program. If you don't have a **Makefile**, you'll need to build one. One of the easiest ways to do this is to use the shell script **xmkmf** (for X Make Makefile). Simply change to the directory where the **Imakefile** resides (the **Imakefile** for the new free software, that is) and run **xmkmf**. If successful, this should build a **Makefile**. If not successful, you can try to create your own, based on the rules in the **Imakefile**.

Summary

Many problems within the X Window System can be solved simply. We cover the most common X problems and convey our solutions.

VI

Programming X

Despite much effort to the contrary, the X Window System (along with Motif and Open Look) tends to be an environment that appeals more to programmers than to users. In this section we cover the basics of programming with Motif and X toolkits. We also discuss common X error messages that are too easily generated by x applications.

Chapter 18

Programming Motif and X Toolkits

As you know, X is basically a programmer's windowing system. This chapter introduces X programming from the perspective of the Motif toolkit. Motif is a toolkit from the Open Software Foundation, and the Motif interface forms one of the two most-used X interfaces. (Open Look is the other.) We use Motif, since X toolkit programming is a lot easier than using only the low-level X library. X application developers need to learn both the low-level calls and the higher-level toolkit calls—and Motif is apparently more widely used than Open Look.

In this chapter we'll introduce the basics of Motif programming. We'll create a Motif program and discuss the format and coding conventions used to develop Motif applications. We won't turn you into expert Motif programmers, but Appendix A lists a number of books that can help in this regard.

To get much at all from this chapter, you should be familiar with C programming on UNIX systems. If you'd prefer to be an X user and not a programmer, skip ahead to the next chapter.

What is Motif?

Motif is:

- A look-and-feel Style Guide for applications.
- A toolkit (C function library) for building compliant applications.
- A window manager, **mwm**, to help enforce the Style Guide.
- A User Interface Language (UIL) interpreter to aid application development.

Motif is based on the X Toolkit (Xt) Intrinsics, much like the Athena widget set (which comes with generic X) and the Open Look Intrinsic Toolkit (OLIT, called Xt+ by AT&T).

Why Use Motif?

Motif presents a *de facto* standard interface, which is in use across many platforms. Many organizations use a Motif interface as a check-off item: If your software doesn't have a Motif interface, you'll have a harder time selling to many larger firms. Motif fits in reasonably well with X standards like window managers and resource files. Finally, using a toolkit—any toolkit—speeds application development.

Still, you should be aware of some trade-offs:

- The Xt Intrinsics enforce an odd pseudo-object-oriented code style.
- Resources and resource files are seemingly impossible to debug.
- Xt-based programs, including Motif, allocate more than 50K of RAM at application start time.
- Motif programs tend to be slow.
- There is a huge overhead per program. (The obligatory Hello World program, for example, takes up one megabyte.)
- No decent C++ interface is available yet.

X programs, and Motif programs in particular, tend toward one megabyte minimum executable size, even for small Motif applications.

Table 18.1 Hello World in Motif.

Program	Size on SCO ODT	Size on Data General Aviion (88K RISC)
hello (text)	28K	35K
hellox (Xlib)	133K	226K
hellom (Motif)	605K	1011K

Programming Motif

There are five basic parts to all Motif programs. First, include the proper header files. Every Motif source file needs to include **Xm.h**, normally from the **/usr/include/Xm** directory:

```
#include <Xm/Xm.h>
```

In addition, each type of Motif widget has its own header file, such as **PushB.h** for the pushbutton widget.

Second, initialize the X Toolkit Intrinsics, using **XtAppInitialize()**, or **XtInitialize()** if you're using Motif 1.0 or X11 Release 3. Motif changed dramatically from version 1.0 to 1.1 and from 1.1 to 1.2. Motif 1.2 works with X11 Release 5.

```
XtAppContext        appcontext;
String              application_class;
XrmOptionDescRec    xrm_options[];
Cardinal            number_of_xrm_options;
Cardinal            pointer_to_argc;
String              argv[];
String              *fallback_resources;
ArgList             args;
Cardinal            number_args;

Widget XtAppInitialize(&appcontext, /* RETURN */
        application_class,
        xrm_options, number_of_xrm_options,
        &pointer_to_argc, argv,
        fallback_resources, args, number_args );
```

You can pass NULL for many of these parameters, as we do below, if you don't need them.

Third, create your **widgets**. A widget is an interface element, like a menu, a scrollbar, or a pushbutton. Inside the C program, the widget is a data structure that can be treated opaquely. Most widgets create an associated window, but some do not. These lightweight, windowless widgets are often called **gadgets** in Motif or **flat widgets** in Open Look.

Some widgets, called **container widgets**, have children, other widgets that the containers control. For example, a dialog-box widget often has child widgets for the OK and Cancel pushbuttons, along with text widgets for user-entered text. In the program below, we'll create five widgets.

The fourth step in Motif programming is to realize the widget hierarchy. After creating the widgets, nothing appears on the screen, because none of the windows associated with the widgets has been created yet. The function `XtRealizeWidget()` recursively creates all the windows for a given container widget and all its child widgets, making the program visible.

Fifth, run the Xt Intrinsics main event-handling loop. X applications are inherently **event-driven applications**. That is, the application runs an event loop that awaits events from the X server. When these events arrive, such as a keypress on the keyboard, the event loop passes off the events to special event-handling routines. This loop goes on forever. In Motif, use the function `XtAppMainLoop()`. If you're running Motif 1.0, use `XtMainLoop()`.

Well, that's all there is to Motif programming. Sound easy?

A First Motif Program

For this chapter, we'll build a very small Motif program, using a pushbutton widget to quit the program, a label widget to display a text string, and a scrolled text widget to show Motif-style text editing. We'll use a class-resource file extensively. In fact, most of the interface definition will be in this resource file. When the user clicks the left mouse button in the pushbutton, the program will exit.

Initializing the Xt Intrinsics

The first call in our program is to initialize the Xt Intrinsics library, which also initializes the Motif widget set. We pass an application class name of **Usingx**, so this will also be the name of our class-resource file. Note how we pass **NULL** for most of the parameters.

XtAppInitialize() returns a top-level shell widget, the container used for the next level of widgets. This top-level shell will also have a window that the window manager will manage.

```
n = 0;
parent = XtAppInitialize(&app_context,
        "Usingx",       /* Application Class */
        NULL, 0,
        &argc, argv,
        NULL,
        args, n);
```

In the code file, below, we show **XtAppInitialize()** in context. In the resource file below we customize some resources for this top-level shell widget. The term *customize* may seem odd, since we didn't set any default values. In a real Motif application, you would.

We gain a benefit from placing all visible text strings in a resource file: internationalization. Users in France can type in French text, instead of the English below, and the program will still work fine.

The **title** resource sets the window title and should appear in the title bar. We also set the **fontList** resource globally for the whole application. (We'll override this for the text widget, below.)

```
Usingx*title:        Sample Motif Program from Using X
Usingx*fontList:     lucidasans-12
```

Creating a Container Widget

Underneath the top-level parent widget, we create another container widget, a paned window widget. We do this because the top-level shell widget can contain only one child widget. The paned window widget, however, can contain a number of children.

The paned window widget divides a window vertically into panes that go across the width of the window. Inside each pane, we'll place a child widget.

We create the paned window widget with **XmCreatePanedWindow()**. This function, as all Motif **XmCreate** functions do, takes four parameters: the widget ID of the parent widget (every widget needs a parent except for the top-level shell), the widget name (to be used to look up resources in a resource file), an array of **Arg** structures (used to pass hard-coded resource customizations), and the number of items in the **Arg** array, which we pass a zero.

The paned window widget requires the **PanedW.h** include file.

```
Widget  pane;
Widget  parent;
Arg     args[10];
int     n;

n = 0;
pane = XmCreatePanedWindow(parent,
       "pane", args, n);
XtManageChild(pane);
```

After creating the widget, you need to manage it, using **XtManageChild()**. If a widget isn't managed, it won't appear.

We also change a resource of the paned window widget in the resource file below. We adjust the sash height to six pixels, which makes the sash smaller and better-looking. This sash allows the user to adjust the size of each pane. Notice the resource-setting command below:

```
Usingx*pane.sashHeight:      6
```

This command sets the **sashHeight** resource on the widget named **pane** in the application class **UsingX**. Thus, only one widget's resources are changed by this command. Throughout the rest of the resource file, we'll use this more complex way of naming which resource to change.

Creating a Pushbutton Widget

The first child of the paned window container widget is a pushbutton widget. This widget performs some action whenever the user clicks the left mouse button in the widget. This action is calling one of your functions, a function you can register with Motif.

We use **XmCreatePushButton()** to create the pushbutton widget and again pass no resource customizations. The pushbutton widget requires the include file **PushB.h**.

```
n = 0;
push = XmCreatePushButton(pane,
       "quit", args, n);
XtManageChild(push);
```

To change the text displayed in the pushbutton, we set the **labelString** resource in the resource file:

```
Usingx*quit.labelString: Quit Program
```

Setting Up a Callback Function

The following code registers our function, **quitCB()**, with Motif as the **activateCallback** function for the pushbutton widget created above. We pass **NULL** as the value for our **client_data**. If necessary, you can pass a pointer to data for the callback. This pointer will be passed on to the callback function.

```
XtAddCallback( push,
      XmNactivateCallback,
      quitCB,
      (caddr_t) NULL );
```

The official syntax for **XtAddCallback()** is:

```
Widget          widget;
String          callback_name;
XtCallbackProc  callback_function;
XtPointer       client_data;   /* passed to callback
                                  function */

void XtAddCallback( widget,
      callback_name,
      callback_function,
      client_data );
```

Format for Callback Functions

Motif callback functions must not return a value, and all take three parameters: a widget ID (of the widget that initiated the callback), the programmer-passed **client_data** (NULL in our case), and Motif-passed **call_data**, which is often a pointer to a complex Motif structure.

```
void quitCB(widget, client_data, call_data)

Widget    widget;
caddr_t   client_data; /* your data */
caddr_t   call_data;/* Motif-passed data */

{         /* quitCB */

          exit(0);

}         /* quitCB */
```

Our callback just calls **exit()**, which quits the program. Since the **XtAppMainLoop()** loops forever, this is how we get out of the loop and quit the program. Notice how we perform no clean-up work in this function—one of the luxuries of small demo programs.

Creating a Label Widget

Next, we create a label widget, also a child of the paned window. A Motif label widget just presents a static text label (or a bitmap picture) and is created with **XmCreateLabel()**. The label widget requires the include file **Label.h**.

```
n = 0;
label = XmCreateLabel(pane,
            "label", args, n);
XtManageChild(label);
```

In the resource file, we also change the **labelString** resource for the label widget:

```
Usingx*label.labelString:    Type Into the Window Below
```

Creating a Scrolled Text Widget

Motif provides a built-in text editor called the text widget. To edit large chunks of text, you need scroll bars surrounding the text widget. We can create both with one function call: **XmCreateScrolledText()**. This function creates a text widget and horizontal and vertical scroll bars.

The code below is very deceptive, since the text widget doesn't really work unless you set a number of resources.

```
n = 0;
text = XmCreateScrolledText(pane,
            "text", args, n);
XtManageChild(text);
```

We need to set these resources in the resource file. First, we change the **fontList** resource to use a fixed-width font. A limitation of the Motif text widget is that it definitely works best with a fixed-width font. You can use proportional fonts, but these fonts are sometimes hard to read in the text widget.

```
Usingx*text.fontList:      lucidasanstypewriter-12
```

Next, we set the **rows** and **columns** resources to determine the size (in characters) of the visible area of the text widget.

```
Usingx*text.columns:      80
Usingx*text.rows:         10
```

The **editable** resource allows the user to edit the text, instead of forcing read-only access (if set to False). The **editMode** controls whether the text widget is a single line text entry field or a multiline text editor.

```
Usingx*text.editable:      True
Usingx*text.editMode:      XmMULTI_LINE_EDIT
```

Finally, we turn on the vertical scroll bar and turn off the horizontal one.

```
Usingx*text.scrollHorizontal:   False
Usingx*text.scrollVertical:     True
```

Realizing the Widgets

After creating and managing all our widgets, we pass the top-level parent widget ID to **XtRealizeWidget()**. This routine then recursively descends the tree of widgets and "realizes" each one.

```
Widget  parent;  /* returned by XtAppInitialize */

XtRealizeWidget( parent );
```

Entering the Main Event-Handling Loop

The **XtAppMainLoop()** function handles all events coming from the X server, which includes keyboard events, mouse events, and redraw request events (called **Expose** events in X terminology).

```
XtAppContext app_context ;
```

```
XtAppMainLoop(app_context);
```

This function loops literally forever. If you want to quit your Motif applications, you must do so from within a callback function.

To quit the program, we use the **quitCB()** function shown above.

Source Code for the Motif Program

The following file, which we name **usingx.c**, contains the source code for our sample Motif program.

```
/*
 *      usingx.c
 *      Motif code to introduce Motif programming.
 *      -E F Johnson
 *
 *      Copyright 1992 Eric F. Johnson and
 *      Kevin Reichard, all rights reserved.
 */

/* Standard Motif include file */
#include <Xm/Xm.h>

/*      Each Motif widget has its own include file. */
#include <Xm/Label.h>
#include <Xm/PanedW.h>
#include <Xm/PushB.h>
#include <Xm/Text.h>

/* Quit callback, quits program. */

void quitCB(widget, client_data, call_data)
```

```
Widget  widget;
caddr_t client_data;    /* your data */
caddr_t call_data;      /* Motif-passed data */

{       /* quitCB */

        exit(0);

}       /* quitCB */

main(argc, argv)

int     argc;
char    *argv[];

{       /* main */
        Widget          parent;
        XtAppContext    app_context;
        Widget          pane, push, label, text;
        Arg             args[20];
        int             n;

        /*
         * Initialize the Xt Intrinsics.
         */
        n = 0;
        XtSetArg(args[n], XmNallowResize, True); n++;

        parent = XtAppInitialize(&app_context,
                "Usingx",        /* Application Class */
                NULL, 0,
                &argc, argv,
                NULL,
                args, n);
        /*
         * Create a paned window frame
         */
        n = 0;
        pane = XmCreatePanedWindow(parent,
             "pane", args, n);
        XtManageChild(pane);
```

```
/*
 * Create a pushbutton to quit the program.
 */
n = 0;
push = XmCreatePushButton(pane,
        "quit", args, n);
XtManageChild(push);

/*
 * Set up a callback function
 * to quit our program.
 */
XtAddCallback(push, XmNactivateCallback,
      quitCB, (caddr_t) NULL);

/*
 * Create a text label.
 */
n = 0;
label = XmCreateLabel(pane,
        "label", args, n);
XtManageChild(label);


/*
 * Create a scrolled text widget for
 * editing text.
 */
n = 0;
text = XmCreateScrolledText(pane,
        "text", args, n);
XtManageChild(text);

/*
 * make the widgets "real".
 */
XtRealizeWidget(parent);

/*
 * Handle events (forever).
 */
XtAppMainLoop(app_context);

}        /* main */

/* end of file usingx.c */
```

Resource Files

Motif uses **resource files**, including class- and user-resource files, just like any other X program. Watch out, though, for some of the odd names Motif uses. For example, Motif uses **fontList** instead of the more common **font** resource. Motif also uses **labelString** instead of the more common **label** resource.

The sample program above won't do much good without the following resource file. Name this file **Usingx** and place it in your home directory.

```
! resource file for Usingx

Usingx*title:              Sample Motif Program from Using X

Usingx*fontList:           lucidasans-12

Usingx*pane.sashHeight:    6

Usingx*quit.labelString:   Quit Program

Usingx*label.labelString:  Type Into the Window Below

!
! Customize the text widget.
!
Usingx*text.fontList:      lucidasanstypewriter-12
Usingx*text.columns:       80
Usingx*text.rows:          10
Usingx*text.editable:      True
Usingx*text.editMode:      XmMULTI_LINE_EDIT
Usingx*text.scrollHorizontal: False
Usingx*text.scrollVertical:  True

! end of resource file
```

Compiling and Linking Motif Programs

Motif programs require the Motif library (usually **libXm.a**), the Xt Intrinsics library (usually **libXt.a**), and the low-level X library (usually **libX11.a**). You can compile the program with the following command:

```
cc -o foo foo.c -lXm -lXt -lX11
```

You might need the **_NO_PROTO** option if your C compiler does not handle ISO/ANSI C function prototypes:

```
cc -o foo -D_NO_PROTO foo.c -lXm -lXt -lX11
```

Some systems, particularly 386-based UNIX systems, require a number of other libraries (usually because networking is considered an option on those systems). SCO Open Desktop, for example, requires:

```
cc -Di386 -DLAI_TCP -DSYSV -o foo foo.c -lXm -lXt -lX11 \
      -ltlisock -lsocket -lnsl_s
```

Interactive (SunSoft) UNIX ver. 3.0 requires:

```
cc -o foo foo.c -lXm -lXt -lX11 -lnsl_s
```

Consult your manuals for any compiling options necessary for your installation.

Summary

This chapter introduced the barest basics of Motif programming. There's a lot more to learn, but we hope we whetted your appetite. In Appendix A we've included a list of books that go into much more detail.

If you plan to release commercial Motif applications, you should purchase a Motif source license from the Open Software Foundation. You really need the source if you encounter problems. The costs start at $2,000. A support or update agreement is also helpful, as Motif updates tend to fix *hundreds* of bugs. Try to avoid Motif 1.0, as it had many memory leaks and other nasty bugs. Motif 1.2 is more up to date.

19

Decoding X Errors

Different computer operating systems treat errors differently. The Macintosh, for instance, displays a cute little bomb with some accompanying text (sometimes relevant, sometimes not), while Microsoft Windows merely tells you something went wrong and advises you to shut down the system as soon as possible; it fails to tell you what caused the error, though.

Similarly, decoding X errors can be as difficult as divining the future from tea leaves. X users and programmers see errors regularly—too regularly. In theory, you shouldn't see X error messages, since X applications should be robust enough to deal internally with low-level X error messages. Unfortunately, that's not the case. And these errors are usually fatal; most X programs simply quit when an X error arrives.

Good X programmers build error-handling mechanisms into their application code, and X provides a number of tools for users to trap errors in programs. Still, dealing with the error and actually solving the problem that generates the error are two different things.

The X server sends X error events to an application whenever it detects a serious problem. These X errors are reported in terms of X protocol, not in terms of X calls or application tasks, so it's hard to determine exactly what went wrong, especially if you don't have the source code for the application. X errors arrive asynchronously—that is, after the fact—which compounds the problem of decoding the error message.

Common X errors include:

- **BadFont**, which indicates that an invalid font was chosen;
- **BadName**, generated when an application tries to load a nonexistent font;
- **BadMatch**, generated when an application tries to copy data between drawables with different depths (a good programmer will avoid this error); and
- **BadAlloc**, the dreaded out-of-memory error.

Most X errors present a message like this:

```
X Error of failed request: BadDrawable (invalid Pixmap or
          Window parameter)
  Major opcode of failed request: 76 (X_ImageText8)
  Minor opcode of failed request:  0
  Resource id in failed request:  0x0
  Serial number of failed request:  12
  Current serial number in output stream:  13
```

BadDrawable tells us that the error involved a bad drawable ID: a bad window or pixmap. In addition, we can guess from the **X_ImageText8** that the error had to do with a call to **XDrawImageString** or some similar function that outputs text. Finally, the resource ID of the failed request is **0x0**, which implies that the bad window or pixmap ID was the constant **None**—an error occurred in creating the window or pixmap and the application didn't check for that error. Later, when drawing to this nonexistent window or pixmap, the application faulted. The serial numbers and minor op-codes don't do you a lot of good.

Heeding Protocol

The protocol number of the failed request was **76**. You can look up X protocol numbers in the file **Xproto.h** in whatever directory your X Window **include** files reside, normally **/usr/include/X11**. About 90 percent of the way through **Xproto.h**, you'll see a listing of the X network protocol-request numbers. Here's some of the more common requests that generate X errors.

```
#define X_CreateWindow               1
#define X_ChangeWindowAttributes      2
#define X_GetWindowAttributes         3
#define X_ChangeProperty             18
#define X_OpenFont                   45
#define X_QueryFont                  47
#define X_CopyArea                   62
#define X_CopyPlane                  63
#define X_ImageText8                 76
```

You can generally associate most protocol numbers with tasks, but a few are tough.

Trapping Errors in Programs

The X library provides two error-trapping functions, **XSetErrorHandler** and **XSetIOErrorHandler**. **XSetErrorHandler** traps normal errors, such as out-of-memory and bad-window-ID errors. **XSetIOErrorHandler** traps fatal I/O errors, such as losing the network connection to the X server. An application generally cannot recover from a fatal I/O error. Programmers pass **XSetErrorHandler**, an error-handling function to be called back when error events arrive.

```
int (*XSetErrorHandler(handler_function))()
        int     (*handler_function)();
```

With X11 Release 4 and later, **XSetErrorHandler** returns a pointer to the old error-handling function. Your **handler_function()** will be passed to the **Display** pointer and a pointer to the error event:

```
handler_function(display, event)
        Display     *display;
        XErrorEvent *event;
```

This function can return if you judge the errors recoverable.

XSetIOErrorHandler sets up a function to be called back on fatal I/O errors.

```
int (*XSetIOErrorHandler(handler_function))()
            int                 (*handler_function)();
```

Your fatal I/O error-handling function should not return, as Xlib terminates your program. (Xlib claims to, anyway. Some versions of Xlib don't.) You may have to look into **setjmp()/longjmp()** to avoid returning. Like **XSetErrorHandler**, **XSetIOErrorHandler** returns the old error-handling function starting with Release 4. Your **handler_function()** is passed to the (now bad) display pointer.

```
handler_function(display)
        Display *display;
```

X Error Events

The X library delivers **XErrorEvent** structures to the error-handling function set up with **XSetErrorHandler**. If you set up an error handler with **XSetErrorHandler** and an X library error occurs, your error handler will be called sometime after the error occurred. These error events arrive asynchronously, which makes it hard to associate the error with the offending routine. You can pull some useful information from the **XErrorEvent** structure:

```
typedef struct {
        int             type;
        Display         *display;
        unsigned long   serial;
        unsigned char   error_code;
        unsigned char   request_code;
        unsigned char   minor_code;
        XID             resourceid;
        } XErrorEvent;
```

The **error_code** tells you what type of error happened. The **XGetErrorText** Xlib function returns the text message for a given error code. The **request_code** is the X protocol request number for the routine that actually caused the error. This number helps when tying the error to the offending part of your code.

   XGetErrorText retrieves an error message associated with an error number and places that message in a character buffer.

```
XGetErrorText (display, error_code, buffer, max_bytes)
        Display *display;
        int     error_code;
        char    *buffer;        /* RETURN */
        int     max_bytes;
```

Watching X Errors with Xscope

Two wonderful programs help to monitor X errors: **xscope** and **xmon**. **Xscope** prints out messages on every X network request. **Xmon** acts much like **xscope**, but it also allows you to filter out events. Once you've got a good idea of what the error is, such as a **BadName** error on a font (trying to load a font that doesn't exist, for example), you can filter out all the unwanted network packets—and there are a lot of X network requests.

Both programs work alike and make use of a clever trick. You configure **xscope** and **xmon** to sit between the X server and your applications. The X server sits at a known socket ID. **Xscope** and **xmon** connect up to that X server as it would to any normal X application. Then **xscope** monitors the known socket ID for the next X server (or any open slot you care to specify). The X applications to be debugged then connect to the **xscope** pseudo X server. **Xscope** then prints out the X network packets and forwards them on to the real X server, so you will actually see your application windows.

For example, if you're using a Sun SPARCstation named **flame** with only one X server running, the default display name would be **flame:0**, for X server **0** on machine **flame**. You configure **xscope** to be a pseudo X server **1**, with a display name of **flame:1**. **Xscope** isn't a real X server, but it looks like one to your X applications. You don't have to do anything special, just tell the application to connect up to the **xscope** server. To start **xscope** on machine **flame**, presenting X server **1** to applications, use:

```
xscope -hflame -i1
```

Then start your application, say **xterm**, with:

```
xterm -display flame:1
```

That's it. Be sure to start **xscope** in its own **xterm** window, so there will be plenty of room for the massive amount of text **xscope** pumps out. You might also want to redirect the **xscope** output to a file for later viewing.

Xmon acts mostly the same, except that it has a graphical interface for filtering out a lot of the unimportant X network packets.

Using Xmon

Xmon allows you to filter X requests, events, errors, and server replies. Since X applications generate a storm of network traffic, **xmon** greatly enhances **xscope**.

The key, of course, is to filter out the unimportant packets so that the important, error-generating packets aren't swamped in the storm of requests.

Xmon requires a more complex command line than does **xscope**:

```
xmonui | xmond -server flame:0 -port 1
```

This sets up the user-interface program, **xmonui**, on the default display (in this case, **flame:0**), and the X monitor daemon, **xmond**, also on the same display. Applications to be debugged should try to connect to server **1** on the host **flame**, as before:

```
xterm -display flame:1
```

Greg McFarlane of OTC, Australia, wrote **xmon**. James L. Peterson of MCC wrote **xscope**. Both of these (pick your favorite) are on our essential X contributed software list (a very short list, we might add). Both programs should be available at any **comp.sources.x** archive site. **Xscope** is also on the X11 R4 and R5 contributed software tapes.

Summary

Users shouldn't deal with errors, but all too often they do. This chapter covers the way X conveys error information to users (cryptically), how programmers can better deal with errors in application code (simply), and how both users and programmers can use two tools, **xmon** and **xscope**, to identify X errors (easily).

VII

Administering X

X is a very popular operating environment in large, networked installations. In the real world, much of the actual hands-on work done with X is performed by system administrators at these large, networked installations, administrators who must balance the needs of the many (the majority of the X users) versus the needs of the few (those quirky users who require unique configurations). The four chapters in this section cover major areas concerning system administration, including:

- Installing X on workstations and PCs;
- Optimizing X performance through hardware and software tricks;
- Configuring the X Display Manager to avoid awful configuration problems; and
- Setting up a user account to use X.

Chapter 20

Installing X on Workstations and PCs

Most UNIX workstations ship with the X Window System already installed. Many users, however, desire the latest and greatest tools, and so they build and install X from the MIT X Consortium source code. You may also want access to the X sources to fix bugs that affect your products. The X source code is written in the C language, the most common programming language on UNIX systems.

X is the most highly portable windowing system we've seen, but it still can be a daunting task to get X built on your workstation. For starters: Be warned that you'll need at least 100 megabytes of disk space for X to work.

The X source code, necessary for building X, is available from a number of vendors, including the MIT X Consortium (the originators of X), on tape, and on CD-ROM. In addition, you can **ftp** (using the File Transfer Protocol) the sources from a number of Internet sites (see Appendix A for more on this).

Unpacking the Sources

If you order the X sources on tape, or **ftp** the sources from an Internet site, you've probably picked up a set of compressed and split files. (The files are split into smaller chunks, which works better for sending many files over a network.) If so, you'll need to unpack the sources. If you have the X sources on a CD-ROM, this should already be done for you.

There are four basic directories, or parts, to the MIT X Consortium release, stored in subdirectories **mit-1**, **mit-2**, **mit-3**, and **mit-4**. To unpack the first part, use the following commands:

```
cd mit-1
cat mit-1.?? | uncompress | (cd mit_src_dir ; tar xfp -)
```

where **mit_src_dir** is the source directory, such as **/usr/local/src**. You then need to repeat this process with the **mit-2**, **mit-3**, and **mit-4** directories. You use a similar command for the contributed directories.

After doing this, read the X release notes. You'll be very sorry if you don't. The instructions in this chapter come from our experiences building X, particularly on Sun SPARCstations. The X source code you get may differ from the version we used, and we hope the problems we faced have been solved, especially if you purchase a tape or CD-ROM of the X sources from a commercial vendor.

Also, a number of fixes have been released by the X Consortium, solving many problems faced by users. You'll want to get the latest set of fixes from the X Consortium as well. (Most X source code vendors include the latest fixes on their tapes or CD-ROMs.)

Note that your release notes may conflict with the instructions presented in the rest of this chapter. When in doubt, use the instructions that came with your X sources. You may very well have a more recent release than we had (we hope so) and the instructions may have changed. As always, common sense helps.

Disk Space

Because the X sources take up so much disk space—over 100 megabytes—we strongly recommend you share the source directories over a network, using NFS or other network file systems. You'll also probably want to build the X sources in a separate set of directories instead of in the default source directories. The **lndir.sh** shell script helps with this.

First, create your top-level build directory, then **cd** to this directory and execute the following command:

mit_src_dir/mit/util/scripts/lndir.sh   mit_src_dir

where **mit_src_dir** is the source directory, such as **/usr/local/src**.

Configuring the Build

Once you've installed the X sources, the next step is to configure X to build on your systems, with any customizations necessary for your site. Most UNIX C software uses a program called **make** to compile and link programs. **Make**, in turn, uses a **Makefile** to tell it which files to compile and how to compile them; it also adds any customizations necessary. X, in contrast, uses a program called **imake** to generate **Makefiles**. **Imake** generates the **Makefiles** from **Imakefiles**, files that tell **imake** what to do. These **Makefiles** generated by **imake** are customized to your system set-up. Then, and only then, **make** uses the newly built **Makefiles** to build the software. To configure the X build for your systems, you need to provide enough information for **imake** to create an **Imakefile** in each subdirectory of the X sources.

In the top-level X source directory, look in the **mit/config** subdirectory. This subdirectory contains a number of vendor-based configuration files for various operating systems, as well a **site.def** file that you should customize for your site. Which vendor-specific file to use should be self-explanatory: Use **sun.cf** on Sun SPARCstations and **sgi.cf** on Silicon Graphics Iris workstations.

In this vendor file—we'll use **sun.cf** as an example—first set up the operating-system version numbers to match the version you're using. On a Sun under SunOS 4.0.3c, for example, set the following variables in the **sun.cf** file:

```
OSName      SunOS 4.0.3
OSMajorVersion 4
OSMinorVersion 0
```

(Before changing any of the configuration files, make a copy.)

Normally you won't have to make any other changes in the vendor file, unless you have a radically different operating-system version than the one listed. There are a lot of differences between SunOS 4.0.3c and 4.1.1, for example, which require changes to the **sun.cf** file. With SunOS 4.0.3c, we had to edit the **StandardDefines** in the **sun.cf** file to include the following:

```
-DX_WCHAR          No wchar_t (wide character) type.
-DX_LOCALE         No setlocale() support.
-DNOSTDHDRS        No standard (ISO/ANSI) C headers.
-DX_NOT_POSIX      Not Posix compatible.
-DX_NOT_STDC_ENV   Not Standard (ISO/ANSI) C.
```

We also had to edit the bootstrap flags entry:

```
#define BootStrapCFlags   -DNOSTDHDRS
```

If you run Motif programs, it's a good idea to allow for backwards compatibility with older Motif 1.1 applications. Set the **MotifBC** directive to **yes**. You'll need to add this line to your **site.def** file:

```
#define MotifBC YES
```

The Site Configuration File

In the **site.def** file, check the **HasGcc** directive. If you use the GNU C compiler (**gcc**), then uncomment this definition:

```
#define HasGcc  YES
```

Otherwise, do nothing. If you use **gcc**, make sure you run the **fixincludes** script to fix the include files for **gcc**, or you'll likely have problems with the way X handles networking.

The **ProjectRoot** directive specifies where the X runtime files should be installed. If you want to use the defaults (**/usr/bin/X11**, **/usr/lib**, **/usr/lib/X11**, **/usr/include/X11** and **/usr/man**), leave **ProjectRoot** commented out between the **/*** and ***/** comment delimiters. If you want to place all X files in a special disk partition or directory, uncomment **ProjectRoot** to read:

```
#define ProjectRoot your_base_directory
```

where **your_base_directory** is the base directory for X files. The X files will be installed in **your_base_directory/bin**, **your_base_directory/lib**, **your_base_directory/include/X11**, and **your_base_directory/man**. In the latter part of **site.def**, there are a number of build parameters you can use to customize which parts of X are built and how they should be installed. The **BuildServer** directive determines whether the X server should be built. This can be overriden, as most parameters can, in the vendor file:

```
#define BuildServer NO
```

The **BuildFonts** directive determines whether to build up the fonts. The PCF format, new in X11 Release 5, allows for sharing fonts between different machine architectures, something that wasn't possible with older versions of X. If you already have a set of PCF fonts built, you can turn off the mechanism for building the fonts again by setting the **BuildFonts** directive to NO:

```
#define BuildFonts NO
```

We experienced many problems building the PHIGS Extension to X, or PEX. If you have problems and cannot solve them, you can build without PEX by setting the **BuildPex** directive to NO:

```
#define BuildPex NO
```

After configuring the **site.def** file, other files you should look over include **Imake.rules**, **Imake.tmpl**, **Library.tmpl**, **Project.tmpl**, and **Server.tmpl**. Edit them, if necessary, *before* you try to build X.

Once you've configured the proper files, the next step is to build the X sources.

Building X

Building X takes a *long* time. We used the following command to build a new X release:

```
make World >& world.log &
```

If you have problems, you may have to use:

```
make World BOOTSTRAPCFLAGS=-DNOSTDHDRS >& world.log &
```

Set the **BOOTSTRAPCFLAGS** to whatever is necessary to get the code to compile. Both make commands above send their output to a file named **world.log**. This file will grow immensely as the build process proceeds. To monitor this file, you can use the following command:

```
tail -f world.log
```

Come back tomorrow. Well, maybe later today. Seriously, the X build takes a *long* time.

Problems Building

On a Sun SPARC, and using X sources on another machine across an NFS link, we got an NFS Ethernet error during the build, since the build process uses so many network resources. The Sun error we saw was:

```
le0: memory error! Ethernet chip access timed out
le0: Reception stopped
```

This happened, ironically, in the middle of the PEX build. If you get errors like this, you'll have to start the build process again. If your Ethernet board doesn't reset back to a good state, you may have to reboot your machine. The PEX code seemed to create the most problems. You may need to build without PEX (see above).

After solving any problems, run the **make World** command, above, again.

When **make** finishes, check the **world.log** file for errors. There's a lot of data to sift through, but check carefully.

Installing X

Once built (successfully), the next step is to install X. Most X files go into, by default, the following directories:

/usr/bin/X11	for X programs
/usr/lib	for X C libraries
/usr/lib/X11	for X configuration, resource, and font files
/usr/include/X11	for X C language include files

All of this takes up a lot of space on your **/usr** partition. You can change the installation using the **ProjectRoot** directive described above. To install X, run **make install**:

```
make install >& install.log
```

If you changed any configuration files, run the following command first:

```
make Everything >& everything.log
```

This will rebuild the **Makefiles** (as well as act much like **make World**). To install the on-line manual pages, run:

```
make install.man >& installman.log
```

Before going on, check all the log files for errors. You may have a problem and not know about it, especially if you let X build overnight.

After Installing X

After installing X, first check to be sure that your terminfo and termcap databases have entries for **xterm**, the most-used X program. If not, look in **mit/clients/xterm** for terminfo and termcap files.

On a SPARC, you need to run **ldconfig**, since X includes a number of shared libraries (unless you chose not to build these libraries). Shared libraries cut down on the amount of RAM used by X, and X is not known for being a lean, mean, fighting machine. To run **ldconfig**, you'll need to be super user (root). Log in as *root* and merely run the following command:

ldconfig

This should alert SunOS to the new shared libraries in **/usr/lib**. If you place the X libraries somewhere else, each user will have to set his or her **LD_LIBRARY_PATH** environment variable to this directory. Use the following command:

setenv LD_LIBRARY_PATH x_shared_lib_dir

where **x_shared_lib_dir** is the directory where you placed the X shared libraries.

When you are done installing shared X libraries, you'll need to compile your X programs that used previous versions of the shared libraries. If you don't, you'll get out-of-sync warnings every time you run these programs.

Building X on a 386

High-volume products usually cost less than special-purpose machines. Taking this to an extreme, there are more than 70 million DOS-based PCs (using Intel 80x86 processors or compatibles) worldwide. Because of this high volume and high availability, many users turn DOS-based PCs into 386 or 486 UNIX workstations.

Unfortunately, UNIX software on this architecture is often problematic, especially in the area of support for the X Window System and for high-end graphics subsystems. Many users attempt to install the X sources on their machines and therefore run the latest (and presumably greatest) version of X. Many vendor-supplied X versions support only a very limited set of graphics adapters and screen resolutions. With the X sources, however, you could write your own drivers and use the ultimate your hardware allows—it's conceivable to do so, anyway, but it's not easy.

X386 provides a framework to set up X on a 386 UNIX workstation (or 486 or 586, and so forth.). Written by Thomas Roell and Mark Snitily, it runs reasonably well on AT&T, Esix, Interactive (SunSoft) and SCO UNIX System V Release 3.2, and AT&T, Dell, Esix, Interactive, and UHC SCO UNIX System V Release 4. By default, the X11 Release 5 implementation of X386 supports the following graphics cards:

Table 20.1 X386 supported video adaptors.

Adapter Card	Chipset	Maximum Resolution
Compuadd Hi-Rez card w/1meg	ET4000	1024x768
Diamond SpeedStar	ET4000	1024x768
EIZO MD-10	ET3000	800x600
GENOA 5300/5400	ET3000	800x600
GENOA 6400	GVGA	800x600
Optima Mega/1024	ET4000	1024x768
Orchid ProDesigner	ET3000	800x600
Orchid ProDesigner II/1024	ET4000	1024x768
Paradise VGA Professional	PVGA1A	640x480
Paradise VGA 1024	WD90C00	640x480
Sigma Legend	ET4000	1024x768
STB PowerGraph w/1meg	ET4000	1024x768
Swan SVGA equipped with VCO chip	ET4000	1024x768
TRICOM Mega/1024	ET4000	1024x768

We've had a lot of problems getting the ET4000 chipset to work in noninterlaced mode at a resolution of 1024x768.

Your UNIX system will require the developer's option (with the C compiler and libraries) as well as a networking developer's option (with TCP/IP socket libraries), as most 386 versions of UNIX treat these as add-on options.

X386 supports the following mice drivers: **busmouse** (Logitech bus mouse), **logitech** (Logitech serial mouse), **microsoft**, **mmseries**, **mouseman**, and **mousesystems**.

Configuring the X386 Build

Much like Sun systems use a **sun.cf** file, with X386 you edit the **x386.cf** file. This file contains a number of new directives, including **X386Server**, which you should set to YES.

#define X386Server   YES

You must put together the **BootstrapCFlags** directive manually. This will be problematic. Your first attempt to build will probably fail, but from this failure you should be able to determine most of the build flags. Look in the **x386.cf** file for more information and plenty of clues.

You'll probably need to use the GNU C compiler, or an ANSI C compiler, to build the X server and libraries. Also, the **make** program on many 386 versions of UNIX is terminally limited, so you may need to use the GNU **make** or another enhanced **make**. The X Window System really exercises your software-development tools.

You'll also need to determine what kind of networking links—including streams or sockets—to support.

Configuring Your 386 Monitor and System

Due to the wide variety of PC graphics hardware, you need to configure your monitor and graphics card for X386. X386 supports only a small number of card/monitor combinations, so check your X386 documentation for the list available in your version.

You'll also soon discover that you need to learn more than you ever wanted to about video circuitry. You'll need to know your monitor's sync-frequency ranges in both horizontal and vertical directions. Since most PC monitors are of the multi-syncing variety, your monitor probably supports a number of frequencies. You'll also need to discover the frequency bandwidth supported by the video card (adapter).

X386 uses the file **/usr/X386/Xconfig** to contain system-configuration parameters. You'll edit this file for your system's set-up, including the frequencies for your monitor. Here are some excerpts from a working **Xconfig** file for the ET4000 chip set with a Logitech serial mouse.

```
Logitech  "/dev/tty00"
  BaudRate        9600
  SampleRate      150
#  Emulate3Buttons


#
# The graphics drivers
#
vga256
  Virtual 1152 900
  ViewPort     0 0
  Modes           "1024x768i" "640x480" "920x690"


#VGA256: et4000 (mem: 1024k clocks: 25 28 37 45 40 33 50 65)


ModeDB
# clock  horzontal timing      vertical timing
  "640x480"    25      640  672  768  800    480  490  492  525
               28      640  672  768  800    480  490  492  525

  "800x600"    33      800  816  952 1056    600  608  610  633
               33      800  832  966  966    600  600  609  631
               37      800  872  968 1104    600  600  606  624
               37      800  864  896 1008    600  600  606  624

  "920x690"    65      920  952 1088 1168    690  688  718  724

  "1024x768i" 40     1024 1064 1224 1264    768  777  785  817    Interlace
               45     1024 1064 1224 1264    768  777  785  817    Interlace
  "1024x768"   65     1024 1092 1220 1344    768  786  791  810
               65     1024 1096 1272 1328    768  776  778  808
               65     1024 1072 1176 1272    768  778  779  804
               65     1024 1072 1200 1240    768  766  782  786

  "1152x900"   65     1152 1184 1288 1360    900  898  929  939    Interlace
```

You'll need to set the chipset to one of **et3000**, **et4000**, **gvga**, or **pvga**. The 1152x900 resolution is a virtual screen size, as the monitor provides only 1024x768 (notice the interlaced mode, too). We haven't gotten X386 to accept this configuration for noninterlaced use.

Summary

Even though the X Window System comes installed on most UNIX workstations, many users choose to build their own X installations when newer versions are released. Most PC UNIX users, unfortunately, have no choice in the matter and must build their own systems. This chapter has covered the installation processes on both workstations and PCs.

Chapter 21

Optimizing X Performance

The X Window System is no speed demon. When graphics on an 8-MHz 68000-based Macintosh SE, however, outperforms a Sun SPARCstation, you know there's a problem, and the problem is X.

Yes, we expect a lot more of the multitasking Sun than a single-tasking Mac. The point, though, is that the X Window System uses far too many system resources.

Don't get us wrong: X works. We'd just like it to work *better*. There are several steps you can take to speed X performance—some involving smarter usage, some involving a hardware upgrade or two. While it's unlikely that you'll be able to adopt all of our suggestions, you'll probably find one or two that will improve your computing life. We base our guidelines on what works for us and what others say works for them.

Memory

For starters: More efficient use of memory. Remember that X applications are huge. Few useful applications use less than 1 megabyte (MB), especially if they use the X Toolkit Intrinsics library, as most Motif and many Open Look applications do. Robust applications eat up RAM quickly.

X performance generally goes down the tubes when your system runs out of RAM and X starts swapping to disk. This is generally the most important impediment to X performance. So: Buy more memory. This sounds simple, but with the ungodly RAM prices charged by workstation manufacturers, you may have trouble with your budgets. It's a question you must answer: Will my life be made easier by a one-time crimp in my budget?

The old standard of 8MB of RAM isn't enough anymore for an X workstation. Sixteen MB is good, but if you develop software, push for 24MB or more. Also, don't buy an X terminal with less than 4MB of RAM, unless you're sure that you can fit your computing needs into less than that. Many X software vendors recommend you have at least 12MB of RAM to run their applications.

We still chuckle when recalling a presentation on performance given at a recent trade show by Hewlett-Packard. The HP machine used for testing had 64MB of RAM—not our opinion of a real-world system, but an indication of things to come.

If you simply can't afford an upgrade (RAM prices are dropping, so keep an eye out for bargains), you must live within 8MB of RAM. (We do.) This isn't optimal, but it works. You probably want to configure your system as efficiently as possible and strip out any frivolous X programs that really just serve to gobble up RAM. Do you really need a pair of eyes (**xeyes**) following the cursor across the screen? Is that windowed clock more efficient than the watch on your wrist? Also, do you really need to run that calendar or calculator program all the time? We can usually figure out what day and time it is.

Avoid needless X programs. Avoid needless bitmaps and icons. And you certainly never need the X logo displayed on your screen unless you're presenting a new X terminal at a sales demonstration (somehow, vendors feel that **xlogo** proves a system runs X).

Configuration Issues

Look over your X display and examine everything on it, every window, every background. Ask yourself whether you really need that giant bitmap showing phases of the moon. Unless you're inflicted with lycanthropy, you probably don't. X supports a lot of neat bitmap backgrounds, but a solid color—while not as pleasing—uses far fewer X server resources than does a large bitmap.

These bitmaps eat resources in a number of ways. First, the X server needs to allocate memory for the bitmaps, and bitmaps eat a lot of memory. Secondly, every time a window (such as a file-selection dialog) goes away or moves, the X server must repaint the screen area with a potentially complex bitmap pattern. Using a solid-color background is much more efficient—though, admittedly, not as cool.

The **xsetroot** command sets up a screen background. We use something like:

```
xsetroot -solid plum
```

This creates a nice solid-color background.

Starting X

Look over how your system starts the X server. Some configurations are set up to call **xinit** at log-in time. **Xinit** then launches the X server and runs a preconfigured list of applications, usually from a **.xinitrc** file. Other configurations (especially X terminals) use **xdm**, the X Display Manager. **Xdm** keeps the X server running all the time, manages the log-in process and launches a user's applications as configured in a **.xsession** file.

Whatever method you use to start your X session, take a look at how many processes are related to X, using the **ps** command.

```
ps -ef
```

works on System V-based systems, and

```
ps -aux
```

on Berkeley UNIX-based systems. You'd be surprised at how many processes X requires (especially when X's designers add additional processes to new releases). You may want to play with your configuration to use fewer system resources. The **ps** command can also help show which processes are in memory and which are swapped out.

Because X is associated with so many processes, and most of these processes share the low-level **Xlib** and **Xt** code, using shared libraries can cut the RAM needed to run all those extra copies of **xterm**. Using shared libraries on a Sun SPARCstation, for instance, cuts some **Xlib**-based programs down to 24KB on disk (not counting the shared library). Many other systems also provide shared libraries.

Unfortunately, though, most commercial X applications are statically linked, voiding the benefit of shared libraries. This may not seem right, but vendors can't be sure whether you've somehow messed up your shared libraries (or didn't apply a key source-code patch). Vendors are sure to be blamed if their applications won't run, no matter who is really to blame. Most vendors skip the shared libraries, with good reason.

Networking

RAM may be a big problem, but usually (and contrary to popular belief) networking *isn't* a problem. Sure, when you move a window about the screen, this generates a flurry of network packets. But users don't spend all day moving windows about. Instead, they do real work. The network bandwidth on Ethernet is typically greater than the ability of the X server to draw dots and the ability of X clients to feed data to the server. Now, with newer RISC processors in the 100 SPECmark range, this may change. And, of course, you should make judicious use of subnets.

Load Balancing

Since X is typically used in a distributed environment, and since X lends itself to distributed processing, you can try to migrate processes from well-loaded machines to less-loaded CPUs. Examine how you access remote machines. Do you use **rsh** or **rlogin** or **telnet**? Changing which machines run the processes you're launching can have a big impact on performance.

NCD, an X terminal manufacturer, has taken this approach one step further by migrating the window manager into its X terminals. (X terminals are looking more and more like workstations, aren't they?) NCD, obviously, likes this approach. Other firms doubt the value of running the window manager locally on the X terminal. One thing is certain: Most window managers are large programs. Perhaps more resource-efficient window managers would make this less of an issue.

For Software Developers

Each X application eats resources. Most applications are 1MB or larger. In addition, most X applications allocate *hordes* of dynamic memory. **XtInitialize()** or **XtAppInitialize()**, called at the start of X Toolkit-based applications, allocate nearly 50K of RAM. Allocating memory takes time and generally slows application startup.

Since each X application eats a lot of memory, there is a lot of incentive for you to find larger, integrated applications. Instead of designing your software with a lot of cooperating X programs, you may want to try writing a large multiwindow application—especially if you use a toolkit. Use multiwindow applications instead of multiple copies of the same application. This may violate the UNIX tradition of creating small programs that work together, but neither the X server nor any modern UNIX kernel can be considered "small" anymore, except on a galactic scale. Moreover, since X toolkit applications allocate a lot of RAM on the fly, usually using **malloc()** or a variant, you might want to find a faster **malloc()** library. SCO Open Desktop, for example, comes with a separate **malloc()** library, **libmalloc.a**. You can link your Motif programs with this to gain better performance, although program size increases slightly. Using the X File Browser application from our *Power Programming Motif* as a test program, shaved the startup time by up to ten seconds, for a twenty-five-second total start-up time. In addition, tasks like deleting and then filling scrolled lists speeded up dramatically.

To speed application start-up time, try to avoid creating all your application's widgets when the application begins. Some of these widgets can be created later. In addition, manage and unmanage pop-up dialog widgets instead of creating and destroying them each time the dialog is popped up.

Gadgets (a form of windowless—lightweight—widgets) and Open Look flat widgets can improve performance by using less system resources, especially X server resources. Gadgets have stirred a lot of controversy, because of extra, unneeded memory allocations in some versions of Motif.

Memory leaks exacerbate dynamic memory allocation. In most versions of UNIX, processes never shrink, so memory leaks translate into a problem that grows larger and larger over time. Motif 1.0, for example, has many documented leaks. If you're still using 1.0, upgrade to a newer version, such as 1.2. If you can, try to restart your X server every day. In some environments, X servers must run twenty-four hours a day and stay on for weeks and months, but in most offices you can simply log out at night and restart the X server in the morning. This diminishes the problem of memory leaks.

Resources

Most X applications use resources to customize their behavior and appearance. These resources are set by commands in resource files, typically text files. Whenever an X toolkit-based application starts up, it must check the X serverwide **RESOURCE_MANAGER** property for resource commands; it also must check a number of places on disk for resource files. Each application is of a certain class, so there can be systemwide, user-accountwide, and classwide resource settings and files.

```
/usr/lib/X11/$LANG/app-defaults/Class, or
/usr/lib/X11/app-defaults/Class
/usr/lib/X11/app-defaults.
$XUSERFILESEARCHPATH/Class
$XAPPLRESDIR/$LANG Class
$XAPPLRESDIR Class
$HOME/$LANG/Class
$HOME/Class$HOME/.Xdefaults
$XENVIRONMENT, or if not set,
$HOME/.Xdefaults-hostname
```

Obviously, the more places you make these programs check, the longer it will take to start up your applications. Many of the environment variables, such as **$APPLRESDIR** and **$XENVIRONMENT**, are optional. You may need to set these environment variables to get programs set up correctly, but watch out for a nasty problem. Most X class names, and therefore class-file names, start with an uppercase letter. Most X programs start with a lowercase letter. But, if you somehow configure your system to look for a class file of the same name as your application, the application will happily read in the entire program binary—usually 1MB or larger—and look for nonexistent resource-setting commands. Generally, you don't want this to happen.

For example, the class of the **xterm** application is **XTerm**, while the program name is **xterm**. Therefore, **xterm** usually looks for a resource file named **/usr/lib/X11/app-defaults/XTerm** (in the default case). If, however, you accidentally set the **$XENVIRONMENT** environment variable to **/usr/lib/X11/xterm**, the program's executable binary, you might be in for a surprise. (This is an extreme example. It's a lot easier to make this mistake with a program stored in the current directory, especially since most UNIX files use all lowercase letters.)

Low-End Hardware

X performance problems hurt the most on low-end systems, like DOS-based 386 PCs turned into UNIX boxes. On 386- and 486-based systems, the PC graphics adapter dramatically effects X performance. Much of the problem lies in the PC's slow bus speeds, which also affect disk throughput. Because the graphics commands must go out over the slow bus, a system can become a lot slower than it has to be. Realizing this, Micronics, an X terminal manufacturer, upgrades its 486-based X terminal into a PC (by adding a disk) and then runs Open Desktop with special graphics drivers and the 32-bit proprietary graphics system from the X terminal, improving X performance a great deal in the process.

The designers of X11 Release 4 removed much of the floating-point code, converting to integer calculations. If you're still using an R3-based server, like the one SCO Open Desktop has, you can speed things up with an 80387 chip or equivalent. With Intel's (and competitor's) price cuts, adding a math chip is a much more viable option.

Summary

The X Window System is not the most efficient graphical environment in the world. There *are* many steps, however, users can take to speed up performance when running X:

- Increasing the amount of RAM on the workstation. A simple solution, but perhaps too expensive for you.
- Use the existing RAM more efficiently. Do you really need that full-color screen background? Probably not. Eliminating it in favor of a solid-color background will free up precious RAM for other tasks.
- Start X more efficiently.
- Use the resources available on your network more efficiently.

We also provided tips for programmers on how to develop their applications to run in less RAM.

## Chapter 22

Configuring the
X Display Manager

The **X Display Manager**, or **xdm**, controls an X session on a given display. For user authentication, **xdm** presents a log-in window where you can enter your username and password. After users successfully log in, **xdm** starts an X session.

Xdm, therefore, acts a lot like the traditional UNIX programs **getty** and **login**. The main difference is that **xdm** is set up especially to work with X terminals.

An X terminal is a kind of smart graphics terminal, but it has limited workstation capabilities. To do any real work, a user at an X terminal must log in to another computer over the network. For reasons of security, this other computer will require the user to log in and provide a password. To do this, users could run **rlogin** or **telnet**, but these solutions don't offer much. Once logged in, the user will have to start manually any X applications he or she wants to run.

Xdm automates this process. Once you've logged in via **xdm**, the display manager starts an X session and launches the X applications you've set up in a **.xsession** file. With **xdm**, users at an X terminal will see pretty much the same things users at an X-based workstation see. And that's the whole point.

Because of all the security issues involved, you'll need to be the "super user" (or root) on your UNIX hosts to set up **xdm**. To set up **xdm** from the X terminal side, you should follow your X terminal's configuration menus, as most X terminals have dramatically improved their user-friendliness over the last few years.

To work with X terminals, **xdm** uses a protocol called XDMCP, the **X Display Manager Control Protocol**. Your X terminals will need to support this protocol, as well as your version of **xdm**. Normally, this shouldn't be a problem, as any good X terminal does this already. The whole point of XDMCP is to make X terminals act a lot like traditional character terminals. When you turn off the X terminal, your X session ends. When you turn on an X terminal, you see a log-in screen. It's **xdm** that manages this feat.

Unfortunately for us (but fortunately for you), there are thousands of ways you can configure your local systems. Because of this, there are thousands of ways you can configure **xdm**. This chapter merely presents an overview of **xdm**. If you're setting up **xdm** on your systems, you'll need to study the **xdm** on-line manual page. Since so much of this set-up depends on your local configuration, you probably won't be able to use this information directly. You'll need to adjust the set-up for your local configuration instead.

Configuring Xdm

Most of the **xdm** files are stored in **/usr/lib/X11/xdm**. A typical installation would include the following files:

```
Xlogin        Xservers         Xstartup          xdm-errors
Xreset        Xsession         Xstartup-remote   xdm-pid
Xresources    Xsession-remote  xdm-config
```

The best idea is to examine these files and then just customize, no more than is necessary to run your desired configuration. Most workstation vendors, such as Silicon Graphics, ship highly customized files in the first place. Since **xdm** configuration is a learned art, it's best to modify as little as possible. All of these files can be configured, and **xdm** can use these files, or any other files, for the same purpose, depending on your set-up. There are literally millions of possibilities.

Xlogin can be used to change the log-in screen background.

Xreset is run as root after a user session terminates but *before* the display is closed. There is often nothing in this file.

Xresources contains resources for the log-in widget. This widget asks the user for a username and password. The most common part to change in this file is the greeting resource:

```
xlogin*greeting:    Good day, oh great one!
```

Many versions of **xdm** require the greeting to be only one line of text. You can also adjust the colors and fonts used by the log-in widget from this file.

N O T E

Xstartup is run by root (so be careful) after the user is authenticated but before the user session starts. You won't need any adjustments here, but you may need to mount directories.

Xservers lists the displays that **xdm** should manage. Here's an example from an SGI workstation:

```
:0 secure /usr/bin/X11/X -bs -c -pseudomap 4sight
```

Here's the more common default:

```
:0 local /usr/bin/X11/X :0
```

A display entry for an X terminal would use something like:

```
ncd:0 foreign
```

If you change the **Xservers** file, **xdm** will not reread this file until it starts again. Since the whole point of **xdm** is to keep it running forever, you can convince **xdm** to reread the **Xservers** file by sending it the **HUP (hang up) signal**, **SIGHUP**. The UNIX **kill** program can send the **SIGHUP** signal using the **-HUP** command-line parameter. (*Kill* is a misnomer, as it really sends a signal to the program. Most programs don't install signal handlers, so they end up "dying" on receipt of the signal.) Use the following command:

```
kill -HUP process_id_number
```

where **process_id_number** is the process ID for the **xdm** program. You can get this number by running the **ps** command and looking for **xdm**'s entry in the process table. On System V-based systems, use **ps -ef**. On Berkeley-based UNIX systems, use **ps -aux**.

You can also use the **xdm-pid** file. This file contains the process ID for **xdm**, unless you change the **pidFile** resource (see below).

The **xdm-errors** file contains any error messages generated by **xdm**, unless you change the error log with the **-errors** command-line parameter to **xdm**. If you're having problems, check here first.

The Xdm Config File

The **xdm-config** file controls how **xdm** acts and tells **xdm** the name of most of the other configuration files. This is where you can change all the defaults. Here's a sample **xdm-config** file that you can use to get started. If your system already has an **xdm-config** file, by all means use that.

```
DisplayManager.servers:         /usr/lib/X11/xdm/Xservers
DisplayManager.errorLogFile:    /usr/lib/X11/xdm/xdm-errors
DisplayManager.pidFile:         /usr/lib/X11/xdm/xdm-pid
DisplayManager*resources:       /usr/lib/X11/xdm/Xresources
DisplayManager*reset:           /usr/lib/X11/xdm/Xreset
DisplayManager*session:         /usr/lib/X11/xdm/Xsession
DisplayManager._0.authorize:    true
DisplayManager*authorize:       false
```

The **_0** is the default display name, **:0**, translated to the X resource-file language. Since a colon has a special meaning in resource files, the :0 becomes _0.

The **Xsession** file controls the user's X session. Normally, this calls **xrdb** to load in the user's **.Xresources** file from the user's home directory, **$HOME/.Xresources**, and often launches a window manager. After that, the user's **.xsession** file is executed. The **.xsession** file acts a lot like your **.xinitrc** file and starts your initial set of X applications; normally, however, you start fewer X clients with **.xsession** than you do with **.xinitrc**. From a user's point of view, you need to check the **Xsession** file to see whether a window manager is launched. If one is, you don't want to start a window manager from your **.xsession** file.

The system **Xsession** file should start your **.xsession** file, if it exists in your home directory, usually **$HOME/.xsession**. Before your **.xsession** is executed, though, the system **Xsession** may have launched some X clients and read in your **.Xresources**, as we mentioned above. Other than that, launch X client programs from **.xsession** in the background, like you do from **.xinitrc**.

An X session ends in one of two ways: when a specific property on the root window is deleted or when a certain process exits. This second method is similar to the way **xinit** terminates your X session—as when your window manager or other last process exits, for instance. To use this method, launch your terminating X process, such as a window manager like **mwm**, as the last program in your **.xsession** file. Your X session will then end when the **.xsession** exits, which will be when the last process exits.

Starting Xdm

Xdm is usually started by **init**. You can place the **xdm** command at the end of **/etc/rc** or another system start-up file, or in your **/etc/inittab** file. You'll need to execute a command like the following:

/usr/bin/X11/xdm

Xdm Command-Line Parameters

Xdm supports a number of command-line parameters. The **-config** parameter tells **xdm** to use a different configuration file from the default. By default, **xdm** uses the configuration file **/usr/lib/X11/xdm/xdm-config**.

-config configfile

The **-error** parameter tells **xdm** to use your file for writing error messages, instead of the default **/usr/lib/X11/xdm/xdm-errors**.

-error error_logging_file

The **-daemon** parameter runs **xdm** as a daemon in the background. (Daemons are UNIX server processes that run in the background.) Most often, you'll use this option. The **-daemon** command-line parameter sets the **DisplayManager .daemonMode** resource to **True**.

-daemon

The **-nodaemon** parameter sets the **DisplayManager.daemonMode** resource to **False**. It also makes **xdm** run in synchronous mode instead of as a daemon. This parameter is often used for debugging.

-nodaemon

The **–debug** parameter sets the debugging level.

–debug level

When you set **level** to a nonzero number (use positive numbers), **xdm** will print out lots of debugging information. If you use this parameter, **xdm** also sets the **DisplayManager.daemonMode** resource to **False**, like the **–nodaemon** command-line parameter.

For More Information on Xdm

Much of **xdm**'s configuration depends on your local system setup. Talk to your system administrator. You can also look up the **xdm** online manual page (**man xdm**) and the XDMCP document, "The X Display Manager Control Protocol."

Chapter 23

Setting Up a User Account for X

M ost UNIX workstations come preconfigured with X. Therefore, your user account is partially set up to run X. It's a good idea to use whatever configuration is already set up and extend that configuration rather than wiping out an existing installation with a new set of customizations.

This chapter will require some discretion on your part. If we show a file and you already have that file installed in your system, just extend the current file—don't wipe it out.

We follow this order when setting up a user account for X:

1. Set up resource files and add to **.Xdefaults**.
2. Edit **.cshrc** (for C shell users).
3. Add (or extend) window-manager configuration files.
4. Create (or modify) **.xinitrc** or **.xsession**.
5. Change **.login** (for C shell users) to call **xinit** or **startx**.
6. Log out and log in again, restarting X.

To take advantage of your system's defaults, it's best to copy system files first and then customize, instead of merely creating your own. This will give you any extra configuration that your administrator has set up systemwide.

Note that the files in this chapter are real X files that we use on a day-to-day basis. Our set-up is probably different from yours, so you probably won't be able to type these files in directly and use them. Use these files instead as a general guide to help you set up your X account. Good luck!

X Resource Files

We always set up a main X resource file, a class-resource file for **xterm**. This file is (surprise!) called **XTerm** and placed in our home directory:

```
!
!        XTerm resource file
!
XTerm*foreground:   black
XTerm*background:   white

XTerm*scrollBar:    True
XTerm*saveLines:    1000


XTerm*font: -adobe-courier-medium-r-normal-14-140-75-75-m-90-iso8859-1

XTerm*vt100.pointerShape:    gumby
!
! The following translations can be used to
! enable copy and paste with OpenWindows programs.
! We comment out this command. remove the
! comment markers, e.g., !, to enable.
!
!XTerm*VT100.translations: #override\n\
!Shift <KeyPress> Select: select-cursor-start() \
!                         select-cursor-end(CLIPBOARD, !CUT_BUFFER0) \n\
!Shift <KeyPress> Insert: insert-selection(CLIPBOARD, !CUT_BUFFER0) \n\
! ~Ctrl ~Meta <Btn2Up>:  insert-selection(CLIPBOARD, !CUT_BUFFER0) \n\
!    <BtnUp>:             select-end(CLIPBOARD, CUT_BUFFER0)
```

We also set up a resource file for the clock program, **xclock**. This file is named **XClock** and also resides in our home directory.

```
!
!       Class resource file for xclock
!
XClock*foreground: black
XClock*background: white
XClock*hands:      black
!
! We don't want a second hand.
!
XClock*update:     60
```

Changing XDefaults

The .**Xdefaults** file below is a catch-all user-resource file. Many of the resources could go into class-resource files. Their placement is purely arbitrary.

```
!
!       Eric and Kevin's .Xdefaults file
!
! Turn on extra debugging messages.
!
*StringConversionWarnings:   on

!
! xlogo program
!
xlogo*Background: magenta

!
! oclock program
!
oclock*update:      60
oclock*background: white
oclock*foreground: black
oclock*hour:       black
oclock*jewel:      gold
oclock*minute:     black
```

```
!
!       xclipboard—used to hold multiple
!       primary selections to aid cut and paste.
!
xclipboard*background:    white
xclipboard*foreground:    black
xclipboard*font: -adobe-courier-medium-r-normal-14-140-75-75-m-90-iso8859-1


!
!       end of .Xdefaults
!
```

You might want to place the above resource-setting commands in your **.Xresources** file instead of in **.Xdefaults**. If you use **xrdb** to load a set of resources into the **RESOURCE_MANAGER** property, use **.Xresources** instead of **.Xdefaults**.

Configuring the Mwm Window Manager

The next step is to configure the window manager. If you're using the Motif window manager, **mwm**, a sample configuration is below. If you're using **twm** or **olwm**, skip ahead.

The **Mwm** file, in our home directory, contains resource-setting commands for **mwm**:

```
!
!  Mwm application defaults resource file.
!
Mwm*moveThreshold:        3
Mwm*buttonBindings:       DefaultButtonBindings
Mwm*resizeBorderWidth:    7

!
! Set up fonts. We use a nice helvetica
! font for the title bars.
!
Mwm*fontList: -adobe-helvetica-bold-r-normal-14-140-75-75-p-82-iso8859-1
Mwm*icon*fontList:        9x15

!
! Set up colors
!
```

```
Mwm*activeBackground:      CadetBlue
Mwm*background:            LightGray

!
! Place icons along the lower edge,
! starting from the left.
!
Mwm*iconPlacement:         left bottom

Mwm*clientAutoPlace:       false
Mwm*positionIsFrame:       false
Mwm*interactivePlacement: false


!
! Use a special icon for xterm
!
Mwm*xterm.iconImage:       /u/erc/bitmaps/mryuk.xbm


!
! We want the keyboard focus to follow the mouse
!
Mwm*keyboardFocusPolicy: pointer

!
! Change the decorations on oclock
!
Mwm*Clock*clientDecoration:     title menu resizeh
!
!   end of Mwm resource file
!
```

The **.mwmrc** configures **mwm**:

```
#
#  Mwm configuration file. Customized from the system .mwmrc file.
#


#
# menu pane descriptions
#
```

```
# Root Menu Description
Menu RootMenu
{
        "Root Menu"          f.title
        "New Window"         f.exec "xterm -geom 80x42 &"
        "Nokomis"            f.exec "xterm -geom 80x42 -name
            nokomis -e rlogin nokomis &"
        "Shuffle Up"         f.circle_up
        "Shuffle Down"       f.circle_down
        "Refresh"            f.refresh
        no-label             f.separator
        "Applications"       f.menu AppMenu
        no-label             f.separator
        "Restart..."         f.restart
        no-label             f.separator
        "Quit"               f.quit_mwm
}

#
#       This menu can be used to launch a number of applications.
#
Menu AppMenu
{
        "Debugger"           f.exec "xdbx &"
        "Clipboard"          f.exec "xclipboard &"
        "Calculator"         f.exec "xcalc &"
        "Select Font"        f.exec "xfontsel &"
        "CPU Load"           f.exec "xload &"
        no-label             f.separator
        "Mahjongg"           f.exec "xmj &"
        no-label             f.separator
        "Edit Resources"     f.exec "editres &"
        "Screen Magnifie"    f.exec "xmag &"
        no-label             f.separator
        "Round Clock"        f.exec "oclock &"
        "Square Clock"       f.exec "xclock &"
        "Digital Clock"      f.exec "xclock -digital &"
}

# Default Window Menu Description
```

```
Menu DefaultWindowMenu
{
        Restore      _R    Alt<Key>F5      f.normalize
        Move         _M    Alt<Key>F7      f.move
        Size         _S    Alt<Key>F8      f.resize
        Minimize     _n    Alt<Key>F9      f.minimize
        Maximize     _x    Alt<Key>F10     f.maximize
        Lower        _L    Alt<Key>F3      f.lower
        no-label                           f.separator
        Close        _C    Alt<Key>F4      f.kill
}


#
# key binding descriptions
#

Keys DefaultKeyBindings
{
        Shift<Key>Escape         window|icon         f.post_wmenu
        Meta<Key>space           window|icon         f.post_wmenu
        Meta<Key>Tab             root|icon|window    f.next_key
        Meta Shift<Key>Tab       root|icon|window    f.prev_key
        Meta<Key>Escape          root|icon|window    f.next_key
        Meta Shift<Key>Escape    root|icon|window    f.prev_key
        Meta Shift Ctrl<Key>exclam root|icon|window  f.set_behavior
        Meta<Key>F6              window              f.next_key transient
        Meta Shift<Key>F6        window              f.prev_key transient
           <Key>F4              icon                f.post_wmenu
}


#
# button binding descriptions
#

Buttons DefaultButtonBindings
{
        <Btn1Down> icon|frame          f.raise
        <Btn3Down> icon                f.post_wmenu
        <Btn1Down> root                f.menu          RootMenu
}
```

```
Buttons ExplicitButtonBindings
{
        <Btn1Down>          frame|icon         f.raise
        <Btn3Down>          frame|icon         f.post_wmenu
        <Btn1Down>          root               f.menu   RootMenu
        Meta<Btn1Down>      window|icon        f.lower
!       Meta<Btn2Down>      window|icon        f.resize
!       Meta<Btn3Down>      window|icon        f.move

}
Buttons PointerButtonBindings
{
        <Btn1Down>          frame|icon         f.raise
        <Btn3Down>          frame|icon         f.post_wmenu
        <Btn1Down>          root               f.menu RootMenu
        <Btn1Down>          window             f.raise
        Meta<Btn1Down>      window|icon        f.lower
!       Meta<Btn2Down>      window|icon        f.resize
!       Meta<Btn3Down>      window|icon        f.move
}

#
#   end of .mwmrc file
#
```

Configuring the Twm Window Manager

The Tab window manager, **twm**, uses a configuration file named **.twmrc** in our home directory. See Chapter 11 for more information.

```
#
#         .twmrc, as modified by Eric, and Kevin.
#
# $XConsortium: system.twmrc,v 1.8 91/04/23 21:10:58 gildea Exp $
#
# Default twm configuration file; needs to be kept small to conserve string
# space in systems whose compilers don't handle medium-sized strings.
#
# Sites should tailor this file, providing any extra title buttons, menus, etc.
# that may be appropriate for their environment.  For example, if most of the
# users were accustomed to uwm, the defaults could be set up not to decorate
```

```
# any windows and to use meta-keys.
#

# NoGrabServer means twm won't grab the server for menus.
NoGrabServer

RestartPreviousState
DecorateTransients
#ClientBorderWidth

#
# Set up fonts.
#
TitleFont "-adobe-helvetica-bold-r-normal—*-120-*-*-*-*-*-*"
ResizeFont "-adobe-helvetica-bold-r-normal—*-120-*-*-*-*-*-*"
MenuFont "-adobe-helvetica-bold-r-normal—*-120-*-*-*-*-*-*"
IconFont "-adobe-helvetica-bold-r-normal—*-100-*-*-*-*-*-*"
IconManagerFont "-adobe-helvetica-bold-r-normal—*-100-*-*-*"

#
# ShowIconManager turns on the icon manager
# when twm starts up.
#ShowIconManager

#
# Set up the icon manager's initial geometry
# to the lower left corner.
IconManagerGeometry "+0+650"

# Moving whole windows instead of just an outline runs
# far too slow on our systems, so we comment this out.
# Comment the following line in to move the whole window.
#OpaqueMove

Color
{
        BorderColor "black"
        DefaultBackground "burlywood"
        DefaultForeground "black"
        TitleBackground "burlywood"
        TitleForeground "black"
        MenuBackground "burlywood"
        MenuForeground "black"
```

```
        MenuTitleBackground "black"
        MenuTitleForeground "burlywood"
        IconBackground "burlywood"
        IconForeground "black"
        IconBorderColor "black"
        IconManagerBackground "burlywood"
        IconManagerForeground "black"
}


#
#       Change the default cursors.
#
Cursors
{
        Frame    "top_left_arrow"
        Title    "top_left_arrow"
        Icon     "top_left_arrow"
        IconMgr  "top_left_arrow"
        Move     "fleur"
        Resize   "fleur"
        Menu     "left_ptr"
        Button   "left_ptr"
        Wait     "watch"
        Select   "question_arrow"
        Destroy  "pirate"
}


#
# The "Tab" part of twm comes from the SqueezeTitle option.
#
#SqueezeTitle
#{
#       "XTerm" left    0       0
#       "oclock"  center        0    0
#}


#
# Xterm doesn't provide its own icon, so we set one.
#
Icons
{
        "XTerm"     "/u/erc/bitmaps/peace.xbm"
}
```

```
#
# Name the windows that shouldn't have a
# title bar.
NoTitle { "xclock" "oclock" "xload" }


#
# Name those applications you wish to raise to
# the top if the mouse is in their windows.
# We don't recommend this option.
AutoRaise { "XTerm" "xmail" }


#
# Define some useful functions for motion-based actions.
#
MoveDelta 3
Function "move-or-lower" { f.move f.deltastop f.lower }
Function "move-or-raise" { f.move f.deltastop f.raise }
Function "move-or-iconify" { f.move f.deltastop f.iconify }


#
# Set some useful bindings.  Sort of uwm-ish, sort of simple-button-ish
#
Button1 = : root : f.menu "defops"

Button1 = m : window|icon : f.function "move-or-lower"
Button2 = m : window|icon : f.iconify
Button3 = m : window|icon : f.function "move-or-raise"

Button1 = : title : f.function "move-or-raise"
Button2 = : title : f.raiselower

Button1 = : icon : f.function "move-or-iconify"
Button2 = : icon : f.iconify

Button1 = : iconmgr : f.iconify
Button2 = : iconmgr : f.iconify


#
# And a menus with the usual things
#
menu "defops"
{
"Modified Twm Menu"    f.title
```

```
"Xterm"              f.exec "xterm -geom 80x42 &"
"Nokomis"            f.exec "xterm -geom 80x42 -name nokomis -e rlogin nokomis &"
"Calculator"         f.exec "xcalc &"
"Magnifier"          f.exec "xmag &"
" "                  f.nop
"Resize"             f.resize
" "                  f.nop
"Raise"              f.raise
"Lower"              f.lower
" "                  f.nop
"Show Iconmgr"       f.showiconmgr
"Hide Iconmgr"       f.hideiconmgr
" "                  f.nop
"Kill"               f.destroy
"Delete"             f.delete
" "                  f.nop
"Restart"            f.restart
" "                  f.nop
"Exit"               f.quit
}
```

Configuring the Olwm Window Manager

The Open Look window manger, **olwm**, defines its root menu in the file **.open-win-menu** in your home directory.

```
#
#       Eric and Kevin's menu file for olwm, the
#       Open Look Window Manager.
#
"Workspace Menu"     TITLE
Applications         MENU
        "Xterm"      DEFAULT xterm -geom 80x44
        "Nokomis"    xterm -geom 80x42 -name nokomis -e rlogin nokomis
        "Calculator" xcalc
Applications END PIN
" "                  NOP
"Refresh Screen"  DEFAULT REFRESH
" "                  NOP
"Restart"            RESTART
"Reread Menu File"  REREAD_MENU_FILE
```

```
"  "                    NOP
"Save Workspace"        SAVE_WORKSPACE
"  "                    NOP
"Exit Olwm"             WMEXIT
"Exit and Quit X"       EXIT


#
#       end of .openwin-menu
#
```

We place the resource commands for **olwm** into our **.Xdefaults** file:

```
!
!       Set up for olwm, Open Look Window Manager
!
olwm.SetInput:          followmouse
olwm.FocusLenience:     true
olwm.WorkspaceColor:    bisque2
olwm.IconLocation:      bottom-lr
olwm.DefaultIconImage:  /u/erc/bitmaps/mryuk.xbm
olwm.MinimalDecor:      xcalc xclock oclock mailbox
olwm.WindowColor:       burlywood
```

Setting Up the C Shell

We normally use the C shell **/bin/csh**. This shell uses a start-up file called **.cshrc**. Watch out with this file: Its syntax is not consistent from program to program, due to different implementations of **csh**. Always copy a system **.cshrc** file first, then extend it.

You might need to check that your **path** is set up correctly, although usually this is done in **.login**. We also add four aliases to **.cshrc**. The first alias, **xcd**, looks odd when printed. (See Chapter 3 for details.) Basically, the ^[means escape (enter it in **vi** with **control-v control-[**), and **^G** means **control-g** (enter it in **vi** with **control-v control-g**). The **xcd** alias sets up the title bar of an **xterm** window when we use **xcd** to change directories.

The **se** alias is used to set the **XENVIRONMENT** environment variable. We normally don't set **XENVIRONMENT** except when using a prototyping tool called Wcl.

The **bitmap** alias increases the speed at which the **bitmap** program is drawn. By default, **bitmap** draws a grid using dashed lines. On low-end hardware, such as 486 ISA systems, dashed lines take far too long to draw. We turn off this mode with the **bitmap** alias. If you have X11 Release 5 or higher, use the **+dashed** version. Otherwise, uncomment the **−nodashed** version and comment out the **+dashed** version.

The **rs** alias should be run after changing the size of an xterm window.

Add the commands below to your .**cshrc** file:

```
alias    xcd    'cd \!* ; echo −n "^[]2;`whoami` @ `hostname`  `pwd` ^G"'
alias    se     setenv XENVIRONMENT
#
# Comment in the next line if you use X11 R4,
# then comment out the other one.
#alias   bitmap   bitmap −nodashed
alias    bitmap   bitmap +dashed

alias rs           'set noglob; eval `resize` '
```

Using Xinit or Startx

If you use **xinit** or **startx** to launch your X session, you'll need a **.xinitrc** file. Watch out, though, if you're already running X from an **.xinitrc** file, as editing this file can result in strange behavior. Copy your current **.xinitrc** file into a separate file, such as **my_xinitrc**. Then edit **my_xinitrc**, adding the lines below. Finally, after you've stopped X, copy **my_xinitrc** to **.xinitrc**. Note: You may want to launch **xconsole** or use the **−C** command-line parameter with **xterm** to capture system console messages.

The **.xinitrc**, which uses the Motif window manager, follows:

```
/usr/bin/X11/xterm −geom 80x40+1+1 &
xsetroot −solid bisque2
/usr/bin/X11/xterm −geom 80x40+300+270 &
/usr/bin/X11/oclock −geom 120x120+900+10 &
exec /usr/bin/X11/mwm
```

Using Xdm

If you're using **xdm**, your **.xsession** file can be much the same as the **.xinitrc** file. We strongly advise you to copy the system **.xsession** file, because there are

usually lots of strange shell commands, such as those found in the following file
from Interactive UNIX's EasyWindows:

```
#
# .xsession, as customized by Eric and Kevin.
#
# Default Easy Windows xsession file, install as $HOME/.xsession
#ident  "@(#)xsession 1.8 - 91/09/15"

# Read the file /etc/TIMEZONE to get the correct timezone value.
# Note that this step is not needed if the file /etc/default/login has
# the correct "TIMEZONE=" line.
. /etc/TIMEZONE

# Get the symbols defined by xrdb so we can determine sizes & colors later.
for x in `xrdb -symbols | sed 's/-D//g'`
do
        echo $x | grep -s "=" >/dev/null
        if [ $? -eq 0 ]        # has an equals sign in it.
        then
             eval $x
        fi
done
unset x

if [ "$WIDTH" -le 801 ]; then    # up to 800 pixels wide
        RES=LOW                  #  is low resolution
elif [ "$WIDTH" -le 1281 ]; then # 801 to 1280 pixels wide
        RES=MED                  #  is medium resolution
else                             # and higher
        RES=HIGH                 #  is high resolution
fi
if [ "$PLANES" -gt 1 ]; then     # more than 1 color plane
        MODE=COLOR               #  assume it's color
else                             # else
        MODE=MONO                #  assume monochrome
fi

# Load .Xdefaults database into the server.
if [ -f $HOME/.Xdefaults ]; then
        xrdb $HOME/.Xdefaults
fi
```

```
# Add any additional fonts to the font path.
fp=
fontdir=/usr/lib/X11/fonts
for i in 75dpi 100dpi bmug info-mac misc oldx10 oldx11 xconq ; do
        if [ -d $fontdir/fonts/$i ]; then
                if [ -z "$fp" ]; then fp="$fontdir/$i"
                else fp="$fp,$fontdir/$i"
                fi
        fi
done
if [ -n "$fp" ]; then
        xset fp= $fp
fi


# Turn autorepeat on, set screenblank time to 10 minutes,
        bell tone & duration.
xset r on s 600 b 100 2500 300


# Turn the CapsLock key into another control key.
# <<UNCOMMENT THIS IF YOU WISH TO USE THIS>>
#xmodmap - << EOF
#remove Lock = Caps_Lock
#add Control = Caps_Lock
#EOF


# System messages window.
if [ -c /dev/osm ]; then
        if [ "$MODE" = MONO -o "$PLANES" -le 4 ]; then
                colors=""
        else
                colors="-fg navyblue -bg lightBlue"
        fi
        xterm -iconic -fn 6x10 -geometry 80x6+0+0 -sb \
                -name 'console messages' -T 'console messages' \
                $colors \
                -e /bin/cat -u /dev/osm &
fi


# Start an xterm.
if [ "$MODE" = MONO -o "$PLANES" -le 4 ]; then
        cursor=""
else
        cursor="-cr red"
```

```
fi
case $RES in
        LOW)   font=ega H=25
               ;;
        MED)   font=vga H=40
               ;;
        HIGH)  font=-misc-fixed-medium-r-normal-20-200-75-75-
           c-100-iso8859-1
               H=40
               ;;
esac
xterm -ls -iconic -fn $font -fb $font $cursor \
        -name nokimis -geometry 80x${H}+0+20 &

# If installed, start looking glass (unless "NOLG" is set in the environment).
if [ -x /usr/bin/X11/lg -a -z "$NOLG" ]; then
        vls -q   # Visix License Server ("-q" tells to not
           display any messages.)
        lg $DIRS &  # Looking Glass
        LG=$!    # Save the process id.
        sleep 5     # Give Looking Glass enough time to
           acquire its colors.
else
        LG=
fi

# Start a clock.
if [ "$RES" = LOW ]; then
        W=100 H=100 X=175
else
        W=150 H=150 X=175
fi
if [ -z "$LG" ]; then    # no Looking Glass - don't offset the clock.
        X=0
fi
oclock -iconic -geometry ${W}x${H}-${X}-0 &

# And invoke the window manager.
if [ -n "$WM" ]; then    # user specified wm using WM=name from xdm
        :
elif [ -x /usr/bin/X11/mwm ]; then# try Motif window manager.
        WM=mwm
```

```
else                    # no Motif, use twm.
        WM=twm
fi

# Run the window manager and wait for it to complete
$WM

# Kill the Looking Glass process, if it still exists.
if [ -n "$LG" ]; then
        kill $LG 2>/dev/null
fi

exit 0
```

The Login File

Like .cshrc and .xsession, you should copy the default .login file and customize that, leaving in most of the system-specific commands. We add the following lines to the end of our .login file, since this installation uses **startx** to begin an X session. If we were using **xdm**, we wouldn't change .login at all.

The following commands set our **DISPLAY** environment variable, update the path to use the X programs (and also the Berkeley UNIX programs in **/usr/ucb**—this is from a System V machine), and start X if we log in at the console.

```
setenv   DISPLAY :0

set path = ( $path /usr/ucb /usr/bin/X11 /usr/local/bin
          /usr/lbin ~/bin )

if ( `tty` == "/dev/console" ) then
        startx
#
# Use xinit instead of startx if that's what you use to
        launch X.
#       xinit

#
# Logout when done with X.
#
        logout
endif
```

## Chapter 24

Compiling Contributed Software With Imake

Most X applications are written in the C programming language, and most of these use a software utility called **make** to control the compiling and linking process of application building. **Make**, in turn, uses a file called **Makefile**, which lists the rules of this building process for particular applications. These rules vary from system to system, particularly with libraries of C language routines heavily used by X applications. Thus the designers of the X Window System include a utility called **imake**.

Imake uses its own rules to build a proper **Makefile** tuned to your own system; then **make** takes over and builds the X application. This chapter shows you how to use **imake** and how to set it up for your system—so you can reap the benefits of hundreds of free X programs.

One advantage of the X Window System is software portability. Programs written on one platform can compute just fine on other platforms—at least on the user-interface (that is, the X) portion of the programs. If the program's developers worked with portability in mind, you can expect to get most X programs running on your platforms with a limited amount of effort. That's an advantage of X. A disadvantage is the difficulty of writing X applications. Add this difficulty to the hundreds of free X programs—including great screen-capture utilities and prototyping tools—and there's a strong incentive to get these free programs working at your site.

The problem, though, is that every operating system works differently. This requires a lot of manual tweaking when you try to compile the supposedly portable X Window applications to your platforms. Part of the answer provided by X is a program called **imake**. (The rest of the answer—as usual—is up to you.)

Make and close variants are available with all C compilers, including DOS, OS/2, and Macintosh platforms.

What Is Imake?

Imake is a simple program that uses the C compiler preprocessor, **cpp**, to generate **Makefile**s. **Imake** builds a **Makefile** from a template file listing variables and rules, and combines this with operating system- and site-specific configuration files. The end result—if **imake** is configured properly—is a **Makefile** that should work on your system to build X Window applications.

There are three main uses of **imake**. First, if you install the X Window System source code and compile your own X server, you'll use **imake** to configure X for your system. Few users need to do this, since X comes preinstalled on many systems, while a number of vendors will sell you precompiled versions of X. If you need to compile your own X source code, there's an extensive set of instructions that ships with the X Window System releases from the X Consortium. Follow these rules and you should do fine. (See also Chapter 20 on "Installing X".)

Second, you can use **imake** to install new X program libraries, like Motif from the Open Software Foundation, also called OSF. If you license Motif sources from the OSF, you'll need to compile the Motif sources into the proper programmer libraries on your system. If you purchase the Motif toolkit precompiled from a third-party vendor, or if Motif already comes with your system, then you won't have to bother with this.

Finally, you can use **imake** to build X applications, especially the free X applications that you can get from CompuServe, from the comp.sources.x Internet newsgroup, and from various program archive sites on the Internet. We'll concentrate on this last case, as it is the most common use of **imake**, especially from a user's perspective.

If you never compile C code into applications, you will never need **imake**.

N O T E

How Imake Works

Imake starts by loading in a master template file called **Imake.tmpl** (the .tmpl stands for template). This file normally resides in **/usr/lib/X11/config**. The master **Imake.tmpl** executes the following steps to build a **Makefile**:

1. **Imake.tmpl** determines what sort of machine you have—let's use Sun SPARCstation, for example—and then executes the rules in a file configured for your operating system. The Sun system file is named **sun.cf** (.cf stands for "configuration"). The Silicon Graphics (SGI) file is named **sgi.cf**, and so on. The **sun.cf** file contains variables to set your version of the operating system. In addition, the file sets special flags, like **HasSaberC**, which should be set to YES if you use CenterLine's CodeCenter (which used to be called Saber C). These commands use the format below:

   #define HasSaberC   YES

   You can replace YES with NO to turn off an option. (Note that **HasSaberC** is the default from the X Consortium, so you might want to define this to YES on Sun platforms even if you don't have the CodeCenter project, because of a bug in the configuration files.) The *system.cf* file (such as **sun.cf** or **sgi.cf**) also contains the standard command-line options to pass to the C compiler, with the variable **StandardDefines**. See Chapter 20 for examples of **StandardDefines**.

   These files, like all **imake** configuration files, are normally located in **/usr/lib/X11/config**. You may need to edit the *system.cf* file when you install the X Window sources, but once you've done that, you probably won't need to edit this file again. On systems where X is preinstalled, you shouldn't need to edit this file.

2. **Imake.tmpl** includes the file **site.def**, also in **/usr/lib/X11/config**. The **site.def** file should have local customizations. For example, if you want X programs to reside somewhere besides the standard **/usr/bin/X11**, you can configure this in the **site.def** file.

3. **Imake.tmpl** includes a project-specific file, named **Project.tmpl**. This is used mainly for building the X Window sources from the X Consortium.

4. **Imake.tmpl** includes a set of rules used to build X programs, stored in a file named **Imake.rules**. **Imake.rules** contains a set of generic rules used by **imake**. You shouldn't need to edit this file, but you might want to take a look at the file to see what sort of rules are defined. The syntax won't make a lot of sense, though, as it uses **cpp** macros extensively.

5. In the last step, **Imake.tmpl** includes the local directory's **Imakefile**. This file describes the high-level rules (using the low-level rules in the **Imake.rules** file) for building a particular X application.

In addition, there's also a **Motif.tmpl** file (a template for Motif programs) and **Motif.rules** (the generic rules for building the Motif libraries and programs that use the Motif libraries).

When all this is done, **imake** uses a program called **makedepend**, along with all the configured rules, for building the **Makefile**.

Configuring Imake For Your System

When you configure **imake**, you'll spend most of your time working with the **site.def** and *system.cf* files. The **site.def** file contains a lot of variables for local customizations, such as **HasGcc**, which you should define to YES if you use the GNU C compiler, **gcc**:

```
#define HasGcc    YES
```

Using Imake

You should configure **imake** only once—if that. Many systems ship with **imake** already preconfigured. (Some systems don't include **imake**, but its sources are freely distributable, so you can pick up a copy from the Internet, on tape, or on CD-ROM if you want. This is shorthand for stating that your vendor left you in the lurch and you're on your own. See Appendix A for more information.) Using **imake** is generally much easier than configuring it.

The purpose of **imake** is to generate a **Makefile** that is configured to work on your system. To do so, **imake** supports the following command-line options:

Table 24.1 Imake command-line options.

Option	Meaning
-D*define*	Define the value following the -D.
-I*directory*	Names the directory for the **Imake.tmpl** file.
-T*template*	Names the master template file, which defaults to **Imake.tmpl**.
-f *filename*	Names the local **Imakefile**, which defaults to **Imakefile**.
-s *filename*	Names the output file, defaults to **Makefile**.
-e	**Imake** should build and execute the **Makefile**; the default is to not execute the **Makefile**.
-v	Turns on verbose mode, which prints out **cpp** commands.

Most users use the **xmkmf** shell script to invoke **imake**.

Xmkmf

X includes a simple UNIX shell script called **xmkmf**, which serves as an easy front-end to **imake**. If you have a directory with an **Imakefile**, you can use **xmkmf** to generate a **Makefile** by changing to the directory with the **Imakefile** and then using the simple command:

xmkmf

If **imake** is set up properly—a big if—then you'll see the following output, and you should now have a **Makefile** in the current directory:

imake -DUseInstalled -I/usr/lib/X11/config

The commands output to the screen are the commands you could use to invoke **imake** directly.

If you run **xmkmf** and there already is a **Makefile** in your local directory, **xmkmf** will save that **Makefile** to **Makefile.bak** before creating a new **Makefile**. Then the command will look something like:

```
mv Makefile Makefile.bak
imake -DUseInstalled -I/usr/lib/X11/config
```

Creating Your Own Imakefiles

The easiest way to create an **Imakefile** is to use an existing working file as a template and then just fill in and/or replace the differences. Most simple X programs can use the file below as a template:

```
#
#     As with Makefiles, lines starting
#     with a "#" are comments.
#
LOCAL_LIBRARIES1 = $(XAWLIB) $(XMULIB)\
          $(XTOOLLIB) $(EXTENSIONLIB) $(XLIB)

CDEBUGFLAGS = -g

SRCS1 = file1.c file2.c file3.c file4.c
OBJS1 = file1.o file2.o file3.o file4.o

INCLUDE_FILES = include1.h include2.h

PROGRAM = xfb

ComplexProgramTarget_1(xfb, $(LOCAL_LIBRARIES1), )
```

The **LOCAL_LIBRARIES1** tell **imake** which libraries are necessary to build the program, using standard X/**imake** macros. The libraries are the Athena widget set (**XAWLIB**), which is normally the library **libXaw.a**, the X miscellaneous utilities library (**XMULIB**, **libXmu.a**), the X Toolkit intrinsics (**XTOOLLIB**, **libXt.a**), the X extension library (**EXTENSIONLIB**, **libXext.a**), and the low-level X library (**XLIB**, **libX11.a**).

The **SRCS1** line lists the C program files used to build the program. The **OBS1** line lists the object modules to be built by the C compiler from the C program files. These object modules will be linked with the libraries listed above to create the X application, named **xfb** on the **PROGRAM** line.

The **ComplexProgramTarget_1** lists the command used to build the C program files into an X application. Unless you have special needs, you can use the **ComplexProgramTarget_1** macro.

The short 400-byte **Imakefile** above generates a 10K **Makefile**, as follows:

```
# Makefile generated by imake - do not edit!
# $XConsortium: imake.c,v 1.51 89/12/12 12:37:30 jim Exp $
#
# The cpp used on this machine replaces all newlines and mul-
          tiple tabs and
# spaces in a macro expansion with a single space. Imake
          tries to compensate
# for this, but is not always successful.
#

#ident  "@(#)Imake.tmpl  1.5 - 91/07/12"


############################################################
# Makefile generated from "Imake.tmpl" and </tmp/IIf.a10734>
# $XConsortium: Imake.tmpl,v 1.77 89/12/18 17:01:37 jim Exp  $
#


############################################################
# platform-specific configuration parameters - edit i386.cf to change

#ident  "@(#)i386.cf  1.15 - 91/07/16"

    ADDRTEXT_X11 = 0xA0800000
    ADDRDATA_X11 = 0xA0C00000
    ADDRTEXT_Xol = 0xA1800000
    ADDRDATA_Xol = 0xA1C00000

YFLAGS =
 STRIP = strip
   AWK = awk
    CD = cd
    LS = ls
    PR = pr
 CHMOD = chmod
 CHOWN = chown
 CHGRP = chgrp
   SED = sed
```

```
##########################################################
# site-specific configuration parameters - edit site.def to change

#ident  "@(#)site.def 1.2 - 90/12/27"

# site:  $XConsortium: site.def,v 1.21 89/12/06 11:46:50 jim
Exp $

            SHELL = /bin/sh

              TOP = .
      CURRENT_DIR = .

               AR = ar cq
   BOOTSTRAPCFLAGS =
               CC = cc

         COMPRESS = /usr/lbin/compress
              CPP = /lib/cpp $(STD_CPP_DEFINES)
    PREPROCESSCMD = cc -E $(STD_CPP_DEFINES)
          INSTALL = /etc/install
               LD = ld
             LINT = lint
      LINTLIBFLAG = -o
         LINTOPTS = -ax
               LN = ln
             MAKE = make
               MV = mv
               CP = cp
           RANLIB = /bin/true
   RANLIBINSTFLAGS =
               RM = rm -f
     STD_INCLUDES = -I.
  STD_CPP_DEFINES = -DSYSV -DUSG
      STD_DEFINES = -DSYSV -DUSG
  EXTRA_LOAD_FLAGS =
  EXTRA_LIBRARIES = -lnsl_s -lc_s
             TAGS = ctags

           MFLAGS = -$(MAKEFLAGS)

    PROTO_DEFINES =

     INSTPGMFLAGS = -m 0555
```

```
    INSTBINFLAGS = -m 0555
    INSTUIDFLAGS = -m 4555 -u root
    INSTLIBFLAGS = -m 0444
    INSTINCFLAGS = -m 0444
    INSTMANFLAGS = -m 0444
    INSTDATFLAGS = -m 0444
  INSTKMEMFLAGS = -m 4555 -u root

        DESTDIR =

   TOP_INCLUDES = -I$(INCROOT)

     CDEBUGFLAGS = -O
       CCOPTIONS =
     COMPATFLAGS =

     ALLINCLUDES = $(STD_INCLUDES) $(TOP_INCLUDES)
        $(INCLUDES) $(EXTRA_INCLUDES)
      ALLDEFINES = $(ALLINCLUDES) $(STD_DEFINES)
        $(PROTO_DEFINES) $(DEFINES) $(COMPATFLAGS)
          CFLAGS = $(CDEBUGFLAGS) $(CCOPTIONS) $(ALLDEFINES)
       LINTFLAGS = $(LINTOPTS) -DLINT $(ALLDEFINES)
          LDLIBS = $(SYS_LIBRARIES) $(EXTRA_LIBRARIES)
       LDOPTIONS = $(CDEBUGFLAGS) $(CCOPTIONS)
  LDCOMBINEFLAGS = -X -r

        MACROFILE = i386.cf
          RM_CMD = $(RM) *.CKP *.ln *.BAK *.bak *.o core
        errs ,* *~ *.a .emacs_* tags TAGS make.log MakeOut

   IMAKE_DEFINES =

        IRULESRC = $(CONFIGDIR)
       IMAKE_CMD = $(IMAKE) -DUseInstalled -I$(IRULESRC)
        $(IMAKE_DEFINES)

    ICONFIGFILES = $(IRULESRC)/Imake.tmpl
        $(IRULESRC)/Imake.rules \
        $(IRULESRC)/Project.tmpl $(IRULESRC)/site.def \
        $(IRULESRC)/$(MACROFILE) $(EXTRA_ICONFIGFILES)

#ident  "@(#)Project.tmpl   1.8 - 91/07/16"
```

```
##############################################################
X Window System Build Parameters
# $XConsortium: Project.tmpl,v 1.63 89/12/18 16:46:44 jim Exp $

##############################################################
X Window System make variables; this need to be coordinated with rules
# $XConsortium: Project.tmpl,v 1.63 89/12/18 16:46:44 jim Exp $

            PATHSEP = /
             USRLIB = UsrLib
          USRLIBDIR = $(DESTDIR)/usr/lib
             BINDIR = $(DESTDIR)/usr/bin/X11
            INCROOT = $(DESTDIR)/usr/include
       BUILDINCROOT = $(TOP)
        BUILDINCDIR = $(BUILDINCROOT)/X11
        BUILDINCTOP = ..
             INCDIR = $(INCROOT)/X11
          USRINCDIR = $(INCROOT)
             ADMDIR = $(DESTDIR)/usr/adm
             LIBDIR = $(USRLIBDIR)/X11
          CONFIGDIR = $(LIBDIR)/config
         LINTLIBDIR = $(USRLIBDIR)/lint

            FONTDIR = $(LIBDIR)/fonts
           XINITDIR = $(LIBDIR)/xinit
             XDMDIR = $(LIBDIR)/xdm
             AWMDIR = $(LIBDIR)/awm
             TWMDIR = $(LIBDIR)/twm
             GWMDIR = $(LIBDIR)/gwm
            MANPATH = $(DESTDIR)/usr/man
      MANSOURCEPATH = $(MANPATH)/man
             MANDIR = $(MANSOURCEPATH)n
          LIBMANDIR = $(MANSOURCEPATH)3
         XAPPLOADDIR = $(LIBDIR)/app-defaults
          FONTCFLAGS =

       INSTAPPFLAGS = $(INSTDATFLAGS)

       TOP_INCLUDES =
     EXTRA_INCLUDES = -I$(INCROOT)  -I$(INCDIR)  -I/usr/include

              FONTC = bdftosnf
           MKFONTDIR = mkfontdir
  INCLUDE_EXTENSION = $(INCDIR)/extensions
```

```
         IMAKE = $(IMAKESRC)/imake
        DEPEND = $(DEPENDSRC)/makedepend
           RGB = $(RGBSRC)/rgb
     MKDIRHIER = /bin/sh $(SCRIPTSRC)/mkdirhier.sh

     CONFIGSRC = $(TOP)/config
     CLIENTSRC = $(TOP)/clients
       DEMOSRC = $(TOP)/demos
        LIBSRC = $(TOP)/lib
       FONTSRC = $(TOP)/fonts
    INCLUDESRC = $(TOP)/X11
     SERVERSRC = $(TOP)/server
       UTILSRC = $(TOP)/util
     SCRIPTSRC = $(UTILSRC)/scripts
    EXAMPLESRC = $(TOP)/examples
    CONTRIBSRC = $(TOP)/../contrib
        DOCSRC = $(TOP)/doc
        RGBSRC = $(TOP)/rgb
     DEPENDSRC = $(UTILSRC)/makedepend
      IMAKESRC = $(CONFIGSRC)
      XAUTHSRC = $(LIBSRC)/Xau
     MALLOCSRC = $(LIBSRC)/Xmalloc
       XLIBSRC = $(LIBSRC)/X
       XMUSRC = $(LIBSRC)/Xmu
     TOOLKITSRC = $(LIBSRC)/Xt
     AWIDGETSRC = $(LIBSRC)/Xaw
    XDMCPLIBSRC = $(LIBSRC)/Xdmcp
     BDFTOSNFSRC = $(FONTSRC)/bdftosnf
     MKFONTDIRSRC = $(FONTSRC)/mkfontdir
    EXTENSIONSRC = $(TOP)/extensions
        ATTSRC = $(TOP)/att
      LOCALSRC = $(TOP)/../local
        PKGSRC = $(TOP)/pkg
        MTGSRC = $(TOP)/mtg
       XMTGSRC = $(MTGSRC)/Xmtg
    XMTGRGBSRC = $(MTGSRC)/rgb
  NAMESERVERSRC = $(TOP)/nameserver
     XOLLIBSRC = $(LIBSRC)/Xol
        BDFSRC = $(FONTSRC)/bdf
    XOLFONTSRC = $(BDFSRC)/Xol
     R2FONTSRC = $(BDFSRC)/r2fonts
        ADMSRC = $(PKGSRC)/adm
```

```
    BITMAPINCDIR = /usr/include/X11/bitmaps
          BSDDIR = BsdDir
       BSDSYSDIR = BsdSysDir
          NETDIR = $(LIBDIR)/net
      STARLANDIR = $(NETDIR)/starlan
           ITDIR = $(NETDIR)/it
          TCPDIR = $(NETDIR)/tcp
          UWMDIR = $(LIBDIR)/uwm
       BITMAPDIR = $(BITMAPINCDIR)

         ARFLAGS =
       CLIBFLAGS =

        XHOSTLOC = $(USRLIBDIR)
      SHLIBFLAGS =   -L $(XHOSTLOC)
      DSLIBFLAGS =

   MALLOC_TO_USE = libXmalloc.a
     XLIB_TO_USE = libX11_s.a
    XtLIB_TO_USE = libXt.a
   XauLIB_TO_USE = libXau.a
   XawLIB_TO_USE = libXaw.a
   XmuLIB_TO_USE = libXmu.a
   XolLIB_TO_USE = libXol.a
  XextLIB_TO_USE = libXext.a
   olcLIB_TO_USE = libolc.a

   XLIBS_TO_BUILD = libX11_s.a libX11.a
  XtLIBS_TO_BUILD = libXt.a
 XauLIBS_TO_BUILD = libXau.a
 XawLIBS_TO_BUILD = libXaw.a
 XmuLIBS_TO_BUILD = libXmu.a
 XolLIBS_TO_BUILD = libXol.a
XextLIBS_TO_BUILD = libXext.a
 olcLIBS_TO_BUILD = libolc.a

     NAMESERVERS =   tcpserver

    EXTENSIONLIB = $(USRLIBDIR)/$(XextLIB_TO_USE)
 DEPEXTENSIONLIB = $(EXTENSIONLIB)
        XAUTHLIB = $(USRLIBDIR)/$(XauLIB_TO_USE)
     DEPXAUTHLIB = $(XAUTHLIB)
      MALLOC_LIB = $(USRLIBDIR)/$(MALLOC_TO_USE)
```

```
            XLIB = $(EXTENSIONLIB) $(USRLIBDIR)/libX11.a
         DEPXLIB = $(XLIB)
          XMULIB = $(USRLIBDIR)/$(XmuLIB_TO_USE)
       DEPXMULIB = $(XMULIB)
        XTOOLLIB = $(USRLIBDIR)/$(XtLIB_TO_USE)
     DEPXTOOLLIB = $(XTOOLLIB)
          XAWLIB = $(USRLIBDIR)/$(XawLIB_TO_USE)
       DEPXAWLIB = $(XAWLIB)
          XOLLIB = $(XOLLIBSRC)/$(XolLIB_TO_USE)
       DEPXOLLIB = $(XOLLIB)
 LINTEXTENSIONLIB = $(USRLIBDIR)/llib-lXext.ln
         LINTXLIB = $(USRLIBDIR)/llib-lX11.ln
          LINTXMU = $(USRLIBDIR)/llib-lXmu.ln
        LINTXTOOL = $(USRLIBDIR)/llib-lXt.ln
         LINTXAW = $(USRLIBDIR)/llib-lXaw.ln

         DEPLIBS = $(LOCAL_LIBRARIES)
        DEPLIBS1 = $(DEPLIBS)
        DEPLIBS2 = $(DEPLIBS)
        DEPLIBS3 = $(DEPLIBS)

#ident  "@(#)Imake.rules 1.15 - 91/09/16"


############################################################
Imake rules for building libraries, programs, scripts, and data files
# rules:  $XConsortium: Imake.rules,v 1.67 89/12/18 17:14:15 jim Exp $

############################################################
start of Imakefile

#A simple Imakefile follows:

#
#       Like with Makefiles, lines starting with a "#" are comments.
#
LOCAL_LIBRARIES1 = $(XAWLIB) $(XMULIB) $(XTOOLLIB) $(EXTEN-
SIONLIB) $(XLIB)


CDEBUGFLAGS = -g

SRCS1 = file1.c file2.c file3.c file4.c
OBJS1 = file1.o file2.o file3.o file4.o
```

```
INCLUDE_FILES = include1.h include2.h

PROGRAM = xfb

 OBJS = $(OBJS1) $(OBJS2) $(OBJS3)
 SRCS = $(SRCS1) $(SRCS2) $(SRCS3)


all:: $(PROGRAMS)

xfb: $(OBJS1) $(DEPLIBS1)
        $(RM) $@; if [ -f $@ ]; then $(MV) $@ $@~; fi
        $(CC) -o $@ $(LDOPTIONS) $(OBJS1)
$(LOCAL_LIBRARIES1)\
            $(MALLOC_LIB) $(LDLIBS)   $(EXTRA_LOAD_FLAGS)

install:: xfb
        $(INSTALL) $(INSTPGMFLAGS)   -f $(BINDIR) xfb
        $(STRIP) $(BINDIR)/xfb

install.man::
        @if [ -f xfb.man ]; \
        then \
        $(INSTALL) -m 0664 -f $(MANDIR) xfb.man; \
        $(MV) $(MANDIR)/xfb.man $(MANDIR)/xfb.n; \
        else \
        echo xfb.man does not exist to install ; \
        fi

depend::
        $(DEPEND) -s "# DO NOT DELETE" — $(ALLDEFINES) — $(SRCS)

clean::
        $(RM) $(PROGRAMS)

##########################################################
common rules for all Makefiles - do not edit

emptyrule::

clean::
        $(RM_CMD) \#*
```

```
clobber::
        $(RM_CMD) \#*

Makefile::
        -@if [ -f Makefile ]; then \
        echo "   $(RM) Makefile.bak; $(MV) Makefile
Makefile.bak"; \
        $(RM) Makefile.bak; $(MV) Makefile Makefile.bak; \
        else exit 0; fi
        $(IMAKE_CMD) -DTOPDIR=$(TOP) -DCURDIR=$(CURRENT_DIR)

tags::
        $(TAGS) -w *.[ch]
        $(TAGS) -xw *.[ch] > TAGS

##############################################################
empty rules for directories that do not have SUBDIRS - do not edit

install::
        @echo "install in $(CURRENT_DIR) done"

install.man::
        @echo "install.man in $(CURRENT_DIR) done"

Makefiles::

includes::

##############################################################
dependencies generated by makedepend
```

We include this **Makefile** because all **Makefile**s generated by **imake** look very similar to it; you can thus easily tell which **Makefile**s are created by hand and which are automatically generated by **imake**. If all goes well, you shouldn't ever have to read the automatically generated **Makefile**, like the file above. Rather, you should be able to just type **make** and the program should be built:

If you build your own **Imakefile**, you should also provide a simple **Makefile**, sometimes named **Makefile.ini** or **Makefile.orig**, for users of systems without **imake**. The whole world doesn't have these neato X utilities, so you should always include a traditional **Makefile**. If users don't have **imake**, they'll have to customize this **Makefile** on their own, but it's a lot easier to customize a **Makefile** than to build a new one from nothing.

For More Information

There's not a lot of information available on **imake**. The best source to start with, though is the online manual for **imake** and **xmkmf**. You might also want to look up a paper titled "Configuration Management in the X Window System," by Jim Fulton. This paper comes with the X Window sources from MIT (see Appendix A).

Summary

The **imake** utility allows you to compile and configure C source code into usable X Window applications. This chapter showed you how to run **imake** and configure it for your particular system.

VIII

Using Motif and Open Look Applications

The two main X Window user-interface styles are Motif from the Open Software Foundation and Open Look from AT&T and Sun. The vast majority of commercial X applications use one of these styles. Until now we've covered how to use X programs in a wide variety of environments and systems. This section extends that coverage to include Motif and Open Look applications:

- Chapter 25 presents the basics of using Motif applications. It covers the standards that Motif programs are supposed to follow and how to interact with these applications;
- Chapter 26 covers X user environments, a new class of application designed to make up for the lack of a decent user interface in the UNIX operating system;
- Chapter 27 introduces Open Look applications; and
- Chapter 28 covers the DeskSet suite of Open Look applications that come with SunSoft's OpenWindows implementation of the X Window System.

Chapter *25*

Using Motif Applications

M otif programs make up the largest segment of commercial X Window applications. These applications bear a distinctive three-dimensional look, which makes them easy to spot on a graphics display. In addition, Motif applications tend to act similarly, which is the whole point of an interface style guide.

One of the main ideas behind Motif is that applications will follow IBM's **Common User Access** (CUA) style and look much like Microsoft Windows 3.x programs. In fact, while the look of Motif applications shows three-dimension accents, the feel of Motif is nearly the same as Windows 3.x. Thus users with experience on Windows or OS/2 should be able to make a running start into the world of X with Motif.

A typical Motif application, shown in figure 25.1, displays a Menu bar with pulldown menus, a scrolled list for making choices, and a scrolled text editing area.

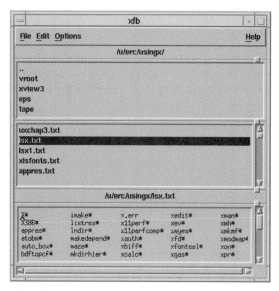

Figure 25.1 A Motif application.

Keyboard Shortcuts

One of the highly touted advantages of Motif is that you often don't need a mouse for casual usage—virtually everything is possible from the keyboard. While this sounds like a great idea, Motif uses a very illogical set of **mnemonics,** or keyboard shortcuts. In the above picture, the underlined letters, like the F in the word File, are Motif mnemonics. Many new users get confused about the underlined letters, and Motif certainly adds to the confusion.

What you can do is type the underlined letter and Motif will act as if you selected the item. The exception is for menus on the Menu bar. In that case, you have to type Alt (or Meta) and the underlined key. This sounds confusing—and it is.

Here's an example: You can call up the file menu from the application above (and from most Motif applications) by typing Alt-F. Alt-F calls up the File menu and you'll see it on the screen. Next, to select a choice in the file menu, such as Save (with an underlined S), you merely type S, not Alt-S. Confused? Just remember that menus themselves require the Alt key, and menu choices don't.

Another handy keyboard shortcut is the Tab key. Using this key, you can move about a window or dialog. Each press of the Tab key moves you forward to the next area that accepts keyboard or mouse input. Using Shift-Tab moves you back.

Calling Menus

As we mentioned above, most Motif menus will provide a keyboard mnemonic so that you can call up a menu without using the mouse. This keyboard mnemonic is activated by typing the Alt key and the underlined letter, such as Alt-E to call up the Edit menu. (You actually type a lowercase *e*, but the underlined letter, *E*, is uppercase.)

Another way to call up a menu is to use the mouse. Simply place the mouse cursor over the name of the menu you want to call up, then click the leftmost mouse button. If you click the mouse button, you'll see the menu. You can then use the Up and Down Arrow keys to navigate around the menu. You can select a choice by pressing the Return (also called Enter) key or click the leftmost mouse button. You can also hold down the leftmost mouse button to display the menu. Still holding the mouse button, move the mouse over the menu choice you want, then release the mouse button. This also selects a menu choice.

You can use the Left and Right Arrow keys to move between Menus on the Menu bar.

Standard Motif Menus

The Motif Style Guide mandates the names and locations of standard menus, although most applications require more than this small set of menus. These menus include File, Edit, View, Option and Help:

Table 25.1 Standard Motif menus.

Name on menu bar	Mnemonic	Purpose
File	F	Operations on files, like saving and opening.
Edit	E	Editing commands like Cut and Paste.
View	V	Options to control viewing data, such as sorting by date or alphabetically.
Option	O	Other program options.
Help	H	Online help.

The View and Option menus are not always available.

The File Menu

The File menu allows you to manipulate files. Since most programs deal with files in some way or another (word processors edit files, spreadsheets manipulate worksheet files, etc.) the File menu comes first on the menu bar. This menu should contain the following choices (or something very similar to the following choices):

Table 25.2 File menu choices.

Choice	Mnemonic	Meaning
New	N	Creates an empty new file
Open...	O	Opens an existing file
Save	S	Saves the current file
Save As...	A	Saves the current file under another name
Print	P	Prints the current file
Exit	x	Exits the application.

If the program supports printing, the print choices should go before the Exit, because Exit must be the last choice of the File menu.

Choosing Files with Motif

Motif provides a standard file-selection dialog, much like that of Windows or the Macintosh. This dialog has two scrolled lists: the one on the left contains a list of subdirectories and the list on the right contains a list of files in the current directory.

Double-click on a file name to select it. Single-click on a file name and you'll see the name appear in the Text Entry window below the lists, and the name on the list will appear in reverse video. Pressing the Return (or Enter) key will select whatever file is highlighted in reverse video. You can also click the leftmost mouse button over the OK choice.

Pressing Escape or clicking the leftmost mouse button over the Cancel choice cancels the operation.

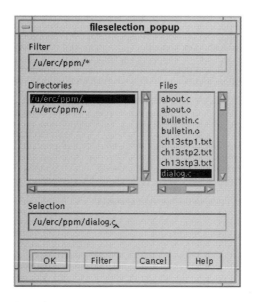

Figure 25.2 Motif's standard file dialog.

You can use the Filter option, with the topmost Text Entry window, to type in a file filter. For example, a filter of ***.c** will filter out all files that *do not* end in .c (that is, it will only include files that end in .c). Thus you'll see a file named **main.c**, but you won't see **program.doc** (assuming these files are in the given directory, of course).

Exiting Motif Programs

Motif programs should have an Exit choice at the end of the File menu. You can select this choice from the menu or use the standard keyboard shortcut: Alt-F to call up the File menu, and then x to select the Exit choice.

Other Motif Menus

The Edit menu allows you to make editing changes and copy and paste data to and from the Motif clipboard.

Table 25.3 Edit menu choices.

Choice	Mnemonic	Meaning
Undo	U	Undo the last user operation.
Cut	t	Cuts the selected text to the clipboard, removing the data from the display.
Copy	C	Copies the selected text to the clipboard.
Paste	P	Pastes the data in the clipboard at the current location.
Clear	l	Clears the selected data.
Delete	D	Deletes the selected data, much like Clear.

Motif supports a clipboard similar to that of Macintosh and Windows. You can copy data to the clipboard and paste in other places in the current program or in other programs. The only problem with the Motif clipboard, though, is that only Motif programs support the Motif clipboard. Thus you'll have difficulty working with other X programs, like **xterm** and the OpenWindows File Manager.

Help Me, Mr. Wizard

All Motif programs with a Menu bar should have a Help menu as the last (right-most) menu choice. Alt-H should call up this menu, which will have at least some of the following choices:

Table 25.4 Help menu choices.

Choice	Mnemonic	Meaning
On Context...	C	Provides help on the current context.
On Help...	H	Tells you how to use the help system.
On Window...	W	Provides help on the current window.
On Keys...	K	Explains the program's use of the keyboard.
Index...	I	Provides an index of help topics.
Tutorial...	T	Provides an online tutorial (not always available).
On Versions...	V	Doesn't provide help, but displays a copyright message.

Unlike Windows, Motif has no standards for how the online help should look. The Motif Style Guide insists that users will be able to get help. Many times, though, you won't get a lot from the online help.

The F1 function key should also call up help in Motif programs—normally the same help as you'd get from the On Window help.

Using Scrollbars

Scrollbars allow you to view a large data set in a small window. You can use scrollbars to navigate through the larger area and selectively view parts of the larger data set.

Motif's scrollbars are fairly easy to operate. Click the leftmost mouse button over one of the arrowheads to move one line in that direction. Grab the **thumb** in the middle of the scrollbar with the leftmost mouse button (that is, hold the leftmost mouse button down over the thumb) and you can move the scroll bar up or down (or left or right on a horizontal scrollbar). Release the mouse button and the scrolled window will display the data at the desired position. (It's easier to use scrollbars than it is to describe them. You'll get the hang of it right away.)

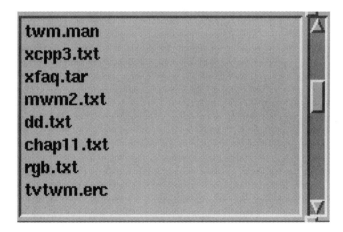

Figure 25.3 A Motif scrollbar.

You can also click in the area above or below the scrollbar thumb. This should move the data up or down one full "page" (the application defines the page size.)

Working with Motif Dialogs

Dialog windows are small windows that allow you to specify options, select files, enter data, and confirm choices. In general, Motif dialogs use the Return key (called Enter on some keyboards) as a shortcut for OK, and the Escape key as a shortcut for Cancel. Most dialogs should have OK, Cancel and Help pushbuttons at the bottom. You can use the mouse or the Return key to select these choices. The Escape key cancels.

The following dialog is called a **prompt dialog** and programs use it to ask the user to type in some information:

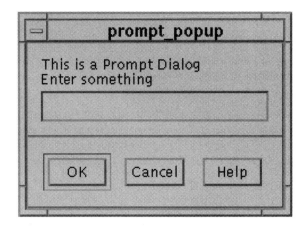

Figure 25.4 A Motif prompt dialog.

N O T E
Note that the use of Return for OK can be tricky. If you have a number of text entries, you cannot press Return at the end of each entry. The first time you press Return, the dialog will go away, before you get a chance to finish the other text entries. This problem often traps new users. Just remember to think twice before pressing the Return key.

When the program is busy with a long, time-consuming operation, you'll often see a working dialog, which should tell you that the program is busy and give you a chance to cancel the long operation, although all programs don't support this.

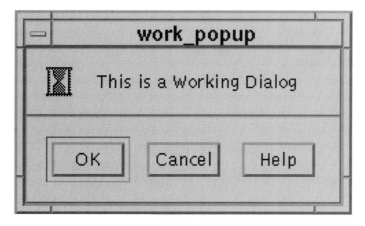

Figure 25.5 A busy or working Motif dialog.

Editing Text with Motif

Text editing with Motif is easy, especially if you're used to cryptic text editors like **vi**. Just point with the mouse, click, then type. You click the leftmost mouse button to place the text-editing cursor, also called the **insertion point**, and then you can type away.

You can select text by dragging the mouse with the leftmost mouse button held down. The selected area should appear in reverse video. The first five lines of the text-editing area are selected in the figure below:

You can double-click (with the leftmost mouse button) to select individual words, triple-click to select a whole line, and quadruple-click to select all the text. You can paste the selected text with the middle mouse button. You can also use the Edit menu to copy the selected text into the Motif clipboard. This two-level paste tends to confuse. Just remember that the middle mouse button pastes whatever text is highlighted in reverse video, while the Paste choice on the Edit menu pastes whatever text is in the Motif clipboard, which may or may not be visible.

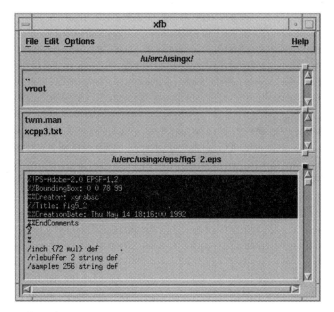

Figure 25.6 Selected text.

Check Boxes

Motif calls check boxes, as shown below, radio buttons. These buttons—which look like diamond-shaped boxes—allow you to choose a single option from a list of many.

Figure 25.7 Motif radio buttons.

The radio button that appears inset is the selected choice. The buttons that appear set out are not selected.

Motif also supports the square-shaped toggle buttons. These buttons allow you to turn on (in) or off (out) a particular choice.

Customizing Motif Applications with Resources

Motif programs use resources just like **xterm**, **xclipboard,** and all the standard X applications. Motif applications, though, use the **fontList** resource to set the font used by an application, and not the font resource used by **xterm**:

Usingx*fontList: lucidasans-12

Motif applications also use the **labelString** resource instead of **xterm**'s label resource:

Usingx*exitbutton.labelString: Exit

Summary

This chapter introduces you to Motif application usage and covers the standard Motif menu choices.

Chapter **26**

X User Environments

S ince the X Window System provides only the most cursory user environment, many vendors layer additional programs on top of X to hide much of the complexity of both X and the underlying operating system (usually UNIX). As we pointed out earlier, the most common X program is **xterm**, which provides an interface to the UNIX command-line shells. As workstations filter into the hands of less experienced users, something is needed to hide the cryptic commands and decidedly unfriendly operating system.

Applications that do this are considered **X user environments**. These applications include Hewlett-Packard's Visual User Environment (or VUE), Visix's Looking Glass, and IXI's X.desktop. SunSoft's OpenWindows includes a DeskSet of applications, which can also be considered an X user environment. The inspiration for these X user environments comes from personal-computer applications like the Macintosh Finder and Microsoft Windows' File Manager.

Most of these X user environments present an clearer view of the UNIX file system. Since the UNIX operating system depends so much on files, a graphical front end to the directory structure goes a long way toward making UNIX easier to use. For example, these user environments present icons for files.

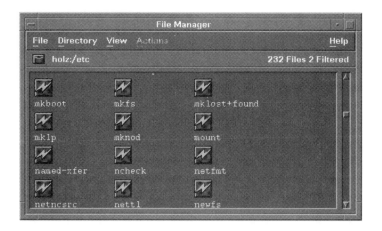

Figure 26.1 The HP VUE file manager.

These packages are far too complex to cover every detail in a book that covers all of X. Instead, we'll cover the main packages and refer you to your system documentation for more information.

HP VUE

Hewlett-Packard provides VUE as an integrated environment for its line of UNIX workstations. (SAIC sells a ported VUE on other platforms, including Sun SPARCstations.) VUE contains six **managers**, which control parts of your system:

- **The File Manager** manages files and directories.
- **The Help Manager** provides online help, including the UNIX online manual pages.
- **The Login Manager** presents a graphical login screen, like that provided by **xdm**.
- **The Session Manager** allows you to log out and then restart your work at the same exact point the next time you log in.

- **The Style Manager** controls parts of the display, such as colors and fonts. It also controls who can access your screen.

- **The Workspace Manager** gives you six workspaces, or virtual screens, where you can divide your work. This also provides a **mwm**-like window manager called **vuewm**.

The main window for VUE is a control panel that appears at the bottom of the screen at all times, even when you're working in a manager. In this control panel, icons represent the time and date, your system's CPU load, incoming electronic mail, and six workspaces. These six workspaces are six virtual screens, where you can organize application windows. You can separate the workspaces; for example, one workspace can be devoted to software development and another to electronic mail. A simple click of the left mouse button in one of the six workspace labels instantly switches to that virtual screen. (A note of caution: The programs in all virtual screens are loaded into RAM, so a series of RAM-hogging programs will cause the system to swap to disk frequently.)

The right side of the main window allows you to print files, view the files and directories in your system, and delete files. The Palette icon at the bottom of the window brings up the Style Manager.

The Style Manager allows you to control the X environment, which includes screen-background patterns (you can have a different pattern for each workspace), application colors, keyboard and mouse sensitivity, and access to the workstation's screen.

Figure 26.2 The VUE Style Manager.

With the Style Manager, you can control colors and fonts for the VUE applications. VUE provides a set of color schemes, a set of eight colors. Once you set a color scheme, all VUE applications adopt this scheme. You can also add your own color schemes, using the Add button.

HP's online help includes all the traditional UNIX manual pages, with complete indexing, as well as individual help files on aspects of VUE.

Looking Glass

Looking Glass is a Macintosh-like front end to the UNIX file system. It also includes an icon editor and an extensive set of rules to bind files to applications, so that you can double-click on a document file icon and launch the proper application.

Because Looking Glass isn't tied to a particular vendor, it supports both the Open Look and Motif user interfaces. Normally, the interface selection will be automatic: If you run the Motif window manager, **mwm**, you'll get the Motif look and feel. If you run the Open Look window manager, **olwm**, you'll see an Open Look application. You can force the issue by using the **-laf** command-line parameter. The following command starts Looking Glass, or **lg**, in Motif mode in background:

```
lg -laf motif &
```

The main directory window then looks like the following:

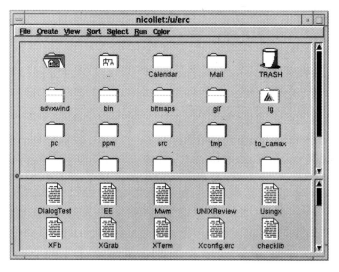

Figure 26.3 Looking Glass following the Motif style.

To get the Open Look style, use the following command:

```
lg -laf openlook
```

Looking Glass supports a desktop panel of commonly used applications. You start these applications by double-clicking on the icon. You can also double-click on programs in the file windows to launch them, but the desktop panel saves you from digging through subdirectories in search of program icons.

Figure 26.4 The Looking Glass Desktop Panel.

Looking Glass sports a complicated licensing scheme. Like many commercial UNIX applications, you normally have to enter a long authentication ID to configure the system. Once, the system is configured, you must run a license server that serves to eat CPU cycles and enforce the Looking Glass license. If you ever have problems running **lg**, chances are you forgot to run the license server, **vls**.

X.desktop

IXI's X.desktop acts much like its direct competitor, Looking Glass, in presenting windows with icons representing files and directories. You also get a Desktop window for commonly used X programs.

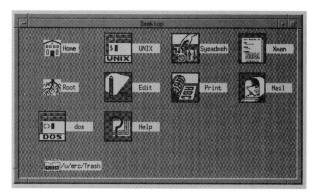

Figure 26.5 X.desktop's desktop window.

As with everything in X.desktop—or **xdt**, as the program is named—you can configure your desktop to add new programs and change icons. Double-click on a program icon to launch the associated application.

xdt displays directories in windows with icons for files. You can display the files as icons or as names, by clicking in the two buttons above the scroll bar on the right side of the window. If you click the left mouse button over a file name, you are presented with a window to rename the file—a very convenient feature.

To delete files, drag their icons into the trash can on the main Desktop window. Double-click on the trash can icon to retrieve files from the trash. To empty the trash, double-click with the right mouse button over the trash can. Watch out! Once you empty the trash, you're out of luck, as the files are gone forever.

The best feature of X.desktop is its rule language for associating files with applications. X.desktop comes standard with the SCO Open Desktop UNIX package for 386 and 486 PCs.

Summary

This chapter covers the basics of three popular X user environments: Hewlett-Packard's VUE, Visix's Looking Glass, and IXI's X.desktop.

## Chapter 27

Using Open Look Applications

Open Look is a graphical interface that ships with every Sun Microsystems SPARCstation. In terms of market share, Sun sells the most popular UNIX workstations. Nonetheless, Sun's implementation of the X Window System is one of the most tortuously off-kilter on the market. This proves that X has not become the checklist item its proponents claim: If people were buying UNIX workstations only for easy-to-work-with X implementations, Sun would not lead the market.

Sun's implementation of X, in some ways, defeats the entire purpose of open systems, because it makes the job of using X in a multivendor environment harder than it should be. Instead of selling X, Sun sells **OpenWindows**, which is structurally similar to X. In fact, OpenWindows supports most X applications and the underlying X protocol. OpenWindows also adds Sun's **NeWS** (Network Extensible Windowing System) protocol and layers the Open Look interface on top. As of this writing, Sun still doggedly clings to Open Look as it battles the Open Software Foundation's Motif (covered in the last two chapters) for the hearts and mice of graphical interface users.

Personally, we think both interfaces have a long way to go before they can be considered good. Computer interfaces in general have miles to go before they can be considered even remotely friendly; computers are still too difficult to use. Aside from these issues, Open Look and Motif both present attempts at making X a lot friendlier, and do in fact present an interface that is much better than the default X programs like **xterm** and **twm**.

Open Look also runs on a few other platforms, notably SPARCstation compatibles, such as from Solbourne and CompuAdd, and any direct derivative of AT&T (UNIX System Laboratories) UNIX.

This chapter concentrates on common features and problems of Open Look applications and SunSoft's OpenWindows environment. The concepts we use should work with any Open Look-compliant applications.

Open Look-compliant applications usually bear a distinctive look and feel, making them instantly recognizable. In the accompanying figure, notice the unique scrollbars.

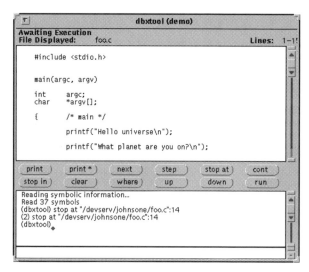

Figure 27.1 An Open Look program.

Open Look was developed by Sun Microsystems and AT&T, based on work licensed from Xerox. Open Look's goals are simplicity, consistency, and efficiency. While the interface doesn't always meet these goals, Open Look applications are generally easy to use, at least as easy as X applications can get.

Using Scrollbars

Open Look scrollbars provide a distinctive **scrolling elevator** that shows where you are in the document you're viewing.

The scrolling elevator allows you to move up or down (or left or right in a horizontal scrollbar) with very small movements of the mouse. Motif menus, on the other hand, require you to move to the far top or bottom of a menu to access the Up and Down arrows. With Open Look, these arrows are right on the scrollbars elevator. You can click or hold down the left mouse button over one of the arrows to move the viewing area in that direction. If you hold down the mouse button, the mouse will move, following the scrollbars elevator, until you've reached the end of the scrollbar.

If you hold the left mouse button over the center of the elevator, you can drag the elevator in either direction. Release the left mouse button when you find the place you want. Unlike Motif scrollbars, the viewing area won't move until you are done and release the mouse button. (Motif scrollbars move the viewing area while you move the mouse, so you can see how far you need to move.)

Open Look scrollbars provide additional controls. You can see how much of the full document is visible by looking at the slightly darker area above and below the elevator. You can click the left mouse button at the top or bottom of the scrollbar and the view will jump to the top or the bottom. You can also click in the area above or below the elevator to move a "page" or screen in either direction.

Open Look scrollbars also provide a menu—and a confusing menu at that. You're presented with three choices:

Table 27.1 Scrollbar menu.

Choice	*Meaning*
Here to top	Moves the line (in the window) next to the mouse to the top of the window.
Top to here	Moves the line at the top of the window down to be next to the mouse.
Previous	Jump the elevator to the previous position.

To make sense of these choices, imagine a horizontal line running across the window from the mouse position. Now look at the line of text that's nearest to this line. The Here to Top menu choice moves *that* line of text to the top of the window. The Top to Here menu choice moves the line of text at the top of the window to the imaginary line level with the mouse position. It's also easy to miss with the mouse and get the line you wanted at the top of the window (Here to Top) invisibly scrolled off the top of the window. It almost seems more work than it's worth, right? The other Open Look menus aren't that confusing.

Open Look Menus

Open Look applications aren't as standardized as Motif programs; thus you'll see a lot of variation. Most applications, though, present at least three menus: File, Edit, and View. There seems to be no standardization on the names or locations of the choices displayed in these menus. You'll have to spend a little time browsing all the menu choices making yourself familiar with each Open Look application.

In any case, most menus are pulled down from what Open Look calls "Menu buttons":

Figure 27.2 Open Look menu buttons.

Note the downward-pointing triangle. That symbol indicates a submenu that the button can access. Just hold the right mouse button down over the Menu button to call up the submenu.

Press and hold the right mouse button to display a menu. Release the mouse over the desired choice. Or, you can click the right mouse button once and then use either the right mouse button (the Menu button) or the left mouse button (the Select button) to choose one of the menu choices.

You cannot use the Left and Right Arrow keys to move between menus. You must use the mouse.

N O T E

In the figure above, the choice inside the over is the default menu choice. If you click the left mouse button (the Select button) over the Menu button from Figure

27.2, the application executes the default menu choice, which is not always what you expect.

Using the Mouse

Open Look defines a consistent use of mouse buttons. Unfortunately, this consistency applies only to Open Look applications. If you're used to Motif or any other X Window interface, you're in for quite a shock when you try to select a menu choice. Motif uses the left mouse button to pull down menus and make menu choices. With Open Look applications, you must always remember to press the right mouse button to pull down menus. Watch out! If you press the left mouse button over something that calls up a menu, the application doesn't display the menu. Instead, the application executes the *default* menu choice—whatever that may be. You can't tell what this default menu choice is without pulling down the menu. But you won't see the menu unless you use the right mouse button—not the left—to pull down the menu. We find this is the most distracting problem when moving from Motif-based applications to Open Look-based programs.

WARNING

Table 27.2 Open Look mouse buttons.

Button	Use in Open Look
Left	Select: selects objects and controls.
Middle	Adjust: extends the number of selected objects.
Right	Menu: calls up menus.

With a two-button mouse, the Adjust function (the middle mouse button) is handled by a keyboard equivalent. With a one-button mouse (popular mainly on Apple Macintoshes), both the Adjust and Menu functions are handled by the keyboard.

Open Look supports a drag-and-drop model for manipulating text, files, graphics, and spreadsheet cells. The process is simple. Use the left mouse button (Select) to select lines of text, file icons, or whatever. Press and hold the left mouse button and drag the mouse over the area you want selected. The selected items will appear in reverse video. Release the mouse button when you've selected the area you want. Use the middle mouse button (Adjust) to change the selection, such as extending it or shrinking it. Finally, press and hold the left mouse button (Select) over the highlighted area, then drag the selected items to wherever you want to "drop" them. You can move text about a window, move files between directories, and drag files into a wastebasket to delete them. If you hold down the Control key while you drag the selected items, you'll make a copy of the selected items.

Calling Menus

The right mouse button (the Menu button) can call menus anywhere. Hold down the right mouse button over various parts of different applications and you'll see a lot of menus—all normally hidden. Open Look supports a lot of hidden menus. Even the scrollbar has a menu. When in doubt, just hold down the right mouse button over part of a window and look at the menu that pops up.

Because they're hidden, these menus tend to be underused, so Open Look supports an amazingly handy feature: **pushpins**. Any menu with a picture of a thumbtack at the top can be *pinned* to the screen. Once pinned, the menu remains visible until you *unpin* it.

To pin a menu or dialog window, click-hold the right mouse button over the pin. Click the left mouse button over the pin to unpin the menu.

Figure 27.3 A pinned menu.

Working with Open Look Dialogs

Open Look dialog windows don't have any means of making them disappear unless you unpin them. Many dialogs even start out unpinned—to get rid of then when you're done, you must first pin the dialog and then unpin it.

The square boxes in a dialog are exclusive choices, sort of like Motif's radio buttons. For each set, you can pick one item. The horizontal lines indicate areas where you can enter text, and the buttons at the bottom show what actions you can perform. Most Open Look dialogs have an Apply button, which, if pressed, will apply the changes you've entered into the dialog, and a Reset button, which will reset the choices to their default settings.

Exiting Open Look Programs

To quit an application, you must access an Open Look hidden menu. Since Open Look defines a popup window menu for each window on the screen, to quit an application you normally must move the mouse to the Title bar of one of the application's windows and then hold down the right mouse button. This will call up the Window menu, and the last choice is Quit. Of course, this menu is not provided by the application itself, but by the Open Look window manager. If you're not running **olwm** as your window manager, you may not be able to quit Open Look applications!

The Close menu choice on the Window menu means iconify, as we described in Chapter 10 on the Open Look Window Manager. For the Motif window manager, **mwm**, the Close menu choice means Quit.

N O T E

If you run under **mwm**, use the Close choice from **mwm**'s Window menu to quit your Open Look applications (see Chapter 9 on the Motif Window Manager). If you use **twm**, use the Delete menu choice to quit programs (see Chapter 11 on the Tab Window Manager).

Open Look Help

You should be able to press the Help key (available on Sun Type 4 keyboards) to get help at any time. If you don't have a key labeled *Help* on your keyboard, the F1 function key may be configured to provide help. In such a case, try F1.

Open Look applications provide a much better help system than most other X applications. Why? Because Open Look requires help to have a certain look and feel, and the Open Look programmer toolkits provide built-in help functions, which encourages application developers to use them. Following is a sample of Open Look help:

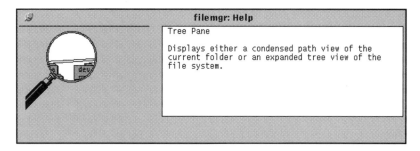

Figure 27.4 *Open Look help.*

Editing Text with Open Look

Open Look text editing is a little on the quirky side. Unlike the active Copy and Paste used by **xterm**, **xclipboard**, **xedit**, and Motif applications, Open Look applications require that you select the text and then use the Copy choice from the Edit menu. Luckily, you can pin the Edit menu to the screen to streamline the process.

Similarly, you must select the Paste menu choice from the Edit menu to paste a text selection. You cannot simply use the middle mouse button as you can with Motif and other X Window applications like **xterm**.

Table 27.3 Selecting Text.

Left Mouse Button	Meaning
Single click	Move text insertion point to mouse location.
Double Click	Select word, the move insertion point to start of word.
Triple click	Select entire line.
Quadruple Click	Select all text.
Drag	Selects text under mouse pointer.
Drag on selected text	Moves text to new location.

You can use the middle mouse button (Adjust) to extend or shrink the amount of text you selected.

Once you select text, you can use the Cut, Copy, and Paste choices in the Edit menu to place the selected text into the clipboard or to paste the text in the clipboard to the current insertion point.

```
All that we see or seem is but a dream within a
dream...
```

Figure 27.5 Text editing.

In addition to using the menu, you can also use the following keyboard shortcuts:

Table 27.4 Cut, Copy, and Paste keyboard shortcuts.

Keys	Meaning
Meta-X	Cut selected text and place it in the clipboard.
Meta-C	Copy selected text into the clipboard.
Meta-V	Paste selected text.

Editing Properties

You can adjust properties (the Open Look term for X resources) in your workspace by using the property editor. You can call up this program from the **olwm** Window Manager Workspace menu or by using the following command:

props &

You can adjust colors, icons, menu settings, and other parts of the display. Only other Open Look applications will use these properties. Even so, this is a much better way to edit X resources than using **vi** or some other text editor to edit a resource file directly.

N O T E

When you choose the Apply button, props will overwrite your **.Xdefaults** file in your home directory. If you placed any comments in this file, you'll lose them.

Use the pushpin to get rid of the property editor.

Customizing Open Look Applications with Resources

Open Look applications are built using a number of programmer toolkits. Depending on the toolkit, you'll find different sets of acceptable resources for Open Look applications.

The best bet for setting resources is to look up the on-line manual for each application for the resources supported by that application. For the OpenWindows DeskSet applications, like **textedit** and **cmdtool**, many of the resources and command-line parameters are described in the **xview** online manual pages.

These XView resources are usually set on a whole class of applications—in this case, the entire DeskSet suite of programs. For example, to set the scrollbars to appear on the left side of the window instead of the right, place the following resource command in your **.Xdefaults** file (see Chapter 6 on resources):

```
OpenWindows.scrollbarPlacement:     Left
```

To place the scrollbars on the right side of the window, the default, use:

```
OpenWindows.scrollbarPlacement:     Right
```

Common Problems with Open Look

We've found some common problems afflict Open Look users. The trickiest problem is remembering to use the right mouse button—and not the left—to call menus. Other problems come about because of the integrated nature of the Open Look support environment, especially with Sun's OpenWindows.

OpenWindows includes a lot more than just the X Window System. The problem is that you cannot use these OpenWindows features on other, non-OpenWindows platforms, which includes just about every workstation made by Sun's competitors. For example, Sun's excellent AnswerBook on-line help program requires the NeWS windowing protocol, in addition to the X protocol. This combination is only available under OpenWindows.

OpenWindows also includes a number of fonts, including scalable Folio (F3) fonts. Few of these fonts are available on other platforms. Thus Sun's Calendar Manager application (which we cover in the next chapter) won't display very well across a network on another X station, including X terminals.

Most OpenWindows applications require you to click the mouse button in an area to type. This click-to-type mode is independent of the Window Manager, which may or may not require you to click the mouse in an application's window to start typing. Since you end up always following the click-to-type mode, this tends to defeat the Window Manager's input control, which you can normally set to follow the mouse or force the click-to-type mode. (See Chapters 9-10 on **mwm** and **olwm** window managers.)

In the next chapter we cover a set of Open Look applications that ships with Sun's OpenWindows. These applications, bundled together in Sun's DeskSet, make using a Sun workstation a lot more convenient. Unfortunately, though, these applications aren't available on other platforms, so you'll still have problems in a multivendor environment.

Summary

This chapter offers some tips on Open Look usage, as well as solutions to common problems faced by Open Look users.

Chapter 28

Using the OpenWindows DeskSet

O
penWindows is SunSoft's powerful X Window environment. Most users run either version 2 or 3 or OpenWindows. Because of version differences, we'll concentrate on common features.

OpenWindows includes the X11/NeWS merged server (which handles X and NeWS windowing protocols), the Open Look window manager (**olwm**), Sun's Folio scaled fonts, three toolkits (the Open Look Intrinsics Toolkit, XView, and tNt), and the DeskSet suite of productivity applications. The total package requires more than 40 megabytes of disk space.

In this chapter, we'll cover the major applications in SunSoft's OpenWindows DeskSet. These applications include a file manager (**filemgr**), a calendar and scheduling program (**cm**), **xterm** replacements (**cmdtool** and **shelltool**), an icon editor (**iconedit**), an electronic-mail program (**mailtool**), and a program to bind document files to the applications that launch them (**binder**).

Getting Started with OpenWindows

The first thing to do before getting started with OpenWindows is to make sure all your paths and environment variables are set up properly. You can store the OpenWindows files in a number of places, but the default is in **/usr/openwin**. You should set the environment variable **OPENWINHOME** to the directory that holds your OpenWindows files:

```
setenv OPENWINHOME /usr/openwin
```

The value of **$OPENWINHOME** is used by several DeskSet applications. These applications themselves are stored in **$OPENWINHOME/bin** and **$OPENWINHOME/bin/xview**, which is normally **/usr/openwin/bin** and **/usr/openwin/bin/xview**. In addition, demo files are stored in **$OPENWINHOME/demo** or, by default, **/usr/openwin/demo**. You'll want to make sure the **bin** and **xview** directories are in your command path. You can use the following command in the C shell to set up your command path:

```
set path = ( $OPENWINHOME/bin/xview $OPENWINHOME/bin $path )
```

This sets the command path to include the location of the DeskSet applications as well as whatever the command path included before.

Since X Window programs in general use an outrageously large amount of RAM, many systems, including SunSoft's Solaris, use shared libraries. These shared libraries save on the amount of memory taken up by the DeskSet suite and other X programs. All X programs require the low-level X programmer library at the very least, and most layer on one or more toolkit libraries. These libraries of prewritten programming functions tend to be huge. Allowing multiple applications to share a large part of their program cuts down on the amount of memory used by the applications, which in turn makes your system run faster.

The OpenWindows shared libraries are normally located in **$OPENWINHOME/lib** or **/usr/openwin/lib** by default. Since normal-system shared libraries in the Solaris environment are stored in **/usr/lib**, you need to tell the operating system to look in another place for shared libraries. The **LD_LIBRARY_PATH** environment variable tells the system where else to look. You can use the following command to set the **LD_LIBRARY_PATH** environment variable:

```
setenv LD_LIBRARY_PATH $OPENWINHOME/lib
```

Once we have these basics set up, we can look in the OpenWindows directories for X and OpenWindows programs, including the DeskSet suite.

The **$OPENWINHOME** directory should contain your X, OpenWindows, and NeWS programs, while most of the DeskSet applications are stored in **$OPENWIN-HOME/bin/xview**.

The most useful DeskSet application is the File Manager, **filemgr**.

The OpenWindows File Manager

The OpenWindows File Manager presents a now-familiar display of files in a directory as icons in a scrolled window. You can select files from their icons, edit the files, delete them, copy them, move them, and change the file's access permissions. The File Manager is normally launched by the default OpenWindows start script, **openwin**, but if you need to launch the file manager, use the following command:

filemgr &

You'll see a window with icons for files and a separate wastebasket window.

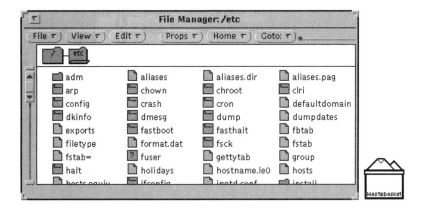

Figure 28.1 The file manager.

A bar of Menu buttons is at the top of the File Manager window. Beneath that lies the file- folder icons showing the directory path, in tiny script, from the root directory (**/**) to the current directory. Beneath that, the File Manager displays the files in the current directory, with icons for directories that look like file folders, as well as icons for program, document, and data files. Application icons look like square windows and sometimes have a picture inside. Document and data-file icons look like a piece of paper with the top right corner folded over. You can drag these file icons into the Wastebasket to delete files.

You can select files by clicking on their icons with the left mouse button. By pressing and holding the left mouse button, you can draw a box and select a group of files a´ la Macintosh. Use the middle mouse button (Adjust) to select more files or adjust the files you have selected. To delete files, drag the files into the Wastebasket. To move files, drag the files to the icon for the directory of the new location. To copy files, hold down the control key while you drag the file icons to their new location. The File Manager copies the selected files to the new location.

To open any file, double-click on the icon with the left mouse button (Select). You can also double-click on Directory File folder icons to open, or view, the sub-directory.

Some of the data-file icons have been bound to the application that edits or creates them. For example, a WordPerfect document's icon could be bound to the WordPerfect application. Once bound, when you double-click on the WordPerfect document icon and open it, the File Manager will launch the WordPerfect application. The **binder** program, covered below, binds document files to programs. The **iconedit** program, also covered below, allows you to customize file icons.

If you double-click on a document or data file to open it, and there is no binding set up, the file manager will launch a text editor, the **textedit** application, to edit the file you tried to open. Since most UNIX files are text files, this normally works well. But, if you try to open a large statistics data file, the text editor won't help much.

Double-clicking on a program or application icon starts the application. Unfortunately, most UNIX applications require command-line parameters to work correctly, so double-clicking is not always the best method of launching an application.

The Menu buttons for the file manager provide the traditional Open Look File, Edit, and View menus, along with menus for editing properties, jumping to your home directory, or jumping quickly to another directory.

The File menu allows you to execute your own commands, if you choose to customize the File Manager (something few users do). In one of its best features, the File menu contains a Remote Copy choice. This allows you to copy files to and from remote machines on a network. This Remote Copy choice replaces the UNIX **rcp** (remote **cp** or copy) command and helps hide **rcp**'s syntax.

The View menu allows you to view the field files as icons, small icons—although the menu choice states that the view is by list—or as a tree structure.

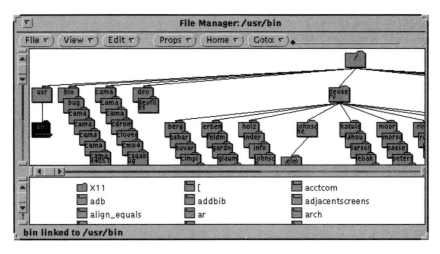

Figure 28.2 The file manager's view of the file system as a tree.

You can sort the files by name, date, size, or type.

If you have problems getting started with the File Manager, you may need to run **install_filemgr**. See your Solaris manuals for more information on **install_filemgr**.

Binding Applications and Data Files

One of the neatest features of OpenWindows is the **binder**, a program that binds together document files and the program that created the document. For example, if you create a user manual with FrameMaker, you can bind the FrameMaker documents with the FrameMaker application itself.

Once bound, you can double-click on a document's icon in the File Manager and then launch the proper editing application. In our example, you can double-click on your user manual's icons in the file manager to launch FrameMaker and configure FrameMaker to edit your user manual.

Start the binder with the following command:

binder &

You could have problems with the **binder** unless you have set the **OPENWINHOME** environment variable. The **binder** window then appears:

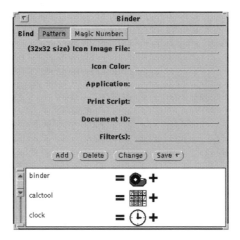

Figure 28.3 The binder.

You'll see an area at the top for creating new bindings and a scrolled list of all the existing bindings below. The file **/etc/filetype** contains the default system bindings for the OpenWindows environment. If you create your own customized bindings, these appear in a file named **.filetype** in your home directory.

To bind a file to an application, you can bind via a single file name, a pattern, such as ***.doc** or a **magic number**. So-called magic numbers are stored in the file **/etc/magic** and contain identification stamps for types of files, including PDP-11 APL workspaces, which should tell you how useful magic numbers are. Use a magic number if you want to bind files of types well-known by the system, such as Sun raster files or PostScript documents. In all other cases, use a single file name or a pattern.

For example, assume you name all your X bitmap files with a **.xbm** suffix. You then want to bind the X bitmap editor, **bitmap**, to these bitmap files. Click the left mouse button over the pattern button in the Bind field. Then fill out the Bind field with ***.xbm**. Finally, fill the Application field with the command to launch the **bitmap** program:

$OPENWINHOME/bin/bitmap $FILE

Note that we placed the full path to the program, since we don't know what command paths will be set up when **bitmap** is first launched. The **$FILE** part specifies that the chosen file name is passed to the **bitmap** editor on the command line.

We must also fill in the icon file name and color. For the color, we can simply make the icon white, using red, green, and blue values of 255, 255, 255 in the Icon Color field. For the icon file name, we can create an icon with the icon editor, **iconedit**, or we can use an existing file. For now, we'll use an existing file:

$OPENWINHOME/include/images/icondoc.icon

You can look in the images directory (**/usr/openwin/include/images**) to see the default set of icon files. When you're finished, click the left mouse button over the Add button. Then click the left mouse button over Save button. You might be asked if you want to overwrite your local binder file, **.filetype**, in your home directory.

The OpenWindows Text Editor

To most UNIX users, text editors consist of **vi** or **emacs**, powerful editors in their own right, but hardly considered easy-to-use. OpenWindows offers **textedit**, a graphical text editor much like the more widespread X program **xedit**.

As text editors, **xedit**, covered in Chapter 13, and **textedit** act much alike. In fact, with most graphical text editors, all you have to do is click the mouse at the desired location in the window and start typing. You can cut, copy, and paste sections of text the same way you cut, copy, and paste files in the File Manager. On a Sun Type-4 keyboard, you'll see a Delete key on top of the Backspace key. With **textedit**, both keys act the same, deleting the character to the left of the insertion point.

You can launch **textedit** with the following command:

textedit &

Sending Electronic Mail

The OpenWindows **mailtool** is an extension of the older SunView application of the same name. Both programs seek to place a graphical front end on the UNIX **mail** program, a program that is not a paragon of user-friendliness.

Mailtool allows you to view electronic mail messages sent to you and to compose messages to send to others.

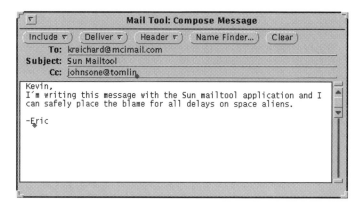

Figure 28.4 Mailtool's compose window.

Most of the operation is fairly easy to grasp. The text-editing acts the same as the rest of the DeskSet applications. To be really useful, however, you need to know how your local system network is set up and how user IDs are assigned to users. You normally don't need to pass any parameters to **mailtool**:

```
mailtool &
```

Working with the UNIX Command Line

OpenWindows provides two replacements for **xterm**: **cmdtool** and **shelltool**. There's almost no differences between the two, except for the default pop-up menus that appear over the command area.

Cmdtool and **shelltool** both allow you to cut, copy, and paste commands, using the pop-up edit menu. This makes working with a command-line prompt much easier, especially with the sometimes long command-line parameters used by many programs. Unlike **xterm**, though, you won't find the convenient single button paste operation (**xterm** uses the middle mouse button to paste). You must use the Copy and Paste menu choices, or their keyboard equivalents (Ctrl-C and Ctrl-V).

You can launch a **cmdtool** with the following command:

```
cmdtool &
```

You can configure **cmdtool** to act as the system console; that is, you can make **cmdtool** display any system-error messages that are normally sent to the system console. Use the following command to launch a **cmdtool** as the system console:

```
cmdtool -C &
```

The default OpenWindows script, **openwin**, launches a **cmdtool** as the system console. We find we use **cmdtool** more than **shelltool**, because **cmdtool** offers several more useful pop-up menu choices:

You can launch a **shelltool** window with the following command:

```
shelltool &
```

Editing Icons

The OpenWindows icon editor, **iconedit**, allows you to edit icons files for OpenWindows applications. Unfortunately, the file format used by **iconedit** is not compatible with the standard X bitmap file format. Thus your use of **iconedit** will be limited to OpenWindows applications. The most useful feature of **iconedit** is that you can edit icons for use with the file manager, **filemgr**. You can then use the **binder**, discussed above, to bind the new icon to a type of file or an application.

The icon editor works with four standard icon sizes: 64 by 64 pixels (for icons), 48 by 48, 32 by 32 pixels (for file manager icons), and 16 by 16 pixel cursors.

You can launch **iconedit** with the following command:

```
iconedit &
```

If you already have an icon file you want to edit, you can use the following command to launch **iconedit** and have the application load in your icon file:

```
iconedit filename &
```

Scheduling Your Time

If you're a type of person who likes to use computer-based calendars to schedule your time, you'll like the OpenWindows calendar manager, **cm**. **Cm** provides a calendar with views of the current year, month, week or day.

You can schedule meetings, appointments, and whatnot for yourself and other users of **cm**. Since **cm** runs only under OpenWindows, you're limited to group scheduling for OpenWindows users—which creates problems in a multivendor environment. (You might not like others to schedule your time.)

To schedule an appointment or meeting, double-click the left mouse button over the desired day. You'll then see the Appointment window:

Like most OpenWindows tools, a simple command launches **cm**:

cm &

The Calendar Manager requires the OpenWindows-specific font set. You'll have problems trying to display **cm**'s output on workstations not running OpenWindows, such as HP 720s or IBM RS/6000s. In addition, you may need to run **install_cmgr** to configure **cm** properly.

Summary

This chapter summarizes the features found in Sun's DeskSet, including a file manager, a calendar and scheduling program, **xterm** replacements, an icon editor, an electronic-mail program, and a program to bind document files to the applications that launch them.

For More Information

The good folks at the X Consortium make it amazingly easy to obtain the X Window System. They also put very few strings on it: You don't need to license X or pay royalties, and developers are encouraged to use X as a development tool.

There are three ways to obtain the X Window System: directly from MIT, through Internet and UUCP, and from commercial consulting firms and vendors.

MIT sells X, along with printed manuals and *X Window System: The Complete Reference to Xlib, X Protocol, ICCCM, XLFD, 3rd edition*. X comes on a set of 1600bpi or QIC-24 tapes in UNIX tar format. You can write:

MIT Software Distribution Center
Technology Licensing Office
Room E32-300
77 Massachusetts Ave.
Cambridge, MA 02139
(617) 258-8330 (the "X Ordering Hotline")

You can also pick up the latest X11 release from a number of archive sites on the Internet or via UUCP from UUNET. It is generally easier on everybody concerned if you pick up X from the closest Internet archive site.

There are many, many commercial firms offering X in one form or another. A quick glance through the ads in *UNIX Review* or another UNIX magazine will yield many possibilities. In addition, the following workstation and software vendors include the X Window System in their products: AT&T, Apple, Bull, DEC, Data General, Everex, Hewlett-Packard, IBM, Motorola, Mt. Xinu, NCR, SCO, Silicon Graphics, Solbourne, Sony, Sun Microsystems, and many more every day.

Obtaining Motif

OSF/Motif is a software product of the Open Software Foundation. You can order a source-code license from the OSF for $2,000 (the price as of this writing).

Open Software Foundation
11 Cambridge Center
Cambridge, MA 02142

Many software vendors offer all or part of Motif with their versions of the UNIX operating system. Vendors like Hewlett-Packard and Data General include Motif with the X Window System, while vendors like DEC and IBM offer Motif as an option. SCO's Open Desktop product includes Motif, and you can order Motif as an add-on for most 386 versions of UNIX, including Interactive UNIX, Destiny, and ESIX.

Many third-party vendors—like ICS, Metrolink, and IXI—offer Motif as a separate product. If you're a Sun SPARCstation owner who wants to use Motif, you have two choices: order the sources from the Open Software Foundation, or buy Motif as a separate product from a third-party vendor.

Obtaining Open Look

Open Look is available with the Solaris operating system on Suns, and also with many versions of UNIX System V Release 4. You can also get Open Look libraries with the contributed sources on the X11 R5 tapes or CD-ROM.

X Programming Books

This book is geared for X users, system administrators, and programmers—with the major emphasis on actual X usage. If you're ready to tackle the sometimes overwhelming task of X programming, here are the essentials:

- *X Window Applications Programming, 2nd edition*. Eric F. Johnson and Kevin Reichard. MIS:Press, 1992. This introduction to X programming covers the basics, including many of the concepts that distinguish X from other windowing systems.

- *Advanced X Window Applications Programming*. Eric F. Johnson and Kevin Reichard. MIS:Press, 1990. Our advanced book takes up where the first book leaves off. We've included long sections on following the rules for well-behaved X applications, opening connections to multiple displays, and interprocess communication using selections.

- *X Window System: The Complete Reference to Xlib, X Protocol, ICCCM, XLFD, 3rd edition*. Robert Scheifler and Jim Gettys, with Jim Flowers and David Rosenthal. Digital Press, 1992. The definitive reference work regarding the Xlib functions and protocol spec, from the principal creators of X. This is essentially an enhanced version of the Xlib manual from Release 5. You won't find any real introductory information here about X, and some of it is written over most users' heads, which makes it ideal for advanced X programmers.

- *Xlib Programming Manual, volume 1*. Adrian Nye. O'Reilly and Associates, 1990.

- *Xlib Programming Manual, volume 2*. O'Reilly and Associates, 1990.

- *X Window System User's Guide*. Tim O'Reilly, Valerie Quercia, Linda Lamb. O'Reilly and Associates, 1990. These three volumes are based directly on the MIT documentation. As a result, some of the prose is lifted directly from the official manuals. *Volume 2*, a reference for all X calls, is probably the best of the lot.

- *Introduction to the X Window System, 2nd edition*. Oliver Jones. Prentice-Hall, 1991. This is another introductory book to Xlib programming by a veteran X programmer. After an excellent introduction, Jones jumps in quickly with some complex programs and examples.

- *Inter-Client Communications Conventions Manual 1.1*, David Rosenthal, 1991. This document describes in cryptic detail how well-behaved X applications should act. Every X application developer should read this, which should be available with the documentation provided by your X vendor.

In addition, we can recommend the following Motif- and Open Look-specific books.

Motif Programming Books

- *Power Programming Motif*. Eric F. Johnson and Kevin Reichard. MIS: Press, 1991.

- *Visual Design With OSF/Motif*, Kobara, Shiz, Addison-Wesley, 1991.

- *OSF/Motif Programmer's Reference*. Open Software Foundation. Prentice-Hall, 1990.

- *OSF/Motif Style Guide*. Open Software Foundation. Prentice-Hall, 1990.

- *OSF/Motif: Concepts and Programming*. Thomas Berlage. Addison-Wesley, 1991.

- *The X Window System: Programming and Applications with Xt, OSF/Motif edition*. Douglas Young. Prentice-Hall, 1990.

Open Look Programming Books

- *UNIX Desktop Guide to Open Look*, Nabajyoti Barkakati. Sams, 1992.

- *The X Window System: Programming and Applications with Xt, Open Look edition*. Douglas Young and John Prew. Prentice-Hall, 1992.

- *Open Look Graphical User Interface Application Style Guide*. Sun Microsystems. Addison-Wesley, 1990.

- *Open Look Graphical User Interface Functional Specification*. Sun Microsystems. Addison-Wesley, 1989.

Index